CALMING YOUR CHILD

Published by Familius LLC, www.familius.com
PO Box 1249, Reedley, CA 93654

Familius books are available at special discounts for bulk purchases, whether for sales promotions or for family or corporate use. For more information, contact Familius Sales at orders@familius.com.

Library of Congress Control Number: 2022935499

Print ISBN 9781641706667
Ebook ISBN 9781641706704

Printed in the United States of America

Edited by Spencer Skeen, Peg Sandkam, and Erin Lund
Cover design by Carlos Guerrero
Book design by Maggie Wickes

10 9 8 7 6 5 4 3 2 1

First Edition

CALMING YOUR CHILD

De-escalating Tantrums,
Anxiety, Aggression, and
Other Challenging Behaviors

Dame Sue Bagshaw, MD
Michael Hempseed

This book is dedicated to all those who served courageously throughout the coronavirus pandemic. It is said that a person can have no greater love than to lay down their life for another. Those who bravely battled the pandemic often did so at a great risk to their own personal health. We want to thank all the doctors, nurses, orderlies, ambulance staff, cleaners, laboratory technicians, researchers, and those who volunteered for human trials. Your valorous efforts have saved many lives.

We humbly thank you for your service.

Contents

Disclaimer

All the information in this book should be considered general advice, and it may not apply in every situation. This book is not intended to replace the advice of a qualified and competent health or helping professional. If any of the techniques in this book cause distress or unpleasant experiences, we recommend that you stop them immediately.

We have made every effort to ensure this information is accurate at the time of writing.

No names or identifying characteristics have been used in the stories of people with mental illness.

Get to Know the Authors

Dame Sue Bagshaw is a medical doctor who has devoted her life to the well-being of as many young people as she possibly can. Sue was born in Hong Kong and gained a medical degree from The University of London. She likes to say that she and her husband, Phil Bagshaw, met over the same dead body while they were both in medical school. (Now there would be an interesting dating TV show!) In 1995, she established "198 Youth Health" (it was called 198 because the address of the building was at 198 Hereford Street, Christchurch, New Zealand). This was a youth one-stop shop with doctors, nurses, youth workers, and counselors all providing free services to those in the city of Christchurch who were most disadvantaged. In 2012, it was renamed "298 Youth Health" when it re-established after the Christchurch earthquakes. In 2019, Sue was knighted (made a dame) for her services to young people. (Damehood is the New Zealand equivalent to the honor of receiving a Presidential Medal of Freedom in the US.) Her husband established the Christchurch Charity Hospital, a free hospital to offer lifesaving medical care to those who were overlooked by the public health system. They have four children together and seven grandchildren. Sue is the founder of The Collaborative Trust for Research and Training in Youth Health and Development, an organization created to promote the training of youth health professionals and to conduct research into the well-being of young people. She is also a senior clinical lecturer of pediatrics at the University of Otago's medical school in Christchurch.

Michael B. Hempseed is an author and professional speaker who aims to take complex scientific information and present it to a popular audience. He gained an honors degree in psychology from the University of Canterbury in 2008. Michael has spent a considerable number of years working directly with young people, including time at 298 Youth Health. Today, he speaks all over New Zealand on topics such as suicide prevention, improving sleep, and understanding and healing trauma. His first book, *Being A True Hero: Understanding and Preventing Suicide in Your Community*, has been used by the New Zealand Police and New Zealand Army medics, among other organizations. He is married to Evita, who he met in 2014. In March 2021, they welcomed their first child into the world. Michael has a taste for adventure, and he has been skydiving and paragliding. He loves to travel and has visited thirty-seven countries. The Chernobyl Nuclear Power Plant, the Killing Fields in Cambodia, and the temples of Angkor Wat in Cambodia are among the many places Michael has visited.

Sue and Michael live in Christchurch, New Zealand. In 2010 and 2011, their city was hit by a series of significant earthquakes that killed 185 people. For several days, Christchurch was headline news around the world. When the media went away, the earthquakes took a massive social and emotional toll on many people. Over the past decade, Sue and Michael have both been heavily involved in trying to offer help to those whose lives were shaken by those events. In 2019, a mosque in Christchurch became the scene of one of the worst terrorist attacks in recent years. Both of these events have led to a substantial number of behavioral problems in many children. Over the years, Sue and Michael have learned what works really well and what does not. Many of the techniques that they have discovered not only work for children who have lived through significant disasters, but they can also work for all children who show challenging behavior. This book is not just Sue and Michael's thoughts on life; it is the result of years of practical experience with young people, as well as careful research.

Introduction

Raising and caring for children today is much more difficult and complicated than it was just a few years ago. Today, many parents and teachers face tremendously challenging behavior from their children. Recently, a teacher with over forty years' experience told us in her whole career she hadn't seen anything like the high rate of students' behavioral problems we have today. We have heard similar statements repeated over and over again from many parents, helping professionals, and other teachers. We will show in later chapters that this is not just their imagination—behavioral problems and mental illness have been increasing in children at an alarming rate in the last decade, and the last three years in particular.

A substantial number of parents and teachers struggle to know how to manage the growing list of difficulties. Parents and teachers can become frustrated and overwhelmed, be at the end of their tether, and even feel hopeless when they try to manage their children. It is our hope that as you read through this book, you will learn immediate techniques to calm and soothe a child in the moment who is upset, but we also want to look at many of the underlying causes of this challenging behavior; ultimately, we want to prevent these issues from arising in the first place.

We are not here to blame you; instead, we want to help you find a positive way forward. Throughout this book, we acknowledge how hard it is to see a child, whom you love, struggle and be in high states of distress.

This book is aimed at parents and teachers who have children roughly between the ages of four and twelve, although we do expect that some parents and teachers of children outside this age range will also find the book helpful. A number of people we sent the draft to said they found it helpful for their children who were in their twenties!

We have divided this book into two main sections. Section one starts with an overview of some of the difficulties parents and teachers experience, what causes challenging behavior, and some key concepts around child development. Then we look at immediate things you can do to calm an angry and upset child.

In section two, we look at many of the major causes of this behavior so we can prevent children from having outbursts and tantrums in the first place. The following story shows our reasons for placing such emphasis on the causes of challenging behavior.

There is a story of a town situated at the bottom of a cliff. Every single day, many cars crash over the cliff. The people in the town lovingly bring ambulances and help to the people who went over the cliff. They do this day after day and year after year.

In this situation, the smart thing to do is to build a fence at the top of the cliff to stop the cars from going over in the first place. That is what we hope this second section will do: help stop children from having explosive outbursts in the first place.

At the end of section two, we have a number of examples that will help you put what you have learned in this book into practice.

Every child is different. We do not offer one technique or method to help children with behavioral difficulties; instead, we offer you a considerable number of ways to improve your child's behavior.

We recommend that you keep a short journal as you go through this book. Record factors that you think may affect your child or techniques you want to try. It may help to order these factors and techniques by which ones you want to address or try first.

Many parenting books that seek to address challenging behavior only focus on the child. Throughout this book, we have tried to see the child within the wider social structure because we believe that, in order to truly help children who show behavioral problems, we must look at the wider family and community.

We are writing this book because we believe that children can overcome some of the substantial difficulties they are experiencing. We have both seen many children with significant behavioral challenges improve and go on to lead positive and successful lives. We want you to know—*there is hope*. We have seen this many times with our own eyes.

One of our key motivations for writing this book is thinking about the kind of world we want our children and grandchildren to grow up in. We don't want children growing up in high states of distress and turmoil, and we don't want to see families come to their breaking point because of children with severe behavioral problems. Life can have many challenges, but overall, we believe life should be full of meaning, enjoyable, and filled with plenty of laughter. It is our sincere hope that this book will allow a growing number of families to experience a more peaceful and stable home environment.

Section One:

What Is Going On?

Part One:

Gaining Perspective on Children's Behavior

Chapter One:
Living in Hell: The Reality of Having a Child with Behavioral Problems

"There is no glory in battle worth the blood it costs."
—*Dwight D. Eisenhower*

An exhausted mother comes home after a difficult and tiring day at the office. She wants to just stop and have a break. She spends an hour lovingly cooking a meal for her son. When she puts it in front of him, he picks up the plate and throws it against a wall, breaking the plate and ruining the meal. He screams at the top of his voice, "I DON'T WANT THIS! I DON'T F___ING WANT THIS!" The tantrum continues for another hour.

A father from a different family desperately tries to coax his son into doing his homework. Once the son finally settles down to do it, he continues to work on it for two hours. He makes a small mistake by putting a black mark on the page; tears the whole thing up, refusing to do anymore; and spends the rest of the evening crying inconsolably under the table.

A different set of parents try to get their daughter to brush her teeth; she reacts with extreme anger and violence. The parents have to hold her down to get her teeth brushed. She bites, kicks, screams, and howls. This family lives in an apartment building where the neighbors have put in numerous complaints about the noise. The parents have been told if it continues, they will be evicted. They live with an unimaginable level of stress. They are beside themselves and do not know what to do.

Bedtimes are also a nightmare. Trying to get their daughter into bed becomes an emotionally draining battle. Once she is in bed, she often screams and will get out of bed and pounds on her bedroom door for up to an hour. Throughout the night at 1, 3, and 5 a.m., she wakes up screaming. This wakes up everyone in the home, and her other siblings' schoolwork begins to suffer. Often, her parents make mistakes at work because they are so exhausted. Their employers have told them to leave their problems at home, but they just can't stop thinking and worrying about their children.

The next day, they start it all over again. The morning is a grueling battle to get their children up and ready for school and get them to eat breakfast and then to brush their teeth. Once again, tantrums, tears, and kicking follow. The child screams, "I don't want to go to school! I don't want to go to school!" They dread a phone call from the school saying what their child has done this time.

They have tried to enroll their children in after-school programs, youth groups, and camps. Every time they do this, their child is asked to leave, even from groups that never ask anyone to leave!

Two other parents have to battle their child every time their child needs to go to the doctor. While in the back of the car, the child screams so loudly that the parents end up with migraines. When they arrive at the doctor's office, the child holds onto everything possible and needs to be dragged from the car to get inside the doctor's office.

Another nine-year-old child who was toilet trained many years ago now soils himself on a regular basis. The parents felt they were making good progress; now they seem to have a nine-year-old who has regressed to the behavior of a toddler.

In another struggling household, a seven-year-old boy repeatedly says, "I want to kill myself." The parents knew that teenagers and adults could experience suicidal thoughts, but they never imagined a child so young would say this and mean it. They hear their child say, "I hate you! I hate you!" This breaks their hearts. The parents often put on a brave face while this is happening, but when it is all over, they often go to their rooms, cry their eyes out, and think, *Why is life so difficult? Why are we in this situation?*

Miles away in a small town, a kind teacher is terrified of a young child. A few days ago, the child got upset, took a chair, and threw it through a window. This terrified the other students, and the teacher just doesn't know what to do.

When many parents in these situations go out socially, they're often told the behavioral problems would be solved "if the child just had less screen time" or "if they ate less sugar," or if the parents "set better boundaries." Little do these advice givers know, the parents have tried all these things and more, and nothing has worked.

Often the parents stop taking their children out. They don't want to be seen in a shopping mall if their child is going to have an explosive tantrum. They stop inviting their friends over because they're worried about what will happen. In many cases, these children scream their lungs out whenever their parents do try to leave their house. They regularly feel trapped. They often order their shopping online and leave the house as little as possible.

Many of their friends and family stop calling or coming over. They often take the lack of contact to mean that the friendship or relationship is over. The parents long to go on a much-needed holiday; however, a holiday is often too much of a battle—it's far easier just to stay home. Many of these parents, older siblings, teachers, caregivers, aunts and uncles, and grandparents are at the end of their tethers.

The examples we've just described are not something out of a horror movie. Tragically, for many families, this is what they experience on a daily basis. Every day has turned into a grueling and heart-wrenching battle. We may associate some of these behaviors with teenagers, yet many teachers and parents are alarmed to see these behaviors in young children.

You may think that some of the examples we have just described are at the more extreme end, or maybe you think they are not extreme enough. Wherever you fall on the spectrum, you are probably reading this book because a child you are working with shows some or all of these behaviors (and maybe more).

This book is here to look at the underlying reasons why this behavior occurs and to find effective, evidence-based solutions to address it. Many parents have tried sticker charts, time outs, time ins, mindfulness, routines, and rewards. These solutions may work for "well-behaved" children, but they don't work for the situations we have just described.

In this book, we won't present just one method for solving the challenges. We will look at a significant number of vastly different strategies. We don't know what will work for your child, but there is almost certainly something in this book that can help or point you in the right direction to find help.

We want you to know there is hope. We have both seen many of the situations we've described, and we know that with the right help and support, these behaviors can be changed and stopped.

Before we can get to some solutions, you need to understand what is behind these behaviors. We will look at this in the next few chapters.

Chapter Two:
The World Through a Child's Eyes

"You never really understand a person until you consider things from his point of view . . . until you climb in his skin and walk around in it."
—*Harper Lee,* To Kill a Mockingbird

I f any of the behaviors we described in chapter one sound familiar, you might be wondering, *What on earth is going on?* When we are confronted with tantrums, meltdowns, and violence, they can seem inexplicable. When we look at these behaviors as adults, we often see children who don't have any respect for others, children who are "out of control" or malicious, or children who are narcissists or even psychopaths.

However, let's stop for a minute. Let's step back. What we're doing is looking at these situations with adult eyes; we're trying to understand this behavior by putting our own interpretation and our own view onto this behavior.

The first step in addressing this behavior is to understand it from the child's perspective.

We were recently contacted by a family with a very "naughty" and "disobedient" son. This seven-year-old had gone to the kitchen, taken a very sharp knife, gone to the garage, and started putting holes in the tires of the family car. Although he was only seven years old and fairly weak, he had managed to do enough damage to make sure that all four tires could no longer be used. The damage cost the parents $600. They were a low-income family and, for them, this was a considerable amount of money. They yelled at, scolded, and smacked the child. But the one thing they didn't do was ask him why he did it.

Eventually, someone had the bright idea to stop and ask, "Could there be a reason for this behavior?" On the surface, a child taking a knife from the kitchen is surely a sign that he is going to become a juvenile delinquent, thug, or psychopath. But when the family started to ask him about this, they found something very different: a friend of the family had been killed in a road accident a few months earlier. When the family took the time to understand what the child was thinking, they realized he was actually trying to protect the family. The child thought that by sabotaging the tires on the car, he would save his family from dying in a car crash. He didn't understand that fatal car crashes are fairly rare. He thought his family was going to die. Although he did a bad thing, he was trying to do something good.

When we see the world from a child's perspective, we see a very different world. Too often when adults see what they perceive as a child misbehaving, they assume that a child is just being naughty.

Mind Reading

In marriage and relationships, one of the biggest causes of arguments—and even breakups—is when couples try to read the other person's thoughts. We call this *mind reading.*

For example, if one person slams the door, the other person might assume, *This person hates me; they did it on purpose to upset me.* But there could be another explanation: maybe there was a gust of wind that forcefully blew the door shut.

Any marriage therapist will tell you that mind reading can be one of the leading causes of breakups. Mind reading usually ends badly because we assume the worst of the other person. Relationship counselors teach people not to put their own interpretation onto a behavior; instead, they encourage their clients to ask what caused the behavior or action. Mind reading can occur in any relationship, and it can happen between parents, teachers, and children.

What Could Be Going on Here?

When it comes to problematic behavior from children, we need to stop and ask, "What could be going on here?" The following stories about challenging behaviors from children will help to show that behavior is a way of communicating.

We heard about two parents who had immense trouble getting their daughter to brush her teeth at night. It always resulted in an aggressive screaming match that often ended in the parents having to hold her down and force her to brush her teeth. Doing this once was bad enough, but this happened night after night.

One day, the father asked, "Why do you not like brushing your teeth?" The daughter said, "I think my teeth are going to fall out when I brush them." Suddenly, the parents started to see this from a different perspective. They began to realize that their daughter was not screaming and yelling for the sake of it. Their daughter did this because she was trying to protect herself. The parents dearly loved their daughter, and they would never let anything bad happen to her; brushing her teeth was meant to give her good oral health, but the child did not see this. She thought her parents were trying to hurt her, so that is why she responded so aggressively.

A different child did not want to take a bath. They used to like baths, but then one day, they suddenly refused to get in and it became a battle to get them to take a bath. Eventually one of the parents asked, "Why don't you like baths?" As it turns out, one day the father had unplugged the bath and jokingly said, "You better be careful that you don't get sucked down the drain." Adults logically know that even the youngest child in the world could not possibly fit down a drain, but this child—with an incomplete view of the world—didn't realize this. The child thought, when going for a bath, there was a danger of being sucked down the drain. This was why they caused so much trouble and made bath time so difficult.

A blog post on boredpanda.com told the story of a child who loved eating cereal. Then one day she suddenly stopped. Years later, she admitted the reason was, as a child, she had heard on the radio that a serial killer was on the loose. She didn't understand that *serial* and *cereal* were two very different things. So she stopped eating cereal.[1]

The children in the examples above were eventually able to tell their parents why they acted a certain way. But not all children will be able to tell their parents what is wrong. It is always important that you ask them, but even then, some children may not know themselves.

The examples we have just given are quite simple, but sometimes the causes are not so obvious. In later chapters, we will look at things that can lead to poor behavior, such as a lack of sleep, sensory issues, and trauma. A tantrum may be a child's way of saying, "I have not had enough sleep," but often they may not know what has caused them to become upset. So, their body tries to show the world.

When we are confronted with problematic behavior, we need to try and understand that a child is trying to tell us something. One of the biggest reasons children act out is because they are fearful.

Afraid of Many Things

Sometimes children's behavior is problematic because they are overwhelmed, stressed, or fearful all the time. Often these children are not just fearful of one thing—such as brushing their teeth—but rather, they become fearful of everything. They become fearful of going to school or the shops, being around new people, trying to learn a new subject—everything becomes difficult for them. We will look at fearfulness, worry, and anxiety in a later chapter.

Perceived Danger

Adults often assume that if they see a situation as being safe, everyone else, including children, will also see it as being safe. If we start to explore the inner world of children, we find something very different.

When we were working at 298 Youth Health, we started asking everyone during their initial assessment, "Have there been any significant events in your life that could have led to how you're feeling now?" When we asked this, we discovered that many people said one of the really traumatic events in their life was a stay in a hospital as a child.

From an adult perspective, we can see that modern hospitals are a very safe, loving, and kind place. If we turn this around and look from a child's perspective, we realize that many children are terrified of hospitals. From a child's perspective, we can easily see that being separated from their parents and in an unusual environment with lots of noisy machines could be very scary. This shows the difference between the way adults perceive the world and the way children do.

Another perceived danger is a bed. Adults often think of a bed as a safe place; however, for many children, bedtime is a really scary time. The reason that many children don't want to go to bed is because they are fearful. They could be fearful that there are monsters under their bed, something is hiding in their closet, or something bad is going to happen to them. We want to be clear: adults logically know there are no monsters under the bed, but children often genuinely believe there are. How would you act if you really thought there was a monster under your bed at night? We used to think that only very young children had these fears, but we have found that older children, teenagers, and some adults experience this fear. We look at ways to resolve this in the chapter on sleep.

Inability to Express Self

In the next chapter, we look more in-depth at child development. But for now, we just want to say that it is important to understand that children do not have fully developed brains and often don't have the ability to talk about or understand how they feel.

Let's go back to many of the behaviors that we talked about in chapter one: screaming, tantrums, yelling at the top of their lungs, kicking, biting, breaking objects, running away, and saying, "I hate you" or even, "I want to kill myself."

It's very easy for adults to look at this and assume that child is malicious. But we now know that often when children do or say these things, they are often not being naughty; rather, they are either scared, distressed, or overwhelmed. We need to see that these children are in a state of fear, panic, or even terror.

Often the way children are trying to communicate is through tantrums or "behavioral problems." They are saying, "I'm scared or upset; I don't know why." Have you ever wanted to hit a computer that won't do what you want it to? This often occurs when adults want to be able to communicate with a computer but are unable to. This is how your distressed child feels.

Many of a child's challenging behaviors are an attempt to communicate. In a previous example, we spoke of a child who didn't want to have a bath because of the fear of being sucked down the drain. The child's screaming and yelling was an attempt to tell their parents, "I don't want to do this. I am scared. I feel I am in danger." This is the secret language of children. By writing this book, we hope to make sure this is secret no longer. The problem is many adults have been taught the wrong language. They have been taught that when a child does not want to have a bath, the child is saying "I'm trying to test the boundaries and prove I am the toughest," "I'm wanting to make your life difficult," or "I'm trying to manipulate you."

Imagine going to a doctor and telling them you have severe back pain. They gently touch your back; you scream in pain, "Stop, that hurts!" Instead of stopping, they press harder and harder. Again, you cry, "Stop!" This only makes them hurt you more. Eventually you realize they think the word "stop" means "press harder." Tragically this is what happens when adults do not understand the language of children. We often try punishments, which make the situation worse, when what we need to be doing is helping children through their difficulty.

Good and Bad Children?

We often use the terms *good children* and *bad children*. Good children brush their teeth silently; they do what they are told; they go to bed when they are asked; they do their work in school; they don't yell; they don't kick; they don't punch; they don't bite.

Bad children, on the other hand, are the opposite of that. They don't like to brush their teeth, cause trouble going to sleep, and are often aggressive, difficult, and disruptive.

We encourage you to change the way you think about children. Instead of seeing children as being *good* or *bad*, we want you to try and to perceive children as feeling *calm, safe, and relaxed* or *scared, afraid, and worried*.

Does this mean children are never naughty? No! An example of a genuinely naughty child would be someone who is deliberately drawing on the walls when they are at an age that they understand what they are doing and they know they should not do it.

Conclusion

In this chapter, we covered that the way adults see the world is often vastly different from how children see the world. It can take a while to start thinking about behavioral problems in a different way. We encourage adults to stop seeing the world from their perspective and with their eyes, and instead try to see a different world. We need to see that if children are acting out, they are usually trying to express themselves to adults, often in the only way they know how. Rather than automatically assuming children are naughty when they display problematic behaviors, we must take time to slowly think about what really lies beneath their actions.

The good news is that if we can understand what is behind these behaviors, we can take steps to prevent and manage them.

Chapter Three:
Understanding Child Development

"Children are not things to be molded, but are people to be unfolded."
—*Jess Lair*

Imagine that you hear about a best selling book. Everyone is raving about it, so you go do wn to your local bookstore and buy a copy. The book is about how to be a success in life. The book says you waste a lot of time traveling each day, but there is a better way: if you flap your arms really fast, you can fly! You're slightly skeptical about this, but you try it. You flap and you flap and you flap, but no matter how hard you try to fly, you just can't. After reading that book, some people would think they're an utter failure, they're useless, and they can't do anything right. However, someone else might ask, "*Can* human beings fly by flapping their arms?" No, it is impossible. Human arms are not *designed* to fly.

It's the same with the advice offered by many parenting gurus. Many books assume children have the same capabilities as adults. They assume children have an adult ability to control and regulate themselves. This means the advice the books offer simply doesn't work and it leaves many parents, teachers, and children highly frustrated. In this chapter, we want to give you a number of key insights into the differences between an adult's brain and a child's brain.

We have looked at many behavioral management books and websites and found that very few mention anything about child development. We also checked Ngram (a publicly available Google tool) for the relative frequency of the word combination *child development* appearing in publications from 1920 to 2019. The image on the next page shows that child development was mentioned more and more until 1970, then it made a significant decline.

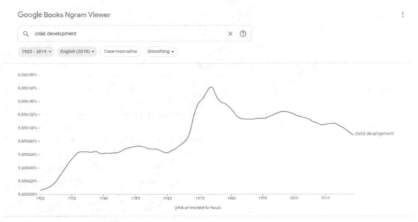

Frequency of the term *child development* as it appears in English-language publications between 1920 and 2019.

Adults often forget that children do not have the same brain that adults do. The human brain takes a very long time to finish developing, possibly as long as twenty-five or even thirty years.[1] We live in a world where we hear messages such as, "Anyone can do anything they want," and, "The only limits are the ones you set for yourself." The problem with many of these popular sayings is that they forget about a little thing called *biology*.

Our biology includes the state of our brain, and a child's brain does not have the capabilities that a fully formed adult brain has. Not looking at biology with child development may lead to an over diagnosis of attention deficit hyperactivity disorder (ADHD) (a condition where children have difficulty regulating and controlling themselves). A group of Harvard University researchers looked at which children, in a single school-grade class, were most likely to be diagnosed with ADHD; the researchers found it was the youngest children.[2] They were careful not to give reasons for this, but it is not too hard to imagine that if we expect the same behavior from the youngest children in a class as we do the oldest, we will get into trouble. A five-year-old with a birthday at the start of the school year will have a lot more brain development than a five-year-old with a birthday at the end of the year. If we forget about brain development, we risk expecting things of children that they are not capable of.

How We Develop

When children are born, they scream, cry, and have little to no self control. This is because they're using a primitive part of their brain. We call this the *crocodile brain* or the brainstem. If you've been around a newborn, you will know there really isn't much the baby can do. They can cry, but they certainly can't have a complex conversation with someone. During the early stages of development, the infant has little control over body movements. As they develop, more and more of the brain comes online* and they are able to perform more complex tasks. But remember: This doesn't happen instantaneously. The whole process of brain development can take twenty-five to thirty years!

One of the last parts of the human brain to fully come online is the prefrontal cortex. This is one of the parts of your brain that you use for self-control, problem solving, and rational decision making. Young children don't have a fully developed prefrontal cortex, so they find controlling themselves (i.e., their emotions, and thus their behavior) more difficult than adults. Sadly, many of the behavioral management books we have looked at don't take this development into account. Some suggest punishing children when they are just trying to do their best with the brain they have.

Books that do talk about child development often rate child development by year. Some books say between ages two and three, this will happen; and then between three and five, this happens; and so on. As a general rule, this is correct; however, within this, we have to be aware there are large differences because children do not all develop at the same rate.

If you've ever been to a classroom of five-year-olds, you will find some who probably have the emotional intelligence of a seven-year-old,

---

* All the parts of the human brain are there when we are born, but not all the pieces come on line until later in life.

and others who have the emotional intelligence of a three-year old.

We sometimes think there is something wrong with children who are a little slower to develop than other children. Often the ones who develop later will catch up and go on to do well in life. As an example, Albert Einstein learned to speak later than many other children his age.[†]

In the following pages, there are a number of principles that will help you to think about child development. We are not going to give you years or ages when this happens, because that can be very misleading. If a parent expects a certain thing should happen by a certain age and it doesn't happen, sometimes the parent can worry there is something wrong when that's just a normal part of child development.

Uneven Development

We must understand that often children do not develop all of their abilities at the same age. For example, we would expect that many seven-year-olds would have a seven-year-old's ability in math, managing emotions, and catching a ball, but some children develop those skills at different times. It is possible to have a seven-year-old with a seven-year-old's ability in math, a ten-year-old's emotional intelligence, and a four-year-old's motor skills (e.g., catching a ball). This can often be normal development.

Self-Control

If an adult is driving down the road and someone cuts them off, most adults may think for a brief moment, "I want to yell and swear at the other driver." Even though we think it, most of us don't do that. Inside your brain, a number of complex things happen. Part of your brain may say, "I want to swear at him," but hopefully another part of your brain will say, "stop, don't do that; it's a bad idea." This happens because one of the control parts of the brain, the *prefrontal cortex*, takes

---

† Many people say Einstein didn't speak until age four, but it was probably closer to two and a half; nonetheless, it was quite a bit later than other children as most children start talking around 18 months.

over and usually stops us from losing our temper. This part of the brain doesn't fully develop until adulthood, which could explain why children are more prone to tantrums than adults.

Let's see what happens when children get upset; maybe a drink is not in their favorite color cup. Because the control part of their brain does not work well, they can get upset more easily. It is natural for children to have one or two tantrums a week. Many parents believe that if a child shows what is normal childhood behavior—such as some tantrums, disagreement, and thinking only about themselves—it is a sign of serious behavioral problems, when in reality, it is just a normal part of childhood development because their prefrontal cortex is not yet fully developed.

Some things, like being the victim of any sort of violence growing up, can slow down the switching on of the connections between the different parts of the brain (especially the connection to the cortex), while other things can speed it up, including being in a safe, loving environment that provides opportunities to contribute, belong, have age-appropriate independence, and participate.

Unable to Think in Their Heads

Another way the lack of the prefrontal cortex shows itself is through the fact that many children need to speak out loud to solve problems. Sometimes adults will think that if children speak their thoughts out loud, they are deliberately trying to irritate an adult, but this is just the stage of development that many are at.

The work of Professor Charles Fernhough, an expert in child development, suggests that younger children have difficulty thinking to themselves in their head and often have to talk out loud to work through a problem.[3] Most adults can add six and seven together silently in their heads, while most children will have to say the numbers out loud. They are not being disruptive—they just need to think out loud to work through the problem.

The Concept of Time

The next concept that children struggle with is a concept of time. Adults are able to think into the future and look back into the past. One of the things that can give us great hope is our ability to think into the future and know that the pain we might be experiencing today may not be there tomorrow.

However, children tend to have a different view of the world. Sue lives next door to her grandchildren. One day she said to her two-year-old granddaughter, "Goodbye, I'll see you tomorrow," and her granddaughter burst into tears. She had no concept of tomorrow. All she knew was that her grandmother wasn't going to be there now.

Adults often get upset when they say to a child, "Come back in five minutes," and the child comes back in ten seconds. The child does this because they often don't have a concept of how long five minutes is. Setting a timer can be a good way to overcome this.

You also can see this in terms of how children process and understand the concept of death. After a funeral, a child may ask, "When is this person coming out of the ground?" They may not understand the concept of eternity and forever.

The concept of time is a good way to understand brain development. This is important to consider when we think about rewards and punishments. If children don't have a very long concept of time and we say, "You can have a reward next week," their brains can't process this and they won't be motivated by the reward. (We will come back to rewards in a later chapter.)

It is crucial that we don't expect children to be able to do tasks that require a complex understanding of the future. We have seen a number of attempts at trying to teach children emotional regulation by trying to get them to imagine a better future or a time when things aren't as difficult. Some children will be able to do this, but for many younger children, it is beyond their stage of brain development.

It's not just children who can struggle with understanding time; many adults do too. Many of us have probably written a list of ten things to do on a Saturday morning and think we will be done by lunch time. But three weeks later we are still working on the fourth item! Time management—in terms of having a good idea of how long tasks will take—is an important skill for children to learn but often only happens as the brain connections become functional during development.

Egocentric View of the World

The next point that's vital to understand is that children tend to have an egocentric view of the world, meaning they focus on themselves more often than they focus on others. To understand another person and to try and understand their thoughts and feelings requires quite a lot of brain development. Most of us do it every day, so we don't notice how much effort it requires. It is quite a complex skill that many children with their developing brain just don't fully have yet.

One of the consequences of children appearing to think the world revolves around them is that children often blame themselves if their parents get angry with each other or even separate and get divorced. They often think, "It was my fault; I caused my parents to split up." To understand why parents get divorced, a child may have to recognize their parents were often stressed about something else, not them. Some children can recognize this, but many can't. So children often assume that if something bad happens, they are responsible.

We are horrified by the number of online articles such as, "Is Your Child a Narcissist?" Many of these articles forget about normal childhood development. They are turning normal childhood behavior into narcissistic behavior. This can significantly disrupt the bond between parent and child. If a parent believes them is a narcissist, they are less likely to want to spend time with their children, whereas a parent who sees this as normal child development will have far more understanding and patience.

When children are quite young, they believe everyone thinks the same way they do. For example, if one child likes chocolate ice cream, they assume everyone does. As the child gets older, they start to understand that other people think differently from them and enjoy vanilla and strawberry.

Children of course do have some capability to think of others. They can share their toys and they can go up to a child who is crying and comfort them, but expecting children to fully understand and appreciate how others are feeling is often beyond their stage of development. Most children are not selfish, narcissistic, or psychopathic; they are just still developing.

Understanding Cause and Effect

Often parents can feel frustrated by some of the advice they get about how to deescalate an upset child. One strategy many parents are given is to help a child work out cause and effect. Parenting advisors try and teach children to recognize what has upset them and do something about it; however, often those connections that allow the brain the ability to show cause and effect just aren't functioning yet. It is better to teach those skills later when the development has happened to avoid getting frustrated and angry with the child. For example, many adults will ask a child why they got upset and threw their toys across the room. They expect the child to be able to tell them exactly what caused this. Many children do not fully understand that one thing can cause another, so they may not know why they threw their toys.

If a child has an explosive outburst, adults often ask "Why did you do this?" We hope the child will be able to identify what led to the outburst; in other words, we hope the child will be able to identify the cause that led to the effect. When children say, "I don't know what caused the outburst," they may genuinely not know. When children say, "I don't know why I got upset," it is not an act of defiance—in many instances, they genuinely don't know.

You may have more luck asking, "How come this happened?" to try to help the child connect the dots to what the child did and felt just before the outburst. As it is slowly talked through, the child may or may not realize and remember. By talking through it, the child may do better next time.

Many adults expect children to recognize complex causes and effects, but that is something often past their brain development. Furthermore, there is another problem with this: adults often assume there was one thing that upset a child, but there could be multiple things, such as lack of sleep, lack of free play, and difficulty making friends. There have been many strategies that try to teach children emotional regulation. They say to children, "If you notice you are getting upset, then you should do something about it," but to recognize that you are getting upset (an example of introspection) takes quite a lot of brain development, and many children don't have this.

It becomes even harder for children to link cause and effect when there is some time between events. We will show you in the chapter on sleep that poor sleep often leads to anger and irritability. If a child gets upset in the afternoon, they may not link it to poor sleep (which, in their mind, happened a long time ago).

There are many things that children do not realize dysregulate them. In a later chapter, we will talk about predatory sounds, such as those of an air conditioner or a ceiling fan. These things can replicate the low growl of a tiger and put children into a state of high alert, but a child probably would not understand that this is what triggered their behavior. Some children can recognize their emotions and respond appropriately, but often the children this book is about cannot. If children are told to do something they cannot developmentally do, they often feel more like failures because they can't do it.

Causes and effects are complex issues, and even many adults don't fully understand this. For example, many people get headaches but may not know what caused them, such as not drinking enough water or not sleeping well.

Sounds

The way we hear sound changes as we age. Adults can usually hear frequencies 0.02 to 16 kHz, whereas teenagers and children can often hear 0.02 to 17.5 Khz. The 1.5 kHz difference may not sound like much, but it could be the difference between adults finding a dentist drill annoying but manageable and a child hating it and needing sedation. If children say they don't like a sound and adults don't find it upsetting, it may be because children hear sounds differently than adults. We will talk about the implications of this in the chapter on sensory processing issues.

Concrete and Abstract Thinking

Children tend to have concrete rather than abstract thinking. Concrete objects and ideas are things you can see and touch. For example, a toy firetruck, a ball, a piece of sporting equipment, and a guitar are concrete objects. Abstract things are real and extremely important, but we can't see them, such as regret, love, creativity, and metaphor. Some people will say, "If you can't see something, it doesn't exist." That is, of course, not correct; we cannot see gravity, or wind, but every single day we can see the effects of these things.

Most adults have abstract thinking. They are able to think about the concept of love very differently from the way a child thinks about it. Often if you ask children what love is, they give concrete examples, such as, "Love is when someone shares a toy with me" or "Love is when someone gives me money." They tend to think in practical, concrete terms. Adults, on the other hand, can think of love very differently. They can think of love involving forgiveness, generosity, and understanding.

Emotions are an abstract concept. We cannot see our emotions, and so for many children, understanding emotions becomes very difficult. We have seen a lot of parenting advice that expects children to understand their emotions, but in many cases, this is well beyond their capabilities. You will find some five-year-olds do have a very high emotional intelligence; they will be able to tell adults exactly what they are feeling, but these children tend to be the exception rather than the rule. In order for a child to understand their emotions, it is very important to help them talk about and name their emotions. This helps them to control their emotions as the connection to the cortex develops.

When asking a child if they feel sad, adults may say to children, "Do you feel blue?" Many children with concrete thinking will take this to mean "Is your skin the color of a smurf?" To "feel blue" is an abstract concept that adults have put onto feelings. If you use terms like that, children may not understand what you mean. Unfortunately, many people who attempt to help children manage their emotions don't understand that children struggle with abstract concepts.

A better way to explain sad might be with a concrete example; you could ask, "how do you feel if you drop your ice-cream cone or if no one wants to play with you at school?" If you give concrete examples like this rather than abstract ones, most children will start to understand these concepts.

Also, it is important to understand that not everyone feels the effects of emotions the same way. For example, some people, if they are emotionally hurt, say they "feel the hurt very strongly in their heart." Other people will feel it in their stomach, while others might feel it in their head. Some will be able to express their feelings in other words and not relate them to a part of the body. It is important to know that there are significant differences in the ways that people understand and express emotions.

Both of us have worked with many adults who do not understand their emotions. When we've asked them how they feel, many have said they don't know. Adults who have experienced trauma often struggle with this because their brain connections may not be working so well.

Many adults try and get children to link their emotions to colors; for example, they ask children "Do you feel blue?" When adults talk about colors and emotions, children often nod their head as though they understand. Researchers have found that when you ask children questions they don't understand, they often assume the adult wants an answer.[4] For example, the question "Which is heavier, yellow or red?" is an illogical question. Most adults would realize this question does not make sense and would say so to the person who asked them that. But children try and give an answer even if they don't understand. They might say, "Well, the sun is really big, so yellow must be heavier."

When children say they don't know how they feel, sometimes adults think they are being difficult, defiant, or are hiding their feelings. But some children genuinely don't know what they feel. In order to look inside ourselves and understand what we're feeling, it requires quite a lot of working connections in the brain, which may not have developed yet in children.

Abstract Thinking and Education

The lack of abstract thinking is one of the key reasons why so many children and teenagers struggle with math. Let's take a look at the Pythagorean theorem; $a^2 + b^2 = c^2$. This is totally meaningless to children.

However, you could visually demonstrate what this means. In the image below, the short side of the triangle—side a—is three boxes long. If you make a square out of it (multiply the number by itself, 3x3), the square has nine little boxes in it—we call this a^2. If you take the next longest side—side b—it is four boxes long; if you make this into a square (4x4), that square now has sixteen little boxes in it—we call this b^2. If you add nine and sixteen together, you get twenty-five, which is how many little boxes are in the square on the longest side—side c—which is 5x5—or c^2.

It is interesting to note that many people say, "Asians are good at math." It has been found that the way many Asian languages represent math is far more concrete.[5] For example, the number "twenty-one" in English is quite hard to understand, but many Asian languages represent it as two sets of ten and then

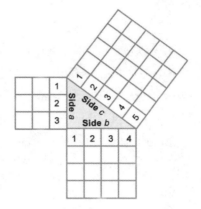

Visualization of the Pythagorean theorem.

one set of one. It has also been found that many Asian schools teach math in a far more concrete way than many Western schools do.[6]

Symbolism

It has been found that many children under the age of four struggle with the concept of symbolism.[7] If you show a three-year-old a picture of a firetruck, they can identify it and say, "Firetruck." If they see a real firetruck and and ask them what it is, they often don't know. The problem occurs because children struggle to connect a picture in a book, which is a symbol, with the real-life object.

Children under the age of five can struggle with this when it comes to emotions. In the Disney movie *Inside Out*, one of the characters is called Anger; he is red and angry. If you ask many children to identify anger on a page with some of the other characters from the movie, they will be able to identify him. Then if you ask them to identify if they are angry, they often have trouble. They struggle to connect the picture with their emotions. Although this mostly affects younger children, it can occur with older children too.

Positives

We have focused a lot on some of the challenges children have, but one thing they do well is react positively. Over the years, Michael has done a lot of team building tasks with people of all ages. One task includes giving a group some objects that they have to use to keep an egg safe when it is dropped from a certain height. Michael almost always sees that the children's groups outperform the adult groups. By and large, children listen to each other, offer help when it is needed, and are encouraging and supportive of each other. Sadly, most adult groups are the opposite.

Conclusion

Child development is a large topic. There is a lot more than what we have mentioned in this chapter; this is just a short summary of some key points. In this chapter, we looked at the ways that children do not have the same capabilities and brain development as adults. When we seek to understand children who show behavioral difficulties, we must examine this through the lens of child development. Hopefully the points we have briefly covered in this chapter will help you to understand the ways children's brains are still developing and what this means for managing and addressing challenging behavior. We hope that with a new understanding of child development, you will have more empathy for children who lack self-control and show some behavioral problems.

Chapter Four:
The Need for Genuine Love

"Where there is love there is life."
—Mahatma Gandhi

The most important theory in all of developmental psychology is probably that of attachment theory, which was promoted by John Bowlby. This theory outlines that when a parent creates a strong sense of attachment from birth by being consistently present and giving comfort when needed, a child will be more secure and will not experience so many fears and tantrums.

If the child's experience from birth has been that their parent does not provide consistent presence and comfort, they can become withdrawn and anxious. If the parental presence is sometimes attentive and sometimes not, the child can become aggressive and angry. Understanding this can help parents prevent tantrums from the start. (We do want to stress that in some cases, children come from very well-connected homes but still develop severe anxiety.)

In this book, we discuss many strategies that can help calm distressed children, but, ultimately, one of the most important in preventing tantrums in the first place is for the child to have strong, stable attachments with parents, siblings, aunts and uncles, grandparents, teachers, and others.

We use the word *attachment*, but why don't we use the word "love?" Ultimately, what children need in order to have the absolute best chances for success in life is to be loved deeply. Too often, the world we live in focuses on what we can gain for ourselves. Love is the opposite of that. Love says, *What can I give to someone else? What can I give to make someone else happy?* There are, of course, limits to this, and some people go too far. But ultimately, what we need is more love. It astounds us that so many parenting books talk about discipline and behavioral management, but they don't talk about the power of love.

Saint Paul writes, "Love is patient. Love is kind. It does not envy. It does not boast. It is not proud. It is not rude. It is not self-seeking. It is not easily angered. It keeps no record of wrongs. Love does not delight in evil but rejoices in truth" (1 Corinthians 13:4–6).

A really interesting way to test how loving you are is to replace the word *love* in that previous passage with your name and measure yourself against it. Many people think life is about trying to take as much as you can for yourself, but love requires sacrifices. Maybe a parent has just come home from work. Maybe they are tired and want to rest or watch a TV program, but their child comes to them and says, "Will you play a game with me?" Love can be sacrificing your own wants and needs for the benefit of others.

We do have to set limits on this. If we are too tired and exhausted, then we cannot help someone else. So there does have to be balance here, but ultimately, love does require sacrifices. Love also requires forgiveness. If you have children, you will know that they do many things to upset and annoy you. But part of love is forgiveness and moving on from that. Forgiveness is accepting that no human being is perfect. It is accepting that people will hurt you, but you still want to love them anyway. (Obviously, this does not apply to situations where there is, say, sexual abuse.)

The fascinating book *Compassionomics*, by Stephen Trzeciak and Anthony Mazzarelli, shows that doctors who have more compassion have lower rates of burnout[1] and patients who recover faster.[2] Love really needs to be in all areas of society.

Many people know Patch Adams as the clown doctor from the movie *Patch Adams* with Robin Williams. The movie is based on the life of Hunter Doherty "Patch" Adams. Comedy is a huge part of Patch Adams's life, but more than that, he has dedicated himself to loving his patients. Adams set up a free hospital that ran for over twenty years.

When patients first arrived, they often had three- to four-hour initial assessments. Doctors are usually in a rush, but this shows how much he loved his patients.

It is important to recognize that love is not really a feeling, but rather a consequence of choosing. When we choose to love often, the feeling follows.

Ultimately, we believe the antidote to anxiety and stress is not Valium. It is family, fun, and friendships. If you are having genuine fun with your children, it is impossible to be stressed or anxious. When you are having genuine fun, all the stress and anxiety melt away.

Mihaly Csikszentmihalyi wrote a great book called *Flow*, in which he writes about how people lose themselves in the joy of what they are doing. For example, an artist may think they have spent twenty minutes painting when it was actually many hours; they lose themselves in the enjoyment of what they are doing.

Ultimately, we think one of the things that children desperately need is more fun. In later chapters, we show the dangers of having too much schoolwork and taking away free play. Children—and even adults—need to have far more fun in their lives.

Both of us regularly work with incredibly distressing situations, such as suicide and sexual abuse. We also read dense scientific papers on a regular basis. But both of us try to make sure we have enough time for fun in our lives. Sue has a large box of costumes she and her grandchildren use to dress up. Michael and his wife cover their house in Christmas lights each year in the hope that it will put a smile on someone's face.

Fun cannot be measured on a standardized test. Fun is done for the sheer enjoyment, to put a smile on people's faces, and to make the world an enjoyable place.

Ultimately, we emphasize that the more time you can spend with your children having fun, the less stress and anxiety they should have.

Fun can be different for different people. Some people's idea of fun is going to the beach and building sandcastles. Other people's idea is going on a bike ride or a hike, while yet other people like to sit at home and play board games.

Most people often think that childhood should be fun and the fun should stop when people become adults; however, we believe this is a terrible idea. Fun needs to continue throughout your life. Sue keeps herself sane by spending lots of time playing with her grandchildren.

Let us think about two children. One has just had a fun day. The child enjoyed making art, going for walks, and spending time with family. Another child has spent all weekend stuck at home doing homework. Which child do you think will be most likely to do the dishes when asked? It is the child who had fun.

Loving your children does not mean buying them expensive presents. It means spending time with them. Building relationships does not happen overnight. It happens in the small but simple actions. It can mean playing one extra game with them or reading them an extra page of a book. Ultimately, family and fun are what will give children the absolute best chances to be successful in life. Love also means remembering the little things young people tell you. When you remember, it tells them that you really listened and that you care.

Chapter Five:
De-escalation Techniques

"To hear the phrase 'our only hope' always makes one anxious, because it means that if the only hope doesn't work, there is nothing left."
—*Lemony Snicket,* The Blank Book

There are a number of techniques that can be really helpful when you are trying to de-escalate an upset child. It is important to know what you can and cannot de-escalate. If a child is moderately upset, you have time to use the techniques that we discuss in this and subsequent chapters. However, if they are in a state of rage, you cannot talk them out of it; they have temporarily lost the power of rational thought.

Giving a Positive Alternative

Have you ever asked a child to stop doing something and he just keeps doing it? Often when he keeps doing it, we think he is being defiant. Our brain can imagine some amazing things, but it is not good at imagining the words *don't*, *stop*, and *no*. If we say, "Don't think of a pink elephant," most people do. Your brain can't imagine the word *don't*, so all we hear is "think of a pink elephant."

Every parent knows that if you ask a child not to cry, the child will immediately burst into tears. If you say to a child, "Stop drawing on the walls," she will only hear "draw on the walls." You need to give a positive alternative, such as, "Go play with your other toys." If you give a positive alternative, she will follow what you say. This is why the American police say, "Stay in your vehicle," rather than, "Don't get out of the car."

Regulate First

Psychiatrist Bruce Perry developed a theory called the Three Rs. The first step in solving behavioral problems is to help the upset person

Regulate (in other words, make them feel calm), then Relate to the them, and then Reason with them. All too often we get it backward: we try and reason with a child before the child is regulated. (It is helpful if you first regulate and calm yourself, and that will help your child.) For example, we say, "If you don't behave, you will get no TV for a week"—this is trying to reason with someone. When someone is distressed, they often don't think about long-term consequences. When we try to reason when someone who is upset, it just doesn't work, and everyone gets more upset.

Let's imagine you have a child and it is past their bedtime. If you say, "You will be tired tomorrow" (Reasoning), this does not motivate them to go to bed at all.

Next, we try bargaining with the child: "If you don't go to bed, you will not get ice cream for desert tomorrow." Statements like this often create more anger. Now you have an even bigger tantrum to deal with.

We write in the chapter on child development that children don't have a good understanding of time; both of these suggestions—the consequences of being tired or having no dessert tomorrow—involve a distance of time that is too great for a child to comprehend.

Instead, you could ask, "Would you like me to read you a story?" Many children love hearing stories read to them, so this helps them relax (or Regulate them). Maybe you could start in the living room, read ten or fifteen pages, stop at an exciting point, and say, "Let's continue in bed."

To Relate to a child, you could say, "I know it can be hard to go to bed at the right time. Even I find it hard sometimes."

Now you can start to Reason with the child. You could ask, "How come you don't want to go to bed?" It often helps to give examples of the kinds of answers you want. "Do you find bed boring?" "Do you not like the dark or your bed?" "Do you hear scary noises?" Once the child is regulated, you can address each of these issues one by one.

Saying "You are not in trouble."

Children often get really upset when they think they're in trouble, even if they are not. For example, if an adult says, "This is your last warning," the adult usually means, "I am trying to stop you from getting into trouble." But children frequently think this means, "An adult is angry with me," "I've failed again," or "I'm no good at anything." When children think they're in trouble, their behavior tends to get worse, not better.

A really good statement to start with is, "You're not in trouble." When children hear this, they are more likely to understand that an adult is trying to help them, which reassures them.

Acknowledging Feelings

Next you need to acknowledge how they are feeling. If you say, "Calm down," children don't actually calm down; often they become more aggravated. An even worse thing to say is, "You're getting upset over nothing." Instead, children often want you to acknowledge how they are feeling. If a child comes into a room and is obviously angry and frustrated, a really good thing to say can be, "You are not in trouble; it looks like things are not going well at all. Please tell me what's been going on—I really want to know."

This shows that we are listening to the state they are in, we are saying, "We are here for you; we want to help you." When you say, "Please tell me what has been going on," it often forces the child to stop and explain what has been going on. This often slows the child down and soothes them.

If you say this in a slow, calm voice, this can also be a good way to de-escalate someone. When it comes to de-escalation, the calmer you are, the calmer the other person will be as well. Even if on the inside you don't feel calm and you're feeling panicky yourself, try and deliberately say your words in a slow, calm voice. This in itself can be very calming and therapeutic. It helps if you are at the same eye level—a child won't feel acknowledged if the other person is towering over him; that can feel quite threatening. Sitting down together so that you are more on the same level is helpful.

Feeling Trapped

One factor that many people do not consider is how far a child is from an exit. If a child feels trapped, he is more likely to become upset and aggravated. Often just knowing that there is an exit that he can use makes a big difference. This doesn't work in every circumstance. For example, if a child is likely to run out onto a busy road, then obviously this is not a good idea.

Many people don't consider how important exits are. When people with high anxiety come into a room, one of the first things they do is look for an exit. If they end up in a part of a room that's away from an exit, that may make them feel trapped. This raises their adrenaline and cortisol levels, which means if something does go wrong, they're more likely to have an explosive tantrum. Consider if there is a way to manage this behavior by putting a child near an exit. It doesn't have to be an exit out of a house onto a road; it could be merely an exit into another room.

Personal Space and Feeling Threatened

Often when children are anxious or have been traumatized, they need a much bigger personal space bubble than other people do. The technical name for this is *peripersonal space*. Most people feel comfortable with someone standing between one-and-a-half and six-and-a-half feet away from them. If it is someone you know really well, the bubble gets much smaller. Researchers have found that people with anxiety or people who have experienced trauma often have a much bigger personal space bubble than those who haven't.[1] Sometimes they prefer a distance of ten to thirteen feet.

When a child is calm, a good question to ask is, "Would you like me to come closer to you? Or would you like me to step further away?"

You will be surprised that often the child will want you to be quite a few feet away. When the child says this, they are not making a joke; it is really how far away they want you to be. Consider that this is the child's safety bubble. If this is a safety bubble, how often does it get violated because we put people too close to the child?

Understanding Shame

Time-outs are when children are sent to their rooms for bad behavior. The problems with these are 1.) children often don't know why they are in time-out and 2.) time-outs can damage the relationship between a child and parent because a child is being separated from their caregiver.

A new version of this is *time-in*, which is when a distressed child stays with a parent or caregiver. This can work well, but there are times when this may not be effective. If a child is crying her eyes out, she may feel embarrassed and filled with shame, and making her stay around an adult can add to the shame; in these situations, allowing her to be by herself can help. There is a difference between sending a child to her room for poor behavior and allowing her to be on her own to cry in private.

Avoid Humiliation

If you are a teacher and a child starts making a paper airplane, one of the tempting things to do is to go over, pick it up, scrunch it up, and yell at the child. However, if you do this, you will humiliate him in front of everyone else. When we are humiliated, we blush and our sympathetic nervous system activates as if we were being chased by a wild animal; people who are humiliated often go into fight mode.

One of the most important aspects of de-escalation, particularly with aggressive children, is not to humiliate them in front of others. If children feel even the slightest bit of humiliation, they may react explosively. If a child is making a paper airplane, a good thing can be to go over to him and say, "That's incredible. As a child, I was never able to make those. Would you be able to show me after class how you made it?" You're affirming him. You're saying that he has a good skill, but you're also saying that now isn't the right time. Often, if you can handle it in this way, you stop an explosive outburst.

It is also worth considering whether there are other things you are doing that may humiliate a child, such as asking them to write on the board. If a child doesn't feel confident about spelling, or he's worried about his handwriting, you can cause an explosive tantrum when you ask him to do this.

Challenging Times

Sometimes children test you. A few years ago, Michael was asked to give a talk at the youth prison. A week before he came in, one of the staff at the youth prison called him and said, "We just wanted you to know we had a presenter in today and she left in tears." Michael thought, *Great. Why did you tell me that now?*

Michael doesn't get intimidated easily, but this really unnerved him. He went in feeling very vulnerable. He started by saying, "Hi, my name is Mic . . ." Before he even finished his name, one of the young people interrupted and said, "Sorry, I'm not trying to be offensive, but do you know you sound like Elmo?" (from Sesame Street)

Often when children say, "I'm not trying to be offensive," what they're really saying is, "I'm trying to offend you as much as I possibly can."

Michael paused for a minute and said, "Thank you. I'll do impersonations later." If he had said, "Shut up, you're being really disrespectful," then that would have become a competition. Or if he had humiliated that person, they'd have tried even harder to throw him off his game.

He doesn't know why that first presenter left in tears, but he suspects that maybe she didn't know quite how to respond to a remark that was actually trying to be offensive, and then the session escalated from there.

Pointing Out Embarrassing Things First

If there is something embarrassing that you worry children might exploit, the best thing is to point this out at the start. For example, Michael's last name is Hempseed. The word *hempseed* is somewhat associated with marijuana. Almost all difficult young people know this. Whenever he introduces himself, he makes a joke out of it. He says, "Hi, my name is Michael Hempseed. I always had this dream to own my own airline. I wanted to be a little bit like Richard Branson. I was going to call this airline Hempseed Airways. And the tagline was going to be, "Hempseed Airways, getting you higher than anyone else."

Most disruptive children love that joke. It also takes away their ammunition. So, if there is something embarrassing, if you make a joke out of it first, then that takes away any fuel they may have.

Conclusion

The strategies we have covered in this chapter are a good start, but they don't work in every situation. In the next chapters, we look at how we can use sensory objects to further de-escalate upset and angry children.

Chapter Six:
The Absence of Soothing Behaviors

"Calmness is the cradle of power."
—*Josiah Gilbert Holland*

Children with behavioral problems can erupt into explosive tantrums. They can yell; they can kick; they can bite. They can throw chairs; they can break property; they can hurt others. It is extremely distressing to watch this.

Often when we try to address this behavior, we say, "Calm down." When a child is distressed, their nervous system is in a state of hyperarousal, their body is flooded with adrenalin and cortisol. When they are distressed, they are acting from a part of the brain called the brain stem; this is the most basic part of the brain. Words have little to no effect when someone is in this state. When a distressed child hears the words *calm down*, this does nothing to bring their body out of the brain stem and back into a calm state. We need to use other methods and other techniques, such as sensory stimulation or physical objects, to try and calm the nervous system. A soothing touch can quickly calm the nervous system in a way that words cannot.

In developmental psychology, there is a concept called *attunement*, which is when a parent recognizes that a child is distressed and they respond to that distress. A parent who is attuned to the child and responds well will go over to that child, comfort him, and do what they can to help soothe him.

What Happened to Soothing Behaviors from the Past?

Unfortunately, many of the modern ideas about parenting have taken away many effective soothing techniques from children and replaced them with ones that are ineffective. For example, when children used to go to the doctor to get an injection, they got a lollipop to self-soothe (or to shut them up!). However, many doctors have now taken this away; they say sugar is bad for children, but they haven't replaced it with anything. Did anyone stop to ask, "Why did we give children lollipops in the first place?" The original purpose was that if a child was distressed, they had something to soothe themselves with or to stop them crying. These physical objects were far better and more effective than just words.

It's not just lollipops at the doctor. A lot of children suck their thumb or bite their nails to manage distress. We now say, "Sucking your thumb is bad. Don't do that. It can damage your teeth." Of course, this is true, but we didn't ask what the purpose of this behavior was. Too often we take away self-soothing behaviors from children without replacing them with other behaviors. This means they don't learn to self-regulate and self-soothe. Sometimes if this distress builds and builds, it can result in very dangerous behaviors, such as head banging.

Conclusion

In the modern world, we have removed so many self-soothing behaviors that children had. The soothing techniques left to us often involve just words. We need to broaden our toolbox and look at other techniques that we can use and include things that stimulate and soothe all five senses. We will look at a wide number of these in the following chapters.

Chapter Seven:
Calming Using Touch

"Touch comes before sight, before speech. It is the first language and the last, and it always tells the truth."

—*Margaret Atwood*

One of the most powerful senses that is able to calm people down is the sense of touch. In the modern Western world, we often greatly underestimate just how important touch is as a way to help calm us down. A researcher in the 1970s, James Prescott, found that societies that had the most physical touch (e.g., hand shaking, hugging) had the lowest rates of violence.[1] It seems that physical contact reduces violent urges in people.

The book *Touching*‡ describes a Philadelphia orphanage where children who did not having loving touch often died, despite having all the food and warmth they needed.[2] Children desperately need cuddles. They desperately need hugs. We must not deprive them of these.

Touching also talks about how important skin-to-skin contact is. There are endless debates about whether breast milk or natural milk is better for children. Almost all these debates look at the quality and substance of the milk yet neglect the most important aspect: that breastfeeding requires skin-to-skin contact.

Before we look at a number of ways touch can be used to soothe children, we first want to look at how touch is processed in the brain. This strange-looking figure on the following page is called a *cortical homunculus*. It is a representation of how much brain power is devoted to the touch sensations in each part of the body. For example, our hands are quite small in real life—they make up only 2.29 percent

‡ This book was published in the 1970s; some of the information is out of date and may not have been written today, but there is still a lot of valuable information in it.

of our bodies[3]—yet there is a large amount of brain power that is involved with processing the feelings in our hands. This is why the hands of the homunculus are six to seven times larger than we would expect, and it means the hands can be a large source of calming information. In fact, the hands receive more sensory information than the entire torso!

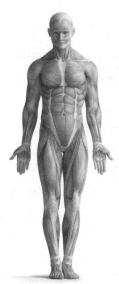

Cortical humunculus, shows the proportion of brain power devoted to different parts of the body versus a correctly proportioned person.

This explains a frustrating problem many of us have. Sooner or later, almost everyone gets a paper cut. We know tiny cuts really hurt. Logically, a lot of adults say, "Why does such a small and tiny cut cause so much pain?" Often a tiny paper cut on your finger hurts more than a medium cut on other parts of your body. The reason is, within your fingertips, you have almost more nerve endings than in any other part of the body. The homunculus shows how much of our brain power is devoted to that small area. People are not overreacting if they have a paper cut—they have just been hurt in a really sensitive area where their brain magnifies that pain.

Sensory Objects

It's really important that we understand our biology. As we said in the previous chapter, just saying "calm down" does little to take someone out of an emotionally charged state. Instead, touch can quickly reach down to the parts of our brain where anger and rage occurs and soothe them. Our hands and fingertips can allow us to receive lots of information very quickly. We can use this knowledge to our advantage when we think about ways to soothe children. Children's fingers can be a source of soothing information, meaning we can use physical objects to help them self-regulate.

We have heard some people say sensory objects don't work. How you use them is very important. If you give a child a smooth pebble and they just hold it, that probably won't do much. Instead, you need to teach them to slowly run their fingers over it and carefully think about all the sensations in their fingers. Often the slower a child does this, the more effective and soothing it is. Calming an angry and distressed brain can take time; it does not happen instantly. This is why sensory objects need to be used slowly, to give the brain time to calm down.

Memory Foam

There are soft toys you can buy made of memory foam. When you press these in, they slowly rebound. When some children are starting to get distressed, you could put this in their hands and press it in a few times. Some children will immediately throw this away, but others may become mesmerized by it. Watching the memory foam slowly rebound gives children a chance to pause, which can take away some of the anger or stress they are feeling. Pushing these in and out becomes very therapeutic for some children.

A mother once approached us saying her daughter had severe sleep problems. We suggested they get a soft memory foam toy. The child took this toy to sleep with her, and she got almost an extra hour of sleep! For some reason, regular soft toys don't seem to work as well for some children.

Fabric

Alternatively, different textures of fabric may be helpful. You can get different types of material at almost every craft store. Let's take bumpy fabric as an example. If a child is getting distressed or upset, they may have a square of it in their pocket or by their pillow at night. If you teach them to slowly feel each and every part of it, this can help regulate a child. If you think this could be a good idea, we recommend taking a child to a craft store to see what different options are out there.

Example of bumpy fabric.

Keys

There are also metal keys that have little cogs or bumps on them. They are often used for scrapbooking (if you Google "scrapbooking keys," some examples should come up). Some children find it tremendously therapeutic to slowly feel a key with their hands, touching the different bits and bumps.

Examples of tactile keys.

Tassels

Other things that can be really helpful are tassels. Unfortunately, a lot of children's toys today are made out of smooth plastic and there's no tactile information. A lot of children find anything that has tassels on it fascinating to play with.

Buttons

Buttons can also be really therapeutic. The buttons that most children like are larger ones that have raised surfaces on them. Children really like to feel the buttons' edges very slowly and feel the holes in the middle.

Examples of tactile buttons.

Finger Painting

Another thing that can be helpful in calming a child is finger painting. Rather than putting paint on the end of a paintbrush, you can get a lot of tactile information out of painting with your fingers. As we said, your fingertips have a lot of nerve endings!

Rubik's Cube

Some children find items such as a Rubik's cube or a Rubik's triangle helpful to calm them and help them focus.

Fidget Spinners

Some parents have found that playing with fidget spinners can be another really helpful tool to help their children self-soothe. Often when we see children with these, we think they must be distracting themselves and not concentrating. But many children, particularly those with ADHD, actually find that doing something like this can help them concentrate.

Other Examples of Sensory Objects

Blu Tack and Play-Doh can be very therapeutic. Many children love to stretch them out and make things.

Also, slowly fingering a smooth pebble they found during a happy time or stroking a piece of soft fabric that someone they love gave them can help calm a child.

You may notice we're trying to suggest things that are silent. A lot of children do say bubble wrap is therapeutic to pop; however, it would not be ideal if a teacher had thirty students popping bubble wrap while trying to teach a class!

It's important that sensory objects are easy to access. We have heard that many schools now have a sensory box in the corner of a classroom. The problem with this is if a student is getting anxious or angry, the student has to recognize they are getting distressed, remember there is a box of calming things in the corner, go over there, and use it. That's far too many steps to remember for someone who's agitated and angry. Instead, we recommend putting sensory objects in front of a child. At school, these should be in or on children's desks; that way, the objects are in front of them and they don't have to think about a box in the corner that they often forget about when they're angry.

Safety Concerns

We do want to stress the importance that sensory objects be age- and developmentally appropriate for children. They can be a strangulation or choking hazard. We urge you to think very carefully about the consequences of using different objects and the effects they could have.

Nature

Too often today, we want children to wear shoes. We don't allow them to be barefoot and feel the grass or sand underneath their feet. By doing this, we're taking away a lot of sensory information from children. We really encourage you to let your children go out into a field, feel the grass between the fingers and toes, play with the dirt.

A lot of children take home things like bark or little rocks and parents think they're just making a mess. But we don't stop to ask what the reason could be that they are bringing these items back. Many of them find things like bark very therapeutic to run their fingers over. The same with water. We need to allow children to dip their hands into water and actually feel it.

Temperature

Many fearful children have *vasoconstriction*, which means they have trouble regulating their temperature. This brings us to another important point: We can regulate our body not just with tactile objects, but also with temperature. Many anxious children find a warm heat pack on their neck or shoulders to be very therapeutic and calming.

Other children find cold objects or water on their skin calming. If you have a child who gets distressed and anxious easily, encourage them to either put a cloth with cold water on their face many times throughout the day or go to the bathroom and place cold water on their face. Cold water applied to the face can quickly help calm and regulate a distressed child by sending safety cues directly to the brain stem. An interesting study found that swimming in cold water could possibly reduce symptoms of depression.[4] *Please note: swimming in cold water should be done with an adult present who can help if something goes wrong; ice swimming is not recommended for children without a discussion with a medical professional first.*

Some children prefer slime to Play-Doh; now, we don't know for sure, but we suspect one of the reasons why might be that slime tends to be colder than Play-Doh; the coldness of it may help regulate some children.

Weighted Objects

Weighted blankets have also become incredibly popular for managing anxiety. Children, and even adults, can wrap themselves in a weighted blanket to help them feel safe and secure. We have used these with many children, and they have been tremendously therapeutic. It is suggested that they should be about 10 percent of a child's weight; however, some children do like heavier ones. *Warning: weighted blankets are a suffocation risk if not used correctly or if they are too heavy for a child,*[5] *so we do urge caution.*

A similar concept is weighted toys. These are like regular soft toys, but they are usually quite a bit bigger and have weights in them. They are useful to cuddle with and hold on the lap.

Many modern blankets are very thin, some children like really thick blankets made out of Dacron (a material like cotton wool that is used for stuffing). They may like blankets that are ten to fifteen centimeters thick; they say they feel safe and secure under them. Adults know that thickness does not necessarily mean an object is heavier or stronger, but children seem to feel safer in thicker blankets, even if this is somewhat of an illusion.

Physical Contact

One of the best and most soothing forms of touch we can have is from a loving adult. Tragically, we live in a world where loving touch is misinterpreted, and many times an adult wants to touch a child, the assumption is that they are up to no good. Obviously pedophilia has a disastrous impact on children and we must work hard to eliminate it, but this constant worldview deprives children of one of the most important aspects of real love—physical contact.

We see that, tragically, these assumptions have even extended to Santa Claus. Around the world, there have been many attempts to stop children sitting on Santa's knee by having them sit beside him. This is tragic because children need the connection of another human being. They need that physical contact.

Obviously, we must not force physical contact on children if they don't want it. But we have gone too far by cutting out almost all physical contact with children.

Safe physical contact is what children need because it helps them regulate. The fact that we have taken this away from many children could be one of the reasons we have such high rates of anxiety today.

Different Needs

Each child is different. If a child does not like any of the techniques you are trying, we suggest you stop using them. What one child may like, another child may hate. A good example of this can be slime. Some children really love playing with slime. Playing with slime can calm and soothe some children, while other children absolutely hate it and can become distressed by it.

It is important to find out what works when a child is calm. If a child is becoming upset and you place something in their hands that upsets them, this will make the situation worse. When your child is calm and peaceful, ask them, "What kinds of things do you like to hold and touch?" It helps if you have a few examples present, such as different fabrics, tassels, bark, or stones.

Putting the Theory into Practice

Let's imagine you have two children, a son and a daughter. You tried out a few sensory objects with both your children when they are calm and discovered your son likes memory foam toys and the sister likes Playdough.

Your son wants to play with one of the toys your daughter is using. You notice he is starting to get upset. You quickly grab a soft memory foam toy and start pushing this in and out in front of him. You place yourself at his eye level and calmly ask what is going on. Then you place the memory foam toy into his hands.

Notice you are not saying, "Calm down" or, "You need to play nicely together," but rather you are subtly getting him to do something that will distract and calm him at the same time. You can also add some of the other de-escalation techniques we mentioned in an earlier chapter.

Conclusion

In this chapter, we have suggested a number of sensory objects that can help with touch. As we said, every child is different. When you find that something works, we suggest you keep using it. You will have to experiment and see what else your child may like. Remember that some children will find sensations very difficult because they have processing issues or are on the autistic spectrum. If a child doesn't like some of the suggestions, then obviously don't continue.

Chapter Eight:
Calming Using Sight

"Many have sight but few have vision."
—*Naren Nagin*

The next sense we want to look at is our sense of sight. One of the significant problems we have today is that many children are over-stimulated by too much information. Sometimes the first thing we need to do is to remove information to calm them down.

Kathleen Liberty did a lot of research into the effects of the Christchurch earthquakes on children. She found that many children were overstimulated in classrooms. Many children found the vast number of pictures and mobiles hanging from the ceiling quite distressing.[1] Some people may say this work is specific to regions where there have been frequent earthquakes, but we have seen children who have not been exposed to earthquakes become overstimulated by too many pictures. We have learned from her work that it's important to ask children if they find too many pictures overwhelming; sometimes removing objects and pictures can be really helpful.

It's beneficial to have some white space; if there are posters everywhere, this can be overwhelming. Have you ever seen a full-page newspaper ad where there's just a few words in the middle? You might think that's a huge waste of space, but that empty space made you notice and read those few words, whereas you may have skipped over many other pages of cluttered ads. Sometimes the power of white space can be hugely underestimated, but it is very important. Some children should not have the walls of their bedrooms covered in posters and artwork; some need blank areas to prevent them from becoming overstimulated.

We also suggest trying to limit the amount of information that children see on screens. If you watch news clips from the 1950s and '60s, they tend to be very slow. The scenes take a lot longer and they don't jump from image to image. One of the problems today is that many TV shows use incredibly quick editing. While this is okay once in a while, we think if some children repeatedly see this, it may over-stimulate them. A study found that children who watch fast-paced cartoons had poorer memory and self-control.[2] It would be really beneficial to have some time with children not in front of screens.

Nature

Ideally children should be spending time in nature. The book *The Nature Fix* by Florence Williams presents hundreds of studies that show just how calming being in nature can be. Real trees emit chemicals called phytoncides. These chemicals help reduce stress, but they also seem to help boost our immunity by increasing natural killer cells in our bodies.[3]

A 2018 study found that when vacant building lots in Philadelphia were replaced with green space, it led to a 9 percent reduction in assaults with guns, as well as reductions in burglaries and vandalism![4]

A review of studies looking at how nature therapy could help people with post-traumatic stress disorder (PTSD) found that when people with PTSD underwent nature therapy, they showed a significant improvement in their symptoms and quality of life.[5]

If people are not able to access nature, putting up pictures of nature—such as forests, seaside scenes, or rivers and mountains—can also be very therapeutic and calming.

Water

Being around water can be very calming and therapeutic. In *Blue Mind*, Wallace Nichols uses a number of studies to illustrate how being around water can be calming. Often people who are stressed find it very calming to go and sit by a lake, a river, or the sea. (This is one of the reasons beachfront property comes at a premium!) Where possible, we suggest taking distressed children to be around water; it can have an amazingly calming effect. Of course, you do need to be careful about water safety with children.

Some households and schools have aquariums. Children can almost be mesmerized when they see the fish silently swimming around. If for some reason you can't have one, you can get aquarium videos on YouTube that can also be quite calming. These are very popular—one video of activity on a coral reef has over thirteen million views!

Color Blue

Water is often related to the color blue; in fact, many people find the color blue itself calming and soothing. Light blue, with some vibrancy, tends to be better than navy or depressing blue/gray colors. Remarkably, researchers have found that placing blue lights in an area where a high number of suicides occur reduced the suicide rate by a phenomenal 84 percent![6] Your child may not get to the point of suicide, but using blue light could be a technique to take them out of an enraged state.

If you would like to know more about the effect of the color blue, you can read the book by Wallace Nichols in which he argues that the color blue is in itself calming.

Fractals

One of the incredible things found in nature is fractals. Fractals are repeating shapes that get smaller and smaller. An example of this is a tree: it starts off with a large trunk, then divides into smaller branches, and those divide into smaller branches, and so on. Scientists have found that fractals are very pleasing to the eye and help us feel calm.[7] We see these everywhere in nature, but they are less common in cities where many things are made of concrete

Example of a fractal found in nature.

blocks. The fact we see few fractals in the modern world may make us more on edge than if we were in nature.

An example of a manmade fractal is the art of Jackson Pollock.

A class of students in front of a Jackson Pollock painting.
Photo credit: TLF Images

To many people, Jackson Pollock's artwork looks like someone threw paint on a canvas, yet art critics insist his paintings are masterpieces (one of his paintings sold for $120 million US dollars!). When Jackson Pollock was alive, the power of fractals was not known. It wasn't until recently that discoveries show he used fractals in his art![8] It turns out one of the reasons so many people like his paintings is because they use fractals, which are calming. So there is more to his work than many realized. Where possible we should try and allow children to look at fractals; this can quickly take away their stress and calm them down.

Coloring

In the past few years, many adult coloring books have been produced. These often involve intricate patterns that adults need to carefully color in. Although these coloring books are designed for adults, many children also enjoy them, or slightly simpler versions. Many children also find doodling—or creating random shapes on a page without trying to draw things accurately—can be helpful.

There is something very powerful about being able to express yourself through art. If this is used as a calming technique, it should not be graded or evaluated in any way. That destroys the value of the activity.

Michael remembers that when he was in school, there was a child who never spoke up and was "never good at anything." One day, the teacher started talking about colors and visual things; this child suddenly came alive and got every single question right. The teacher was astonished at this. She realized that the student needed to be taught with visual aids. After this discovery, the child did much better in school.

Photographs of Family

A technique that isn't utilized often is to have a child keep a picture of anyone who they find calming. Sometimes this can cause children more stress because they miss their loved one, but for others, it is really helpful. As we say multiple times throughout this book, there is no one-size-fits-all solution. It's about adapting and trying to work out what may work for your child.

Putting the Theory into Practice

You have a child who needs to go to the doctor to get an injection. The last time you tried this, they screamed their lungs out for an hour beforehand. They kicked you and, when you tried to take them by the hand, bit you.

This time you do things differently. Their injection is at 4:30 p.m. After school at 3 p.m., you take them to a beach, a calm river, or a small forest or green area. You encourage them to walk with you in nature, suggest they walk around and collect sticks and stones, or get them to splash their feet in the river. We recommend allowing them to have a good hour in nature to significantly reduce their stress levels—five minutes won't be enough time. After this, you can take them to the doctor. The time in nature should have reduced their stress levels considerably. They may still get upset when they go to the doctor, but they should be far less upset than without the time in nature.

Chapter Nine:
Calming Using Sound

"Music has charms to soothe a savage breast,
to soften rocks, or bend a knotted oak."
—*William Congreve*

When we become angry, we lose our ability to understand words such as *calm down*. However, that does not mean to say that we cannot use sound to soothe people who might be distressed or anxious. There can be other sounds that people find very therapeutic.

Music

When some people get upset, they are not sure how to release these feelings in a positive way. Some people find that listening to tranquil music takes away a lot of their anger and rage. It seems to help lower people's blood pressure and distract them from the thing that has upset them.

Creating music can also be a fantastic outlet for a lot of people. In his book *Scattered Minds*, Dr. Gabor Maté shares the story of when he was asked to teach a very difficult map reading class. Many teachers had tried with this class and failed. On the first day, he gathered all the musical instruments he could find. He took the children to the workshop, where they spent an hour making as much noise as they possibly could. The only rule was if you were there, you had to take part. The next day, he was able to teach map reading. No other teacher had been able to get anything out of the group. After that one day of musical stimulation, the group came back and was able to learn.

Music can be a fantastic outlet for many people. If people are creating music to be soothing, it's really important that this is not graded or judged in any way. As soon as that happens, it often adds to stress and renders the exercise useless.

Nature

In the last chapter, we talked about how the sight of nature can be calming. As well as the sights, the sounds of nature—such as whales or birds—are also very calming. Many of these sounds are available on YouTube; for example, you can find "eight hours of whale sounds" or "eight hours of forest sounds." It can be best to download these because YouTube can be interrupted by ads (not helpful if you are trying to stay calm). Playing this around a child can immediately help them to regulate their system.

Sound and Sleep

When children have poor sleep, they tend to be much more angry and irritable. We have a whole chapter on sleep, but for now we wanted to cover two points. Some people say they can only get to sleep with the sound of white noise. Sometimes children say they want to sleep with a fan on. They don't necessarily want the warm or cool air from the fan; rather, they want the sound that it makes. If you look on YouTube, sometimes there are eight-hour playlists of just white noise. This can be really helpful for some people. As we've said throughout this book, some of these techniques will work for some people while others will find they won't be able to benefit from those same techniques. There will be some people who find it harder to get to sleep with noise in the background, but for other people, it really helps them.

Scientists have found that a type of "pink noise" (a bit like static but sounds more like a waterfall) also helps. You can also find eight-hour videos of pink noise on YouTube. Pink noise is similar to white noise, but it has different frequencies. The article in *Time* magazine called "The Sound of 'Pink Noise' Improves Sleep and Memory" has a good overview of this.[1] If you have a child who struggles to sleep, you could try playing both white and pink noise while they sleep to try and help them sleep more peacefully.

Mindfulness

One other thing that can be helpful for some people is mindfulness. There are several places in this book where mindfulness could go, but we decided to put it here because many people listen to guided mindfulness exercises that involve tranquil music.

Mindfulness is a type of meditation. There many websites that offer free or guided meditations that are often accompanied by calming music or sounds.

A simple form of this is to breathe in slowly and breathe out slowly; imagine you are breathing in calm and breathing out anger. You might repeat this ten or fifteen times. Breathing out creates a chemical called GABA, or gamma-aminobutyric acid. This is one of the naturally calming chemicals in your body. This is why mindfulness can be effective.

Someone we saw at 298 Youth Health was so anxious with the thought of going to school that she vomited uncontrollably. We gave her some mindfulness exercises to do, and, after using them for a few days, she was able to go to school.

For some people, mindfulness can have an extraordinary effect on their well-being. It can help them calm down and remove a lot of stress or worry; however, mindfulness does not work for everyone. One study found 25 percent of people who try mindfulness have unpleasant experiences with it. The results also suggest that mindfulness could increase anger and even cause PTSD-like symptoms in some people.[2] Mindfulness can be helpful for some people, but if it is causing a child distress, we urge you to stop immediately. Mindfulness is not a magic cure that will work for everyone.

Putting the Theory into Practice

It is the last few days of the school break. Your child really doesn't like school. You know they start to have more tantrums in the lead-up to school returning. Find some cheap musical instruments—even toy ones will do—and let your child play them. Encourage them to make noise for the fun of it (but remember to respect the neighbors!). Remind your child that this is just about having fun; there is no assessment. They can just play random sounds.

The less planned and rigid this is, the better. Hopefully doing this should start to release a lot of the tension and worry they have about school. It can give the child something to distract themselves from the worry. If we sit with our worries, we tend to make them bigger and bigger. When we distract ourselves, we stop the worries from growing.

In this chapter, we have shown how sound can be used to calm children. We really encourage you to explore other ways that sounds might be able to help regulate your children.

Chapter Ten:
Calming Using Taste

"Laughter is brightest in the place where the food is."
—Irish Proverb

We previously showed you the image of the cortical homunculus—the image of how our brain represents parts of the body according to the attention it devotes to touch. As well as having large hands, the homunculus also has large lips. We gain a lot of sensory information from our lips and tongue, so it is worth considering oral techniques to help regulation.

First of all, it's important to know just how relaxing the method of chewing can be. We are hard-wired to stay alive. If we don't eat, we start to feel anxious, because we eat to stay alive. The action of chewing and eating is naturally self-soothing and calming.

Many people will be horrified to hear this because they say food should never be used to soothe. They say, "We have an obesity epidemic." Rather, we urge caution using some of the things we are about to suggest rather than removing this way to self-soothe altogether.

Anxious people frequently have trouble regulating their temperature when they feel hot. When people are too hot, they get angry more easily. Sucking on ice may help with this. The cold sensation of ice is not just helpful to calm anxiety; many schools have begun giving popsicles to children who are having panic attacks. The act of licking something cold slows down a person's breathing and stops the panic and distress; it can also help soothe an overactive brain stem. If you're worried about the sugar content of popsicles, just sucking on ice cubes can be helpful (although the ones adults put in their drinks are often too big for children, but you can buy molds to make smaller ones).

In her work with children who experienced the Christchurch

earthquake, Kathleen Liberty found that having cold water bottles on classroom desks also helped to regulate anxious children. When we get anxious, we get a dry mouth because the body's emergency response diverts saliva away from our tongue. People who are anxious often need more water to regulate themselves.

Another thing Kathleen Liberty found helpful in regulating children was having a snack after play time. Many children have morning tea during the break, but she found that having it when the students returned to class after playing was more soothing and helped regulate problematic behavior.[1] It is hard to know why this worked, but it could be the act of chewing helped calm and regulate the students after they were active during play time.

You can buy a product called "chewable shark teeth"; these are nontoxic toys that children can chew on. Many children say chewing or sucking on one of these helps them to feel calm and regulated.

Putting the Theory into Practice

You have a twelve-year-old son who seems to be anxious about everything. At night, you put two or three bottles of water in the fridge and some ice cubes in the freezer. When he wakes up, you give him a glass of cold water with ice in it. Throughout the day, make sure he has a bottle with him that keeps water cold. (Plastic water bottles are not good at keeping things cold. There are insulated water bottles that are not too expensive that can keep drinks cold.) You can also encourage him to put a cold face cloth on his face several times throughout the day. You should find that after a few days of doing this, he will become less anxious and agitated.

Conclusion

Many children naturally find the acts of chewing, licking, and sucking to be therapeutic. As much as possible, we must try and make opportunities for this to happen in a safe way.

Chapter Eleven:
Calming Using Smell

"Smell is a potent wizard that transports you across thousands of miles and all the years you have lived."
—*Helen Keller*

We don't need to explain how the other senses work; most people understand them at least a little. But when it comes to smell, many people don't understand how it works, so we start this chapter with a few interesting facts about the way we process smell, and then we look at how we can use smell to calm a child.

Your other four senses (sight, sound, taste, and touch) all have to go through a part of the brain called the *thalamus*, but smell goes directly to some of the emotional parts of the brain: the amygdala and the hippocampus. This means that for many people, smells bring on

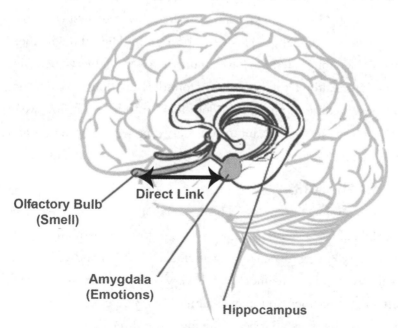

The route smell signals travel through our brain.

strong emotions. The fact that our sense of smell is directly connected to the hippocampus—which is one of the memory bits of the brain— also means that smells can conjure up strong memories. Many people who smell Play-Doh say it instantly reminds them of their childhood.[1] Therefore, we believe that smell could be one of the most underutilized techniques helping children stay calm and relaxed.

We tend to think that some animals, such as dogs, have a strong sense of smell, while humans have a weak sense of smell.[2] Yet researchers are discovering more and more that humans do have a strong sense of smell and that smell can have a profound effect on us, even if we don't realize it.

A group of researchers from Stony Brook University in New York asked first-time skydivers to place sweat pads under their arms.[1] As they were first-time skydivers, they were very nervous. Next, the researchers asked people who were calm and well-rested to inhale the smell of the sweat through a nebulizer. (They didn't tell the subjects what was being inhaled.) They found that the subjects had elevated stress levels just by smelling the sweat. When this study first came out, many scientists thought, "This can't be right." They thought there wouldn't be enough sweat to have an impact on the subjects' behavior or emotions. And yet, this is what they found. Even though we may not consciously realize it, often smell does have an impact on how we're feeling. This is very important to consider when we are trying to calm anxious children.

How Smell Works

Smell is extremely complex. The makers of perfumes often have great difficulties because it is not as straightforward as many people assume. If you mix two colors together, such as blue and yellow, it is easy to predict the outcome. Smell is very different; if you mix three sweet smells together, you may assume you would get a sweet smell. But strange things can happen—mixing those three sweet smells may produce something that smells like vomit! Later we will suggest using different smells to calm your child; just be aware that mixing pleasant smells together may have unintentional results, so it is best to stick with one.

It's important to know that when it comes to smell, there is no hard-wiring. With all the other senses, everyone around the world interprets them mostly the same way. If you take someone from any place in the world and put sugar on their tongue, they should taste sweetness (unless they have experienced a brain injury or something).

Michael was speaking about this in one of his seminars when a woman interrupted him and said, "I like the smell of cow dung." Michael paused and looked curiously at this woman, as did everyone else. They were wondering, "Is this a joke or is she serious?" Then she said she grew up on a farm. As paradoxical as it sounds, she found the smell of cow dung calming because it reminded her of home.

Smell and Dysregulation

We have seen examples where children who smell unpleasant things seem to be difficult to calm down and often remain agitated for a long time. For example a child who walks into a room with an unpleasant smell may complain about it 20 minutes after they walk in. Many adults think the child is being deliberately disruptive, but maybe they are far more distressed by the unpleasant smell than we realize.

A fascinating study published in 2020 found that when people felt disgust, they were more likely to smell unpleasant smells, even if there wasn't an unpleasant smell present!.[3] Tragically, many instances of bullying revolve around body odor. We often think that children are being rude if they point out someone else has body odor, but perhaps they're trying to say, "I find the smell unpleasant; I would like you to do something about it." Bullies who bully about smell could be one of the most misunderstood groups in society.

It's important to remember that smells that can be calming for one person may cause the opposite reaction for another. When trying to use smell to help a distressed child, listen to them carefully when they tell you if it helps or not.

Using Smell to Regulate

In the past, people who were anxious were given Valium to sniff, which often calmed them down. Today, the power of smell has been somewhat rediscovered with aromatherapy. You can now buy diffusers that put certain smells into the air. A possible way to use this is to find out what type of smells your child finds calming (for example, lavender). During a situation that a child finds challenging, such as taking a bath, you could have a diffuser in the bathroom spraying lavender, which may help to calm them down.

Again, aromatherapy does not work for everyone, but there are several smells that some people find really helpful. One study claimed the smell of jasmine was just as therapeutic as taking Valium.[4] Other people find the smells of lavender or peppermint really helpful.

In a later chapter, we show that disrupted sleep from nightmares can increase behavioral problems in children. Smell may be an innovative way to address this.

Perhaps the most promising study looked at the effect of pleasant smells on PTSD.[‡] People who had severe PTSD were given pleasant smells to sniff at night and reported better sleep and fewer nightmares. While this study was conducted with participants aged twenty to fifty-nine,[5] this could potentially be a useful strategy to help children who have PTSD, because their brains are not typically developed enough for many other forms of therapy to work well.

One of the most powerful techniques with smell might be having a parent or caregiver carry a piece of cloth around with them during the day. This will get the loved one's scent on the material so an anxious child could carry it at school.

While we are not aware of any studies on this, many hospitals employ this technique when children have to stay at the hospital by themselves. Putting the cloth under the child's pillow often helped them sleep well. The reverse of this also seems to work; many new parents become distressed if their children end up in incubators and they can't hold them. Getting parents to have something with the child's scent can help calm the parents.[6] A calm parent is imperative, because if they are not calm, how can they calm a child?

Putting the Theory into Practice

You have a child who seems to cope well at school. The teachers report no outbursts or behavioral problems. Yet, when the child comes home, they throw countless tantrums. They may be overwhelmed at school and hold it together until they come home, then all that stress is released. When you pick them up, you could have a handful of real jasmine in the car. Away from the school, pull over and ask your child to spend ten to twenty minutes sniffing the jasmine on the car ride home. This may help take away a lot of the stress from school. You should find that after doing this, the child will be much calmer at home and have fewer tantrums.

Conclusion

We often think about our other four senses to calm distressed children, but the sense of smell is often neglected. Hopefully, in this chapter we have encouraged you to think about a number of different ways in which smells may aggravate or calm your child. One of the reasons many people don't think of smell as a calming technique is because we can't see it, so we often forget about it. As we have shown, though, it can be a powerful tool for some children.

Chapter Twelve:
The Soothing Power of Animals

"Animals are such agreeable friends—they ask no questions; they pass
no criticisms."
—*George Eliot*

A nimals can have a tremendously calming influence on children. There's a form of therapy called *animal-assisted therapy*. This has been developed for people who have experienced significant trauma and developed PTSD. One study found that people who have PTSD experienced less hypervigilance and a better quality of life with the presence of animals.[1] Animals are not just a way to calm people who have PTSD; they can be a way to calm dysregulated and aggressive children.

Animal-assisted therapy was developed for people who struggle with trusting anyone, which often happens when a child has been through a significant trauma, such as abuse. The therapy involves learning to look after and care for an animal. This process can be tremendously therapeutic. It can teach empathy and have a fantastically calming effect on some people. Sometimes people don't need full therapy; having a pet or being around animals will do.

We have suggested to several parents of children with severe anxiety or PTSD that they get a pet. It was a carefully thought-out decision and, for some of these children, changed them dramatically. After they got a pet, they've had far fewer tantrums and explosive outbursts and are now a lot calmer, even when they are not around the animal. Many children find it very calming to have an animal in their room at night, which helps them go to sleep (we will discuss sleep in a later chapter).

It is also important to think about the disadvantages. Owning a pet is a big responsibility. You need to think about whether your child really wants a pet for the lifespan of the animal or if the child will lose interest in it after a few days. Think about the costs associated with a pet in terms of food and vet bills, and whether your child might be allergic to the pet.

Some of the pets that tend to be really calming for children are cats, dogs, and rabbits. It's important to think carefully about your situation before you choose a pet. We have mentioned that children and young people under the age of twenty-five often hear higher-pitched sounds than adults do. If children have sensory issues (discussed in a later chapter), getting a dog with a high-pitched yelp is probably not a good idea. It is really important to think very carefully about the type of animal you want to choose. By and large, we recommend animals that are really calm. It is also worth considering the age of an animal; puppies and kittens are cute, but they are more hyperactive.

If you are considering getting a pet for a child with behavioral issues, we strongly encourage you to include the child in the decision-making process rather than making it a surprise.

Dogs

There are multiple dog breeds that can be particularly good: Irish setters, beagles, Labrador retrievers, and golden retrievers. It's important to make sure the kind of dog is something your child wants. Some children like to have dogs for protection, but if the dog is aggressive, this choice may backfire and ultimately cause the child more distress.

Cats

Cats can be tremendously helpful as well. We have found that pedigree cats—although typically more expensive—are often a lot calmer than mixed-breed cats. For example, mixed-breed cats may scratch and bite, whereas pedigree cats are often much gentler. They are less likely to bite or scratch if they're treated well. Older cats tend to be calmer than younger cats. Some really good pedigree cats that can have calming influence on children are Siamese cats, Ragdolls, and Maine Coons.

Rabbits

And, of course, there are rabbits. As these are smaller, they are usually easier to take care of, and children often love to cuddle them. Also, they tend to move a bit slower and are often more placid than cats or dogs.

Can't Have Pets?

We are aware that not everyone can own a pet. Maybe you have a small or rented house, or maybe you don't have the finances to support a pet. There are many programs where children can volunteer to look after animals. Maybe there is a local petting zoo or animal shelter. These organizations are usually looking for people who can volunteer to look after the animals. See what is in your area with a Google search.

There may also be some cat or dog breeders who would be willing to help. If you explain to the breeder that this opportunity could help a child with behavioral issues, they might be able to let you come over once or twice a week. Even this quantity can be really helpful. The fact that you aren't able to afford an animal shouldn't stop a child from getting the help they need.

Conclusion

Having something in your arms that you can stroke, pat, or cuddle can be amazingly therapeutic. It's important to teach children how to look after an animal, how to hold them in ways that don't hurt or upset them, and how to feed them. Pets can be a tremendous tool for managing children who easily become distressed and upset.

Chapter Thirteen:
Conclusions for Section One

In this section, we have looked at some of the reasons why children misbehave and throw tantrums. We covered the fact that many children who act out are distressed and fearful. We hope that after reading this section, you will perceive children who act out as feeling distressed and unsafe rather than naughty. Just understanding this often means that you have a better knowledge of how to address many of the challenges that you have in front of you.

Next, we looked at child development and how understanding the abilities and limitations of a child's brain will help you find effective strategies in helping calm distressed and upset children.

After this, we looked at a number of de-escalation strategies, such as saying, "You are not in trouble," and really acknowledging children's feelings and emotions.

Then we looked at the ways the five senses and animals can be used to calm a child.

These are things that can be used to help calm a child who is already upset or distressed. This is about twenty-five percent of the book.

The next, much larger section looks at the underlying causes of problematic behavior. We don't want you to have to use these de-escalation techniques multiple times a day. We want to look at why children become upset in the first place and how to address these issues so they don't keep having tantrums.

In the final chapter of this book, we have worked up some examples that show you how to put everything you have learned into practice.

In the first part of this book, we looked at what you can do if you have an angry and upset child in front of you. Now we want to look at some of the significant, underlying causes of this behavior.

Section Two:

What Can Cause This Behavior?

Chapter Fourteen:
The Importance of Good Sleep

"That we are not much sicker and much madder than we are is due exclusively to that most blessed and blessing of all natural graces, sleep."
—Aldous Huxley

If you take a child with moderate behavioral problems and add poor sleep into the mix, the child's behavior will deteriorate dramatically. Exhausted children can become even more angry, tearful, aggressive, and exceptionally challenging to manage.

There is no one magic cure when it comes to behavioral problems in children; however, improving sleep can make a huge difference for many of them. We are surprised how many modern behavioral books don't mention sleep. It is a sad omission in the light of what we have learned in the last thirty years. If you are not sure where to start to improve a child's behavior, we suggest trying to improve your child's sleep as a first step.

The tips in this chapter are not just for children; many adults reading this chapter will find it really helpful to improve their own sleep and, therefore, well-being. Adults who are well-rested have far more tolerance and ability to manage challenging children.

When we talk about health and well-being, we often emphasize eating well and exercising. But researchers now believe that sleep could be more important than eating well and exercising. Every single biological process in the human body improves with good sleep. This includes digestion, immunity, memory, self-control, blood flow, and circulation.[1] It is staggering just how many processes are affected by sleep.

If you take a perfectly healthy person with no history of mental illness and you deprive the person of sleep for two or three days, the person may start to hallucinate.[2] Even if children don't get to the point of having hallucinations, poor sleep starts to cause significant problems. In fact, sleep deprivation has such a negative impact on our well-being that it was used as a form of torture in the past!

Sleep Cycle

There are five main stages of the sleep cycle. Stages one through four are called NREM, or non–rapid eye movement; stage five is called REM, or rapid eye movement. NREM sleep is important in helping with memory and increasing well-being, while REM sleep helps a person processes a lot of their memories from the previous day.[3]

A person goes through a complete cycle of these stages roughly every 90 to 120 minutes. Someone with good sleep should cycle through these stages four or five times. Scientists have found that the last stage of REM sleep is deeper and longer than the others and seems to be more restorative than the other phases.[4] If we wake someone up an hour before they finish their natural sleep cycle, we often think, "Oh, it's just an hour, it doesn't matter," but we are depriving them of the most critical and restorative part of their sleep. We cannot neglect that final hour or two.

Sleep Pressure

One of the most important concepts to understand is sleep pressure (the technical name for this is *homeostatic sleep drive*). We often hope that if we put children to bed at a certain time, they will fall asleep. We assume that if we can eat whenever we want, then we should be able to sleep whenever we want. But sleep does not work this way. Sleeping and eating are very different.

In order to get to sleep, quite a few complex processes need to happen within the body. Sleep is largely controlled by a part of the brain called the *suprachiasmatic nucleus*. We can't just turn on sleep when we want it; we need sleep pressure and melatonin. For most people, this needs to build up during the day. If we have a short nap two hours before we go to sleep for the night, we reduce the sleep pressure and it takes us longer to get to sleep when we want to sleep for the night.

Sleep pressure can be affected by cortisol. If we have too much cortisol in our system, it is hard to sleep. Cortisol can be brought on by stress and anxiety.

If we try and put children to bed when they are not ready to fall asleep, their biology will prevent them from sleeping. We often get upset with children who don't go to sleep when we want them to; more often than not, it is not their behavior, but rather their biology.

Sleep pressure can also work in the opposite way. If we have not had sleep, the need builds up and builds up until it forces us to sleep. This is why some children fall asleep during class; despite desperately trying to stay awake, their bodies demand sleep.

How Much Sleep Do You Need?

Most adults need between seven and nine hours of sleep. Children, depending on their age, need two to four additional hours. Some people say, "I don't need that; I can survive on four." Researchers have found that, although some people say they can manage on less, they don't actually realize how much of an impact sleep deprivation has on them. A large study by Michigan University suggested the effects of sleep deprivation have been greatly underestimated. The study found people who are sleep deprived are much more likely to make mistakes on tasks that require multiple steps to complete, such as following a recipe.[5] A 2019 study found that people who suffered from insomnia performed more poorly on a test than people who were well-rested, which refutes the idea that people adapt to sleep deprivation.[6]

Consistent Sleep

Scientists have also found that consistent sleep is really important for well-being. Erratic sleep tends to cause severe mental health problems.[7]

An example of erratic sleep would be someone who goes to sleep at 7 p.m. one night, 2 a.m. the next night, and 10 p.m. the night after that. Ideally, we need consistent times of sleep.

Broken Sleep

Researchers have also found that broken sleep is far worse for our well-being than short naps. Broken sleep occurs when we go to sleep for, say, an hour, then we get woken up, then we go to sleep for another hour and get woken up. Eight single hours of sleep are not the same as eight continuous hours of sleep. Full and complete sleep is important. Scientists have found that people who experience broken sleep tend to have higher rates of mental illness and other negative outcomes.[8]

Too Much Sleep

We will talk about problems with lack of sleep, but we want you to know that hypersomnia, or sleeping for longer than is normal on a regular basis, can also cause very similar problems to the ones we will mention. If this affects you or your children, you should get help from a health professional.

Effects of Sleep Loss

Mental Illness

Studies have found a significant relationship between poor sleep and mental illness. We used to think sleep problems were a result of mental illness, but we now believe it may also be the other way around. We now believe that poor sleep can trigger, cause, or exacerbate mental illness.[9]

Two very interesting studies found that when people are sleep deprived, they find it harder to remember good or happy memories, but they remember bad memories quite strongly. The researchers also found that poor sleep is associated with a rise in depression and anxiety.[10]

A study found that after just one night of poor sleep the amygdala, one of the parts of the brain associated with processing fear, showed 60 percent more activation![11] The researchers also found that the prefrontal cortex, a part of the brain that regulates and calms fear, did not work as well when participants were sleep deprived.

A study of adults found that night owls (people who naturally have a later sleep cycle) have a 12 percent higher rate of depression than morning people.[12] The world is designed for people who function well in the morning and those with an earlier sleep cycle. (We are both night owls, so we want more people to know about this research! We should start a group called the The Society for the Conservation and Preservation of Night Owls!)

Sickness and Injury

Cortisol is one of the stress- and anxiety-inducing hormones. You naturally get this at different times during the day and night. Your cortisol levels are supposed to rise in the morning, which helps you wake up, and then gradually drop away throughout the day and into the night. However, researchers have found that if you are sleep deprived, this process is disrupted and you tend to have more cortisol in your system later in the day. You tend to feel more anxious and it becomes a vicious cycle: poor sleep causes your anxiety to rise, and anxiety makes it harder to get a good night's sleep.

Cortisol can also suppress the immune system. If you have more cortisol in your system because of poor sleep, this increases your chances of catching colds and getting sick. Researchers have found that poor sleep also seems to disrupt T cells, which help fight off diseases.[13] If our T cells have been disrupted, it makes us far more vulnerable to illness.

Researchers have also found that when people are sleep deprived, they tend to feel pain more intensely than people who are well-rested.[14] If someone has moderate back pain and sleeps well, they may be able to go to work or school, but if they sleep poorly, that same injury may mean they need to stay home. Poor sleep often makes a moderate pain an intolerable pain.

Weight Gain

Poor sleep is also associated with weight gain. You have two hormones in your body called *ghrelin* and *leptin*. When you eat, they are supposed to send a signal to your brain saying, "I'm full; stop eating." Scientists have found that if people are sleep deprived, this hormone doesn't activate.[15] People eat and eat, and they feel hungry even when they're full.

There may be another way sleep affects the way we eat. Two interesting studies suggest that we feel more pleasure when we see food when we are sleep deprived than when we are well-rested.[16] In other words, when we are well-rested, we may have a moderate desire to eat a chocolate bar, yet when we are sleep deprived, we may see it as irresistible.

Teenagers

We may think teenage brain development starts at age thirteen, when children become teenagers, but in reality, it could be five years earlier for some children, so it is important that parents of younger children are aware of this. Many teenagers have a different sleep cycle from adults.[17] We call a natural sleeping pattern a *chronotype*. Often, teenagers naturally want to go to sleep two to three hours after an adult. They're not being difficult or defiant when they want to stay up late. This is what their biology is programmed to do. Furthermore, they probably need an extra two hours of sleep.

In the United States, there is a movement called Start Schools Later (see their website at www.startschoollater.net). The movement's aim is to ensure that secondary school start times are informed by the latest and most up-to-date scientific research. Generally speaking, they have found that if high schools start later, to give students full and complete sleep, students perform much better academically and have far less sickness. This is mostly for high schools, but some primary schools may need to start looking at this for their older students.

An American study suggested that the US economy could save $9.3 billion a year and $140 billion over fifteen years if we could help students get better sleep.[18]

School start times and teenagers are a little bit more complicated. One study gives a deeper overview of the research, suggesting that chronotype (whether you are a morning or evening person) and stress levels play a role in how sleep affects academic performance.[19]

Difficulty Learning

Many behavioral modification techniques rely on teaching children new skills, such as remembering to breathe slowly when they are distressed. One possible reason why so many children forget these new skills could be because of poor sleep.

A number of interesting studies show just how much of an impact sleep has on our memory.[20] Researchers have found that if you sleep poorly, it's much harder to remember things you've learned the previous day.

An intriguing study found that if children are trying to learn a new skill involving movement and coordination, such as playing the piano, they need a good night's sleep after learning the skill to master the task.[21] We now know that good sleep helps save memories into the brain.

Similarities to ADHD

The behaviors associated with ADHD can be displayed in people who sleep poorly. A 2020 study found that poor sleep seems to alter the parts of children's brains associated with impulse control.[22] Scientists have also found that when people sleep poorly, they want to move around a lot more and generally find it harder to concentrate.[23] Both of these behaviors are among the classic symptoms of ADHD.

ADHD is supposed to be a diagnosis by exclusion, which means that clinicians are supposed to rule out any other possible explanations; if they don't find anything else, only then are they supposed to diagnose ADHD. Tragically, we often see clinicians diagnose ADHD as the first option and they don't look at poor sleep as a possible cause of these behaviors.

Bullying and Aggression

In the last thirty years, schools have realized how devastating bullying can be to student's well-being, so they have invested large sums of money in anti-bullying programs. Unfortunately, anti-bullying programs often don't really work in schools.[24] Researchers have found that bullying and domestic violence tends to increase when children are sleep deprived.[25] It's entirely possible that anti-bullying programs don't work because they don't look at some of the key causes of bullying, including poor sleep.

A study of 202 college students in the United States found that students reported much more anger after a night of poor sleep.[26] We know that when we are tired, our tolerance for problems and things that annoy us decreases dramatically. This may be one reason why bullying and domestic violence increase when people are sleep deprived.

Another study may have found an explanation of why bullying and domestic violence may increase when we're sleep deprived. The researchers showed people pictures of different human faces. When people who were well-rested saw an expressionless face, they saw it as a blank face. But when people were sleep deprived, they saw this expressionless face as an angry face. So poor sleep changes our perception of the world.[27] If we want to get on top of bullying and aggression, one of the things we need to start looking at is poor sleep.

An interesting analogy is the length of a fuse on a stick of dynamite.

We often say when people get angry, they "have a short fuse." Good sleep may give us a long fuse and more patience for things that upset us.

Suicide

Suicide rates for ten- to fourteen year olds tripled between 2007 and 2014.[28] One significant factor many people don't consider in terms of suicide is sleep deprivation. Several studies have found that many suicides happen between 12 and 3 a.m., particularly in younger people.[29]

A different study found that many suicides also happen in the afternoon, often when people had been sleeping poorly beforehand.[30] If people have been up all night worrying, studying, or gaming, this may explain why the afternoon is a risk.

There could be other reasons why poor sleep is related to suicide. Researchers found that if we sleep poorly, we tend to have lower self-esteem.[31] Another study suggests that when we are sleep deprived, we tend to feel loneliness far more intensely than when we are well rested.[32]

We all know that when something goes wrong when we're sleep deprived, it often seems much worse than it actually is. If we want to get on top of suicide, then we need to get on top of sleep problems.

How Do You Know If Your Child Is Getting Enough Sleep?

Children probably need between nine and thirteen hours of sleep, depending on what age they are. A good way to know if you or a child is getting good sleep is to ask, "When I wake up, do I or does my child feel exhausted, or are we ready to go?" If you consistently wake up feeling exhausted, you may not be getting good sleep. It is normal after a long week to have one or two days where you may wake up feeling tired, but if this happens on a regular basis, then you are probably not getting the sleep you need. There are professional sleep tests you can take, but this question gives a good indication of the quality of your sleep.

Improving Your Sleep

We have shown many ways that poor sleep can affect our well-being. Now we want to look at how sleep problems can be addressed. Some people believe there are a number of lucky individuals who are born with good sleep and there are others who have bad sleep and there is nothing you can do to change this. This is not the case at all; the overwhelming majority of sleep problems can be addressed and improved.

Sunlight

There's a very interesting book by Linda Geddes called *Chasing the Sun*, which talks about how natural sunlight greatly improves the quality of our sleep because natural sunlight helps with melatonin production later at night. Often, we think of sleep preparation as something that we need to do just before bed, but really, we have to get the body ready for sleep during the day.

In Finland, a country where students perform better academically and have lower rates of mental illness, children have at least an hour outside every day.[34] Tragically, there are many Western schools where they have almost no time outside. This is a mistake and significantly disrupts the natural process of sleep. If we want our children to get more sleep, they need time in the sun and time to run around.

Cut Back on Caffeine

Caffeine is a stimulant, a chemical that wakes your body up. A study found that drinking 400 milligrams of caffeine (roughly 1 1/2 cups of coffee) up to six hours before bed reduces the average amount of sleep by one hour![35] Many energy drinks have high amounts of caffeine in them. So, if you have children who are having energy drinks at seven or eight o'clock at night, they're going to find it very hard to get a good night's sleep. Ideally, there should be no caffeine within six hours before bedtime. Even if people can sleep with caffeine in their system, it disrupts the quality of sleep.

Fear of the Dark and Noises

One of the biggest causes of sleep loss in children is fear. It can be fear that there are monsters under their bed, fear that the creaking sound is someone trying to break into the house, or just fear in general. Most adults know a dark room is fairly safe, but we need to look at this through a child's eyes. Often the reason children have tantrums before bed is because they're terrified of their bedrooms. Many adults like their beds; they think it's a safe place where they can finally relax, but a lot of children don't see it like this.

If children fear monsters under their bed, we suggest parents place bricks or other large objects under the bed so they know nothing can hide there. If children fear monsters in their closet, we suggest putting bells over the door to act as an alarm to wake the child up.

If children really don't want to go to bed, we have to ask why. For example, if a child hears a creaking sound, they may think it is a burglar or someone coming to attack them. Sometimes talking to children about how a house is made of wood and will naturally make some creaking sounds helps ease their fear. It can be worth taking a bit of time to stop and listen for some of these sounds during the day. It can really help to teach children the difference between the normal sounds that a creaking house makes and the sounds that an intruder would make.

We talked about pets in a previous chapter and have found some children do have a better time getting to sleep if they have an animal in the room; it makes them feel safe.

Nightmares

Many children with behavioral problems have nightmares, which disrupts their sleep and, in turn, becomes a vicious cycle. A few nightmares here and there seem to be part of normal childhood development, but it is important to know that if children are having nightmares every night, or multiple times a night, it needs to be addressed with a healthcare professional.

Dr. Justin Havens, a psychological therapist, created a short video available on YouTube called *From Nightmares to Peaceful Sleep with the Dream Completion Technique*. He uses a technique where, if people do have nightmares and they are woken up by them, he gets people to imagine the dream being completed in a way they would like. For example, if a child dreams they are always being chased by monsters, they could imagine turning into a large dinosaur and eating the monsters. The way people imagine the dream to finishing does not need to be realistic. This has mainly been tested on adults, but it may work for some children as well.

Sleep Apnea

Sleep apnea occurs when people have disrupted sleep because of breathing problems. They are often not aware that they have woken up, but their sleep cycle has been disrupted. A possible indicator that you have this is if you think you had a good night's sleep but you woke up exhausted.

We often associate sleep apnea with middle-aged men, but researchers are finding that a considerable number of children experience this.[33] If you think children seem to be sleeping well but they are waking up exhausted, it is worth getting this looked at.

Many people don't want to get help for this because they believe the masks to manage sleep apnea are really uncomfortable, but modern masks are much more comfortable than the older ones.

Atonia

An unusual condition that affects more children than many people realize is sleep atonia, which is when people violently move their arms and legs around at night. This condition is often linked to having severe nightmares. Sleep atonia requires specialist help from a doctor, but it is worth being aware of it because children could harm themselves at night.

Bladder Issues and Bed Wetting

Many parents are surprised to find that children who have been toilet trained for years start wetting the bed. The chapter on anxiety shows that the digestive processes are shut down when we become anxious. Adrenaline and noradrenaline stimulate the bladder to empty.

If children do have bladder issues, there are several things that can help, but it is good to check with your doctor because sometimes infections can cause problems too. A medical doctor should check for other causes, such as concentrated urine produced with too much fluid restriction, which can often irritate the bladder and lead to wetting as well.

Limit Phone and Screen Use

There has been a huge focus on the problem of blue lights and phones. The problem with any computer screen is that your eyes perceive it as a blue light. Although a 2019 study suggests that the effects of blue light have been overestimated, it is still not ideal to be looking at screens late at night.[36]

Blue light aside, one of the problems with phones is being woken up multiple times throughout the night by notifications. We previously said broken sleep is worse than short sleep.[37] Notifications from phones disrupt our sleep. Ideally children should not have a phone in their room at night, but if they do, they should have it on airplane mode or on silent. (Some people worry that if their phones are on silent, the alarm won't sound. Yes, the alarm *will* still sound.) We believe one of the strong reasons why mental illness has risen is not just because blue light disrupts our sleep, but because phones cause broken sleep from being woken up many times.

Dark Rooms

Ideally, a room should be as dark as possible for good sleep. We are aware that some children find it very difficult to sleep unless they have a nightlight. A nightlight should ideally be fairly dim and have a red light (which can be less disruptive to sleep). However, we do understand that some children have such a fear of the dark that they will only sleep with a full light on. Unfortunately, this does disrupt their sleep, so it's really important to try and look at the causes of this fear and address it.

Reading

Studies also show that reading a physical book, not a book on a screen, can be really helpful in calming the mind so that sleep can happen. Studies by David Lewis show that people who read a book before bed have a 68 percent reduction in stress.[38] One of the sad things that's happened in the last few years is that we've lost the idea of children's bedtime stories; this tradition can be a fantastic way to help a child relax. When they are older, they can start to read on their own.

Don't Stare at a Clock

We also know that if a person has a visible clock in the room at night, this often adds to their anxiety because they just stare at the clock and think, "It's 1 a.m. I should be asleep right now." Sometimes turning the clock away or taking it out of the room can be a helpful step.

Try to Stay Awake

Another technique for older children and adults is something called *paradoxical intention*. When many people try and go to sleep, they often find it very difficult. But if they try and stay awake (doing the opposite of what they are trying to do), they usually just fall asleep. Mary Poppins does this when the children don't want to go to sleep. She sings "Stay awake, don't close your eyes." The children fall to sleep almost immediately.

Writing

One of the biggest causes of insomnia is what we call *racing thoughts*. This is when people can't turn their brain off; their mind is always active. A person may think, "What about the test tomorrow? What about this? What about that?" And they can't switch their brain off, so they often stay awake for hours and hours worrying. There's a technique called *expressive writing*, where you write down whatever is on your mind on a piece of paper for a few minutes before bed. It's important to remind children that this doesn't have to include correct spelling and they can even draw pictures. For some, it can be a really helpful way to calm their racing thoughts. We recommend you teach your children this technique, but if it doesn't work, do understand that some children don't have the language capacity or the brain development to be able to do it.

Medication

Ideally, you should try the strategies we have previously mentioned before trying medication. We want to be clear: we are not telling your doctor what to do; they need to make that decision themselves. But two medications you can talk to your doctor about are melatonin and sleeping pills.

Melatonin is a naturally occurring chemical in your body that tells your body when to switch off and go to sleep. Scientists have produced artificial melatonin. In most countries, this product is available as an over-the-counter medicine, while in other countries, you need a prescription. Even if it is available over the counter, we do recommend that you talk to your child's doctor before starting to medicate. Giving melatonin to children who don't need it often results in the children becoming hyperactive, and it may cause headaches and nausea in a few people. There are some other rarer side effects too.

Melatonin doesn't help everyone sleep, but it may be worth trying. We have worked with a number of families who say it is absolutely brilliant and changed their lives because their children now sleep. We've also worked with other families who say it does nothing. One of the central themes of this book is that there is no one-size-fits-all solution, and melatonin does not work for everyone. *Please note that there are different types of melatonin: some are fast acting and some are slow acting. Often the fast-acting ones help people get to sleep quickly, but they don't help people maintain good sleep throughout the night.*

Some foods contain natural melatonin. Some people have suggested that melatonin-rich foods are a way to get the melatonin people need in a natural way. Unfortunately, a 2020 paper found that the amount of melatonin in food is not enough to affect the quality of our sleep.[39] The best way to make melatonin is to be outside for at least an hour a day.

Some people will ask about sleeping pills. The problem with sleeping pills is that they don't actually put your body to sleep. They tranquilize your body. All the healing processes that are supposed to happen when we have genuine sleep do not happen when we are tranquilized. This is why most people who are on sleeping pills wake up feeling tired and exhausted. The fact that they've been unconscious does not mean they have had a good night's sleep.

Professional Help

If you do have a child who is just not sleeping and you've tried these strategies, we recommend you take them to a sleep specialist. There are more and more sleep specialists who specialize in children's medicine. If a child is not sleeping well, it is vital to get this addressed. If we want the behavioral problems that we talked about in chapter one to go away, then we have to get on top of sleep. There is no use trying to look at behavioral management techniques if you have a child who is exhausted; they just can't think clearly and often become more aggressive and hostile.

Counseling for Insomnia

There is something called CBTi, or cognitive behavioral therapy for insomnia. In other words, counseling to help you get to sleep. It's mainly been tested on adults; however, we do know some children who have had success with it. CBTi helps people calm down their thoughts and get into a good state of mind ready for sleep. There are many counselors who offer this, but there are also online courses available for purchase.

Putting the Theory into Practice

When it comes to sleep, it is important to try and work out what the problem is rather than guessing and applying random solutions in the hope that they work. If you give a child with sleep apnea melatonin, that may make them hyperactive and not actually address the sleep issue.

A good way to start to addressing sleep problems is to asking a child why they aren't sleeping; their response should tell you what to target. If they say they go to bed and just lie there without being able to get enough sleep, that may indicate a lack of melatonin; in this case, maybe they need to spend more time in the sun or try the medication melatonin. If they say they can't turn off their brain when they go to sleep, this may indicate anxiety, and expressive writing or CBTi may help. If they say they have constant nightmares, you could try the dream completion technique or seek therapy.

It is all about trying to understand the problem and respond with the right solution.

Conclusion

Sleep is vital to our well-being. Throughout this chapter, we have shown that sleep improves overall health, including reducing excessive weight gain, improving immunity, reducing the chances of developing mental illness, and greatly reducing bullying and behavioral problems. Good sleep has so many positive benefits. If you are not sure where to start helping your child with behavioral problems, we strongly recommend improving their sleep. It will almost certainly improve many behavioral challenges.

Chapter Fifteen:
The Power of Play

"We don't stop playing because we grow old; we grow old because we stop playing."
—*George Bernard Shaw*

Y ou might ask why we have include a chapter on play in a book about calming aggressive children. The research around play reveals just how powerful the link between aggression and a lack of free play is.

In 1966, the Texas Tower Sniper opened fire on a large number of people, killing sixteen and wounding thirty-one. Dr Stuart Brown, a psychiatrist, began to look into what could have caused this behavior. He also investigated other criminals who had been convicted of violent crimes. He discovered almost all of them had two things in common: the lack of a stable attachment growing up and growing up with a lack of free play. Does this mean that if your child has had a lack of free play that they are likely to become a mass murderer? No, not at all, but they may be more likely to have tantrums.

As further evidence supporting this, an interesting study found that if you take young rat pups and deprive them of free play, they grow up to be angry and aggressive.[1] This is exactly the sort of behavior we described in chapter one. So free play is not a waste of time at all; it is a vital part of helping children self-regulate and they should not be deprived of it. In his book *Free to Learn*, researcher Peter Gray suggests that free play helps with confidence and navigating conflict, and, in some cases, the lack of it can contribute to an increase in mental illness, which may underlie challenging behavior.

A fascinating study found that play seems to strengthen the prefrontal cortex, the part of the brain associated with control.[2] The more of the control part of the brain that is working, the less likely children are to become upset when something goes wrong.

In the United States, the decline of free play started in the 1990s. American leaders realized that academic standards were not measuring up to that of other countries. To try and change this, they made a number of dramatic policy changes, such as getting younger and younger children to start learning, in the hope it would give them an academic advantage later in life. They did this by reducing the amount of free time children have in and out of school. Instead of having American children playing in kindergarten, it was decided the best thing they could do is start learning math, English, and science to help children get ahead in life. While this sounds like a good theory, the consequences have been disastrous. We believe the lack of free play for children is a significant factor in the rising rates of mental illness.[3] On top of this, there has been a significant decline in creativity and interpersonal skills. We will come back to this later.

Tragically this emphasis on reducing free play did not stop in America; it has gone around the world. In 2010, New Zealand introduced national standards that emphasized standardized testing in primary schools. This was removed in 2018 though, when the harm it was causing became apparent.

Play and Achievement

Many adults think that playing is a waste of time. They think we need to get rid of soft subjects like art and music and have children concentrate on the hard and important subjects, like math, English, and science. However, this is a short-sighted view.

The Nobel Prize is the most prestigious academic prize in the world; surely, the winners of this would have not wasted time on art or music? Professor Robert Root-Bernstein studied Nobel prize winners and revealed something rather surprising: almost everyone who has won a Nobel Prize in the sciences also has an artistic or musical hobby.[4] The article from *Inside Science* called "To Win a Nobel Prize in Science . . . Make Art?" has a good summary of Root-Bernstein's work; it is worth reading in full.[5]

Art and music are not a hinderance to great discoveries—rather, they are an essential part. For example, Albert Einstein played the violin, Max Planck (Nobel Prize-winning physicist) played in concerts, and the New Zealand Nobel Prize-winning physicist Earnest Rutherford wrote songs. Even many other high-achieving scientists who did not win a Nobel Prize had artistic hobbies, such as Galileo, who wrote poetry. That seems very surprising. One of the things about music and art is that it teaches you to solve problems and think creatively.

Sir Arthur Conan Doyle created Sherlock Holmes, one of the most famous fictional detectives in history. Holmes is a genius; in his first book, *A Study in Scarlet*, Holmes figures out a way to test for the presence of human blood. It is an early example of forensic science. Holmes isn't just obsessed with science; he also plays the violin and enjoys the opera. Sir Arthur Conan Doyle seems to have known about the connection between science and the arts. In fact, in classical education, art was considered an essential part of a full education.

The opera *La Bohème* starts off with two very poor students in Paris in 1830. One of them burns a play he had been writing to keep warm. In this opera, the very last thing a student burns is his creativity. It's used to show how much creativity was valued in the past. Today, this scene may not have the same impact because we may not prize creativity so highly.

It may seem that it's a waste of time playing dress up, building forts, and having make-believe tea parties. But these skills are absolutely vital. When children do things like this, they learn how to solve problems. Problem solving is something we cannot just teach people. It is something children have to learn in the real world. Take, for example, playing dress up: many serious adults think it is a total waste of time to have a box of costumes in a classroom; children should be focusing on far more important things. But when children play dress up, they have to use a lot of their brain power to imagine things that are not there. The power of imagination is really important.

In fact, one of the most famous scientific discoveries of all time came about when a person was playing. Albert Einstein came up with his famous theory of relativity when he was trying to imagine what would happen if he followed a beam of light around the room. In other words, his ability to play and use his imagination led to one of the most important scientific discoveries in history.

Problem Solving

In his book *Play*, Stuart Brown talks about engineers at the National Aeronautics and Space Administration's (NASA) Jet Propulsion Laboratory (JPL). JPL is one of the most respected aerospace companies in the world and has had a major role in every American space launch. The head of the company, Nate Jones, discovered there were many new engineers coming through who had top marks from the most prestigious colleges in the United States. But despite this technical knowledge, they weren't very good at solving problems in real-life situations. He discovered the engineers who were the best at their job didn't just have prestigious academic degrees; as children, they'd played with radios and gadgets. The ones who'd played with radios and taken them apart and (hopefully) put them back together were the best at real-life problem solving.

One of the most important skills you can ever teach a child is problem solving. Michael spent a number of years in the UK running school camps. They always did a number of team-building exercises. One of them involved having to get a class of children from one side of a field to the other. They weren't allowed to step on the ground. The groups were given tires, planks of wood, and bits of rope to make their way across.

It was very interesting to watch how some teachers managed this.

There were some teachers who would do this for them; they would say, "You take this rope, put it here. Now, you take this tire, put it here. And now you take this log and put it here." They would do it all for the young people.

Other teachers would stand back and let the children figure it out for themselves. The teachers who told the children exactly what to do were more interested in getting the right result rather than having the children learn anything.

Problem solving does not involve standing over people and giving them the answer. One of the reasons we believe so many children hate math is because most math books give a worked-through example and then students are expected to copy the formula. Most math books supply only the relevant information that is needed; you don't have to go hunting for it and you don't have to sift out irrelevant information. This is not problem solving—this is copying. "Monkey see, monkey do" is not real problem solving.

Following Google

We often talk about free play in regards to children, but it is also really important for adults. One of the reasons Google may be so successful is because they allow their employees to have 20 percent free time during their workdays to do whatever they want. This can include taking a rest and not working.

When adults at Google have free time, they start to fix problems. They think "I've got some time now; I could fix that bug on the software that's been driving everyone crazy." So, having free time as adults often leads to some really good ideas. Gmail was one of the ideas that came out of this free time.

So, it's not just children who need free play. We should really encourage this in adults. We've got to get away from this idea of always scheduling things and always having things happen. Sometimes just having a bit of freedom is a fantastic way to relieve stress and get really good ideas.

The Right to Free Play

The American Academy of Pediatrics and the United Nations both consider the importance of free play as a childhood right. The United Nations gives free play the same emphasis as stopping child labor and preventing sexual abuse!

Article 31 of the United Nations Convention on the Rights of the Child states:

> That every child has the right to rest and leisure, to engage in play and recreational activities appropriate to the age of the child and to participate freely in cultural life and the arts.
>
> That member governments shall respect and promote the right of the child to participate fully in cultural and artistic life and shall encourage the provision of appropriate and equal opportunities for cultural, artistic, recreational and leisure activity.[6]

The American Academy of Pediatrics released a report called "The Importance of Play in Promoting Healthy Child Development and Maintaining Strong Parent-Child Bonds." The report says, "Play is essential to development because it contributes to the cognitive, physical, social, and emotional well-being of children and youth. Play also offers an ideal opportunity for parents to engage fully with their children."

Where are Break Times?

In the relentless battle to improve academic achievement, schools have offered less and less free, unsupervised time. Interestingly, many governments insist that prisoners must have at least one hour of outside activity every single day. Many children don't even have the same rights as prisoners!

One of the reasons many people give for not having breaktimes is that children will have more injuries and will bully others; yet studies suggest the opposite is true. Swanson Primary School in New Zealand found that allowing children to climb trees, ride skateboards, and do other dangerous activities resulted in less bullying and fewer injuries![7] When children have more free play, they learn safe boundaries for themselves. Sure, they may fall out of a tree once, but they learn from that.

When children are extremely stressed and overwhelmed, they are more likely to bully others. Swanson Primary School found that bullying decreased when there was free play in breaktimes. If children have free play, they have a chance to let off some steam and they don't get so angry with other students. Furthermore, free play teaches negotiation skills and how to express feelings.

Studies have shown that when children do have more breaktimes and more physical activity, they learn much better.[8] It is absolute nonsense to expect children to be able to sit still in class all day absorbing information. They need time to process all that they learn, and they need time to stop. Finland insists on children having at least a fifteen-minute break after every hour of learning. Unsurprisingly, Finland tends to have some of the best educational achievements in the world. The authors of *Let the Children Play* talk about this in a lot more depth, but it is absolutely vital that we look at countries that are doing well and ask what they are doing.

Exhausted Parents

Two of the most common complaints we hear from parents is that they are exhausted and have no time to do anything. If parents need to supervise their children 24/7, then no wonder they are exhausted and have no time. In the not-too-distant past, it was common for children as young as five years old to leave the house at 7 or 8 a.m. on the weekend and not come back until the evening meal. There were no cell phones to check up on children. When children learned how to play by themselves, unsupervised, the parents had more time to relax and get things done. However, there are more things that can go wrong in the modern world, so there need to be some safe boundaries. The website freerangekids.com helps parents to have safe guidelines for allowing children more freedom, such as saying it is okay to speak to strangers, but if a stranger wants to take you somewhere, you need to stop this at once.

Homework

Many young children often spend two or three hours after school completing homework. It may seem that if you want your children to be successful in life, then you need to make sure they do lots of homework. There are two good books that challenge this assumption: *The Case Against Homework*, by Nancy Kalish and Sara Bennett, and *The Homework Myth*, by Alfie Kohn. The authors argue there is very little scientific evidence that shows the more hours of homework someone does, the better the person performs in school. This will surprise many parents, but it is true.

Homework often leaves students highly stressed and upset, causes significant arguments in households, and often causes students to hate the subjects they are learning. In the previous chapter, we explained how high stress is related to poor sleep; too much homework can also affect sleep. Homework often takes away a love of learning rather than inspiring it. Teachers need to be careful what tasks they set, because homework tasks, such as reading a chapter of a book and circling the nouns, take away their ability to follow the book and decreases their love of learning.

One of the biggest problems is that homework removes so much of the time a child would naturally have to play and, therefore, all the significant benefits from play we have stated in this chapter. Worse yet, if children stay up until two or three in the morning to finish assignments, they are destroying their sleep. Homework often doesn't just happen on weeknights; many schools now give large amounts of homework on the weekends and even during holidays. This means that young people are in a constant state of stress and they never have time to relax.

Self-Directed Learning

An important aspect of free play is that it is self-directed learning.

Too many modern toys take away all the fun from children. In the past, children might have had a cardboard box to play with, but now they have toys that make sounds and do all the playing for them. In fact, a child doesn't need to play with the toy at all. We really encourage parents to buy toys that don't make sounds and don't have lights on them. In other words, toys that require children to use their imagination. Some of these toys can include simple wooden blocks and cardboard boxes.

Playgrounds

There has been a huge focus on wrapping children in cotton wool and protecting them from all the difficult things in the world, and we see this clearly in the design of playgrounds. In the past, playgrounds used to include two-story forts, flying foxes (or ziplines), and high slides. Now, their drawbridges are just a few centimeters off the ground. They are plain boring. No wonder we have so many anxious children; if they are only allowed to play on "safe equipment," they aren't challenged until they get out into the real world, and then everything becomes scary. We must let children climb trees, build campfires, and take appropriate risks.

Older style playground vs. modern "safe" playground.

Boredom

We have been surprised to see that during the COVID–19 lockdown, many people have reported feeling bored. This is somewhat unbelievable, given that we live in the most entertaining and stimulating world that has ever existed. We believe that the lack of free play was partially responsible for this boredom; people don't know how to entertain themselves.

Declining Resilience

Free play researchers such as Peter Gray believe that resilience is declining at an alarming rate amongst young people.[9] In the past, many students would be satisfied if they got a B or a C on a test, but today, this is not good enough for many people. For many students, an A- is a catastrophe; some even consider suicide because it is not an A+. When children have free play, they learn that life does not always go according to plan. Gray suggests that free play helps build resilience.

Importance of Failure

Sometimes really anxious children are too afraid to try anything in case they get it wrong. Sometimes if an adult demonstrates failure, this can help children learn. For example, you may try and create a device to stop water getting into your mailbox; maybe you could first deliberately make one that doesn't work so you will need to try again. If children see that adults fail, it will encourage them to risk failure to solve a problem. Too many children today are afraid of failure and therefore, are not willing to try. We have to encourage a culture where failure is acceptable.

Hopefully you are reading a nicely edited book. Some people might imagine that we just sat down and wrote this book. We can assure you that it does not always go well. The process of writing a book involves immense frustrations. You write something down, it sounds good, and then you read it over the next day and realize it makes no sense, so you have to rewrite it. This is all part of writing: it involves many false starts, many failures, and many attempts at rewriting.

What is the antidote for all the fear of failure? The antidote is to teach children (and adults) free play. When you play, it doesn't matter if you fail. Let us imagine that a group of children are making a fort out of blankets; if it all falls down while they are playing, it is not a problem; in fact, they may laugh at it. Learning how to fail safely when we play allows us to overcome the bigger failures in life, such as not getting the grade we want.

Playful Parenting

A brilliant book for parents who are struggling with difficult behavior is *Playful Parenting*, by Lawrence Cohen. Michael believes that this is one of the best parenting books he has ever read.

If a child says a bad word, the traditional way to manage this is to yell at the child, punish the child, or take the child's stickers away from a sticker chart. This often causes tantrums. Often if you tell children not to say a word, they'll say it more and more. Cohen suggests that if you don't want a child to say a word, the best thing to do is make a game out of it and say, "Try really hard not to say *cheezled schezers*" (made up words). It doesn't matter if the child keeps saying this. The child will repeat this word and forget about the other word you don't want them to say. Furthermore, the more you both laugh at this, the more enjoyment you will have.

For example, if trying to get children to brush their teeth becomes a major battle, try and turn it into a game and say, "Who can create the most foam?" Sometimes this can turn a traumatic and agonizing battle to get them to brush their teeth into a fun game where they laugh and giggle.

Encouraging Problem Solving

When people learn problem solving, they can learn how to manage challenging situations. The best way to learn problem solving is during free play. Perhaps a child needs to make a rocket ship out of popsicle sticks and cardboard. The first ideas they have may not work so well.

We suspect that many children become anxious because they are not good at solving problems. For example, a child who is not so good at problem solving may panic if they forget their lunch, but a child who is good at problem solving may calmly work through some options.

There are many ways to encourage problem solving. For example, go to a thrift store and find an old radio. Encourage children to take it apart and learn how it works. Things like this can be great to pull apart because it involves real problem solving. If it comes from a charity shop, it doesn't really matter if they break it. This can also allow children to learn other valuable life skills, such as the difference between a Phillips and a flat-head screwdriver.

Most "problem solving" tasks we give children are boring. If you want to make a bird house, you can go down to a hardware store and buy one that is pre-cut with the holes drilled into it. Where's the fun in that?

YouTube has some amazing how-to videos. We encourage you to spend some time with a child looking on YouTube to learn some basic DIY skills, like how to cook, sew a button back onto a shirt, or mend things that are broken. If an electronic device stops working or slows down, it can be worthwhile to teach children how to Google the model number and the problem to see if other people have found a solution. Sometimes this requires patience to work through the steps.

We encourage you to give children real problems to solve, such as creating a device for watering potted plants when you are away or a device to stop things from falling down the edge of a car seat. Could they create a smoke alarm that is easier to get off the ceiling for changing the battery? Maybe you know someone who finds it hard to get things that are dropped under a bed; could your child create something to help? Try and look for problems in the real world and see if children can come up with solutions.

Problem solving does not involve getting the right answer the first time; it involves a lot of frustration. This means people may fail or get it wrong, but that is how you learn. The culture of always focusing on success deprives many people of the importance of problem solving. Part of problem solving is getting stuck and feeling frustrated. At first, children may think they can't do it; they will feel frustrated and may even have tears. Sometimes problems in real life take several days, weeks, or months to solve. But then, once the child does come up with a solution, they feel good about themselves and often want to find more problems to solve.

Conclusion

Free play may not de-escalate an upset child in the moment, but in this chapter, we have shown that children who have more free play experience less anxiety and aggression. If we allow our children to have more free play, it should prevent or lessen the anxiety and anger many children feel.

Play is a powerful tool in addressing challenging behavior; we must try and use it more often.

Chapter Sixteen:
Understanding Mental Illness

*"I have never been remotely ashamed of having been depressed. Never.
What's there to be ashamed of? I went through a really tough time and I
am quite proud that I got out of that."*

—*J. K. Rowling*

Before we can look at the way mental illness affects children, we need
to first understand what mental illness is and how it often presents
in adults. This chapter is about understanding mental illness, the next
chapter is about how anxiety presents in adults, and the following chapter is about how anxiety presents in children. Some will ask why we can't
just go straight to child anxiety. In order to understand how anxiety
affects children, we first need to understand how anxiety affects adults
and then see how this differs in children. The reason anxiety often presents differently in children is because their brains are still developing.

When we talk about mental illness, this can include, but is not limited
to, depression, anxiety, eating disorders, and addiction. Throughout
most of this book, we focus on anxiety because it is a significant cause
of behavioral problems in children. Of course, some of the other
mental illnesses do play a role as well.

Difference between Normal Life and Mental Illness

We all feel a bit worried from time to time; does that mean we all have
anxiety? Let's use the example of someone who feels nervous about a
job interview. Almost all of us will feel nervous before going to a job
interview. This is normal; if we can still go to the interview, then we do
not have anxiety. If someone is so nervous that they throw up before
the interview or they cannot leave the house, then that is probably be
anxiety. It becomes a mental illness when it stops someone living a
normal, happy, or productive life.

Is Mental Illness Real?

Some people believe that mental illness is imaginary. They believe people are just making it up to get out of school or work. We now have some amazing technology that allows us to see what is happening inside the brains of people with mental illness. One piece of technology is called fMRI, or Functional Magnetic Resonance Imaging. This allows scientists to see which parts of your brain are performing various tasks. fMRI has allowed us to see what is happening in the brain of someone with anxiety.

There is a part of the brain called the *amygdala*, which is partially responsible for detecting danger and creating a feeling of fear. Many people believe it is just the amygdala that is responsible for processing fear; however, that is a much more complex process that involves many more brain parts. To learn more, Joseph LaDoux, a leading neuroscientist, explains this in his book *Anxious*. Scientists have found that the amygdala is much larger in people who have anxiety.[1] If the part of the brain that detects danger is bigger in people with anxiety, it means they can feel fear more easily than others. Often the brains of people with anxiety are far more sensitive to threats than those without anxiety. Can you imagine how difficult life would be if your fear center was always going off at the wrong time?

It is not just anxiety that involves significant brain changes; it can happen with depression too. In 2018, researchers found that the *hypothalamus*, one area of the brain that contributes to the production of stress, was 5 percent larger in people with depression. When someone without depression has a stressful event, their brain will activate the stress response system, but after the event, the brain turns it off. This returning to baseline process doesn't seem to happen as quickly with people who have depression, meaning they often remain in states of high stress even when they are not in a stressful situation.[2]

There is another part of the brain called the *medial prefrontal cortex*, which is the part of the brain we use to think about ourselves.

Researchers have found that if someone has depression, this part of the brain seems to work harder and has stronger control over other parts of the brain, and these people think more negatively about themselves.[3] Scientists still aren't entirely sure whether this is a result or a cause of depression. Many people with depression may think, "I'm such a loser." If the part of the brain that is responsible for how we think about ourselves is working in an unusual way, that may explain why people with depression have such strong negative thoughts about themselves. We also use this part of the brain to think about how we are feeling. We often tell children to recognize their emotions and respond to them, but if the part of the brain associated with thinking about ourselves is not working so well, then it can be really hard to recognize our emotions. We will come back to this in later chapters.

The good news is that, by and large, these brain changes are not permanent. If someone gets the right help, then the affected parts can change back.[4] We will talk about lots of different options for help as we go through this book.

Is Mental Illness New?

Some people believe that mental illness is new. Numerous people may have only heard about it in the last few years, so they assume it is new. This is not the case at all. Although many ancient writers did not have the scientific terminology we use today, they reported symptoms that were very similar to what we call mental illness. Here are some examples through history:

- The Hindu text *Ramayana* (a collection of Hindu stories) talks about what we would call anxiety and PTSD.[5] It was written seven thousand years ago; this predates early Western writings on mental illness by almost four thousand years!
- In the Bible, Elijah describes symptoms that we could describe as depression today, and it was written about 2500 years ago. "He [Elijah] came to a broom bush, sat down under it and

prayed that he might die. 'I have had enough, Lord,' he said. 'Take my life'" (1 Kings 19:4–5).

- Hippocrates (460–370 BC), the Greek father of Western medicine, also wrote about symptoms we would call depression.[6] For example, ". . . there was aversion to food, despondency, and insomnolency [trouble sleeping]; irritability, restlessness; she was of a melancholic turn of mind."[7]

- In 1621, Dr. Robert Burton published *The Anatomy of Melancholy*. *Melancholy* is another word for depression, so there is a scientific book about depression from the seventeenth century. It has almost never been out of print since its publication.

- Abraham Lincoln is considered one of the greatest presidents of the United States because he played a major role in abolishing slavery in America. Lincoln experienced depression for a large part of his life. This is presented in the book *Lincoln's Melancholy: How Depression Challenged a President and Fueled His Greatness* by Joshua Wolf Shenk. Shenk suggests Lincoln's depression may have made him more empathetic to the suffering of slaves.

- In 1861, after the death of her husband, Prince Albert, Queen Victoria seemed to fall into a deep depression. She recovered for a while, but it resurfaced at the end of her life.[8] That is why she wore black for much of the later part of her life.

- In the book *The Wind in the Willows* (1908) by Kenneth Grahame, we read that Mr. Toad has all the symptoms of addiction to motor cars and extreme mood swings, which today we might label as bipolar.

- Eeyore, who features in the Winnie-the-Pooh books (first published in 1924), has symptoms of depression.

- It is particularly interesting that in the early part of the twentieth century, there was a considerable number of children's books that featured characters who displayed signs and symptoms of mental illness. Mental illness in children's books, by and large, seems to be used as a plot device to teach friendship and compassion. Books from the early twentieth century that were written for children were designed to teach children character and morals.

These are just a few examples of historical records of mental illness, but there are countless others. Although the terminology and understanding has changed over the years, the basic experience of mental illness has been there throughout human history.

Mental Illness is Increasing

There are many people who say the rates of mental illness are the same as they have always been and the reason we seem to have more mental illness today is that we are just better at recognizing it. While this is partially true, there is a general consensus among researchers that mental illness is rising at an alarming rate.

Most of the studies are from North America, but many countries around the world have seen a similar increase, even in countries that were previously considered to have low rates.[9] The following studies do have different dates, so the rising rates are not always perfectly consistent, but overall the following studies show a strong trend that mental illness is rising.

One of the first studies, looking at historical rates of mental illness in the US population is the Epidemiological Catchment Area study. This study interviewed almost 9500 adults and was published in 1978. Researchers asked people who were born between 1905 and 1925 if they ever experienced any episodes of depression. It was found that 1 percent of the studied population reported having experienced an episode of depression. The researchers then asked people born in 1950 and the rate of depression rose to 9 percent.[10]

Professor Jean Twenge, who is a well-respected researcher in youth development, looked at rates of mental illness in teenagers between

1938 and the year 2000. She found a fivefold increase in mental illness in that time.[11] Today, researchers think 26 percent of the adult population may experience mental illness in any given year.[12]

Another report by Jean Twenge suggests the average young person today is more stressed and anxious than psychiatric patients were in the 1950s and '60s.[13] We have presented this research to many teachers; they are shocked, but they all agree that rates of stress and anxiety today among students is exceptionally high.

So far we have presented a lot of statistics; sometimes seeing them visually helps. The study below shows an alarming rise in mental illness in the United States, particularly in young people (eighteen and under), starting in the year 2010.[14]

In New Zealand, we have given roughly 8500 high school students a well-being survey every few years called the Youth 2000 Survey. In 2001, 11.6 percent of those surveyed reported depressive symptoms. In 2019, 22.7 percent reported depressive symptoms. The rate of New Zealand high school students reporting depressive symptoms has almost doubled in the last twenty years.[15]

The COVID-19 pandemic has led to a staggering rise in mental illness. In the United States, before the pandemic, 8.5 percent of the population reported depressive symptoms at any one time. During the first six months of the pandemic, 27.8 percent of adults reported depressive symptoms.[16] That is almost a threefold increase. Severe depression rose from 0.7 percent to 5.1 percent during the first six months of the pandemic. Those most affected were eighteen- to twenty four year-olds, women, parents with young children, and low-wage earners.[17]

Not all health statistics are rising so sharply though. In fact, many statistics show the opposite trend. Between 1950 and 2016, there has been at least a 75 percent decrease in deaths by heart disease and stroke in most industrialized nations.[18] So why it is the brain that is suffering most? What's going on?

One suggestion is that in the last five hundred years, there have been huge changes in society. The number of people we have face-to-face interactions with has gone down; for example, there are now many families with only one or two children, and grandparents and other relatives live separately. In the past, there may have been ten children and extended family living in the same house. In the 1500s, there were roughly twenty people in a household. In 1860, that number declined to ten, and today it is about three or four people.[19]

Children and Mental Illness

Until now, the majority of writings and research on mental illness has focused on adults and teenagers. Worryingly, we are seeing a sharp rise in mental illness in children.

A report from the Centers for Disease Control (CDC) found that between 2007 and 2017, there was a threefold increase in suicides of ten– to fourteen-year-olds in the United States.[20] Another study found that suicidal thinking in children was far more common than previously thought and family conflict was a significant cause of this.[21] We will come back to this in the chapter on dangerous behaviors.

The following Ngram shows that between 1800 and 1985, anxiety in children was almost never written about. Even after World War II, it was rare. Then we see a significant increase starting around the year 1993.

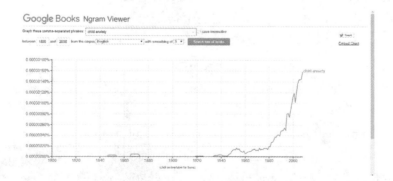

Frequency of the term *child anxiety* as it appears in English-language publications between 1800 and 2008.

Some may think that authors didn't use the word *anxiety* until the last thirty years, and this explains the rise. But if we look at an Ngram of just anxiety, we see the word has been used a lot since the 1800s.

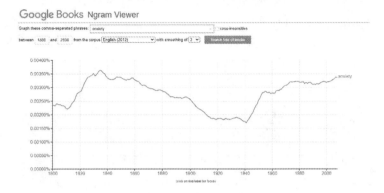

Frequency of the term *anxiety* as it appears in English-language publications between 1800 and 2008.

We now believe a staggering one in five children in the United States aged two to eight has a mental illness or diagnosable behavioral problem[22] and 6.2 percent have anxiety.[23]

Some people will ask, "Are the high numbers of children who report mental illness really experiencing mental illness or are they just a bit angry or sad sometimes?" It is normal for children to have some tantrums, feel shy, and be nervous to try new things. It can be normal for children to get really upset over something small, such as when their sandwiches are cut into the wrong kind of triangles or a drink is in the wrong color of cup.

The behaviors we describe in chapter one (constant tantrums, biting, kicking, screaming, and violence on a regular basis) are well outside the range of normal childhood behaviors. We say a behavior becomes a mental illness when it has a negative impact on the person or others. The behaviors described in chapter one have a devastating effect on not only the child, but also on siblings, parents, teachers, and others.

It is important to understand behavior within the context of culture. There can be strong cultural differences in acceptable ways for children to behave. A child saying "I hate you" to a parent in the Maori culture (the indigenous people of New Zealand), where there is often great respect for elders, is often considered more significant than in some European cultures. However, the behaviors we described are not cultural differences; they are a sign a child is upset, scared, or distressed.

Many people ask what children have to be upset about. They don't have the stress of paying rent or a mortgage, getting or keeping a job, and paying bills. In other chapters, we suggest there are indeed good reasons why even young children experience mental illness; these include the lack of free play, trauma, intergenerational trauma, and poor sleep.

Conclusion

We hope you now understand that mental illness has been recorded for a lot longer than many people realize and that it is very real; a lot of people have or have had it, and it is becoming more common. In the next chapters, we look at how mental illness affects patients.

As you go through this book, you may wonder if you have a mental illness yourself. We know it can run in families, and if you become aware of this for the first time, it can be quite disconcerting. Try and remember that if you discover this from a professional diagnosis, you will be able to get help and greatly improve the situation. We never encourage you to self-diagnose.

Those who have been diagnosed with mental illness can go on to live positive and meaningful lives. The book *A First-Rate Madness: Uncovering the Links Between Leadership and Mental Illness*, by Nassir Ghaemi, looks at this in a different way. The book suggests that people with mild to moderate mental illness and people who have recovered show more empathy and make better leaders in times of crisis than those who have never experienced mental illness. He uses the examples of Abraham Lincoln, Martin Luther King Jr., Mahatma Ghandi, and Winston Churchill. They all experienced depression, yet they may have had more compassion and a drive for social justice because of it.

Now that we know a little bit more about what mental illness is, we can start to look at a very common one: anxiety.

Chapter Seventeen:
Understanding How Anxiety Affects the Mind and Body

"What else does anxiety about the future bring you but sorrow upon sorrow?"

—*Thomas á Kempis*

Some people think the behaviors we described in the first chapter could only happen after prolonged and significant abuse. We will certainly talk about the effects of trauma in another chapter, and yes, unquestionably trauma can cause these things. However, we must be very careful to not assume trauma is always the reason. We have worked with many families where there is no evidence of trauma; the children come from loving family homes, and yet we sometimes still see children behave in aggressive and disruptive ways. In many cases, this behavior is caused by anxiety.

Emergency Response

In order to understand anxiety, we need to understand how humans respond when they are in danger of being seriously injured or killed. Human beings are hardwired to survive.

People often think that fear is a bad emotion, but that is not the case at all. Fear is a really good emotion. It is designed to warn us that we are in danger, so we want to feel this in some situations. For example, if you are walking along a street and a large car comes towards you, you want to be filled with fear and terror. You don't want your body to take time to look at the car and examine what make it is. You want your body to realize this car could kill you.

In this situation, you need your body to activate the emergency response immediately. A few milliseconds of delay could be the difference between life and death. As your body responds, it activates the sympathetic nervous system, causing your brain to send a signal to the adrenal glands to start releasing the emergency chemicals. The adrenal glands are just above your kidneys in the middle of your body. This is really well-placed; if they were in the head or the feet, it would take longer for these chemicals to get through the whole body. Being in the middle means these chemicals can deploy as quickly as possible.

The emergency response will fill your body with adrenaline, noradrenaline, and cortisol; these chemicals get your body ready for action.

Adrenaline, noradrenaline, and cortisol make:

- you breathe faster, so you get more oxygen to make more energy for your body.
- your heart beat faster, so the oxygen can get to all parts of your body and you have the energy to attack or run away.
- your muscles stronger, so you can fight with more force or run faster.
- your pupils dilate (the irises pull back, letting in more light), so you can see better.
- the levels of glucose (sugar) in your system rise for more energy.
- your body shut off the digestive system so it can devote all its energy to staying alive. The chemicals stimulate the bowel and bladder to empty so you will be lighter and can run faster (which is why anxious people may soil or wet themselves).
- your body divert saliva away from the mouth. If you need to stay alive in an emergency, you do not need to eat, so there is no need for saliva to help you swallow (this is why many people get dry mouth before public speaking).

Before you have even consciously realized you are in danger, your body has activated its emergency response mechanism. Dr. Stephen Porges came up with the term *neuroception*, which means your brain detects a threat before you consciously do.[1] This system is designed to be exceptionally fast rather than accurate. Imagine you are in a jungle and hear rustling leaves: the sound could be a tiger or just a bird. The cost of waiting and making a mistake could be fatal, so the system is designed to be overly sensitive, which means it is not always accurate.

Generally speaking, the emergency response is a powerful system and, in many instances, keeps us alive if we are in physical danger. There are just five things the emergency response can do: flee (flight), fight, flock, freeze, and faint.

Flee/Flight

If you are attacked by a lion, a bear, or another ferocious animal, usually the best strategy is to run away. If you are fast enough, running away is the best option because fighting could leave you severely wounded. The chemicals we previously talked about will increase the strength in your body and help you run faster.

Fight

If you are not able to run away, the next best strategy is to try to fight off the predator. Again, the chemicals we talked about will strengthen your body so you are stronger. The term *hysterical strength* describes people full of adrenaline who can perform superhuman feats. There are reports of people having the strength to lift cars in this state, such as in 2015, when Shea Heights lifted a car off a child who was trapped.[2]

Flock

This is when we move toward the people we know and love. Many children may run away from school to be with their parents; this could be both the flight and flocking responses. Usually there is safety in numbers; the more people that are present, the more people there are to attack or defend against a predator.

Freeze

We previously talked about the sympathetic nervous system; this strengthens and speeds up your reactions. Another part of the nervous system is called the *parasympathetic nervous system*, which slows things down. If you can't remember which is which, remember the parasympathetic nervous system is like a parachute; it slows you down. If you are bleeding heavily, you don't want your body to be pumping blood out of your body at a fast rate, so to stop this, your body slows everything down to conserve energy. However, it can slow things down so much that we freeze.

A number of animals freeze or become motionless when they are under attack. As a survival mechanism, some animals pretend they are dead. If predators think their prey is dead, they may leave it alone. It is helpful to freeze when animals are attacking because some animals often have eyesight that only detects movement, so if you don't move, they can't see you.

Freezing may be the most common emergency response; up to 70 percent of people in earthquakes freeze. But there are other ways the freeze response can come out. A lot of victims of sexual assault say, "It was my fault I froze." They think they were cowards, when in reality, it was a biological response that they could not control. When we have explained this to people who have experienced sexual assault, it took away some of their guilt.

We mean *freeze* as in becoming motionless, not feeling cold, but it is worth mentioning that some people with anxiety frequently feel cold. If you are under threat, your body can take energy and heat away from your arms, legs, hands, and feet and divert it toward your vital organs, such as your head and chest. Therefore, anxious and stressed people often find it difficult to regulate their body temperature.

Faint

Fainting is a more extreme form of freezing. In some situations, your body decides to shut down its system to protect you, and thus faint. This is why some people faint when they see needles or blood.

The Polyvagal Theory

Dr. Stephen Porges, a highly respected researcher in physiology and psychology, has done a lot of research into what makes people feel safe. He came up with something called the *polyvagal theory*. We believe this is one of the most important theories in trauma work because it is about what makes a person feel calm and safe.

The theory involves a part of the body called the *vagus nerve*, which runs from the base of the brain stem through the spinal cord and is connected to many of your vital organs, including those responsible for breathing and digestion. When the vagus nerve is well-regulated, it helps us feel calm and safe and form positive relationships. But when this nerve is set off, it puts us into the emergency response mode.

Dr. Porges found that predatory sounds—such as the low growl of a tiger—can put the emergency response system into a state of fear and panic. Such a sound warns us that we are in danger, so we go into emergency response mode. The problem is that there are many sounds in the modern world that replicate the low growl of a tiger, such as the hum of an air conditioner or computer fan. These sounds are not dangerous, but the vagus nerve may misinterpret these sounds and put our system into emergency response mode. In other words, some people become as dysregulated by the sound of an air conditioner as they would if they were in the presence of a tiger.

Dr. Porges has a number of good talks freely available on YouTube that go into this in more depth. He has also written several books that explain this in more detail. His first book is called *The Polyvagal Theory*; it is quite technical, and you need a good knowledge of anatomy to understand it, but it gives an excellent overview of all his research. He wrote a much simpler version of it called *The Pocket Guide to the Polyvagal Theory*.

What Is Anxiety?

Anxiety is that same fear response you get when you are in danger, but it happens when there is no danger, like the same way your smoke alarm can go off if you singe a bit of toast. A smoke alarm doesn't know the difference between a false alarm and a real emergency. This is the same with your brain. Often, it's not very good at knowing the difference between a genuine life-threatening emergency and a false alarm.

For example, many people fear public speaking. When they give talks, they can feel anxious and afraid. Giving a talk in public is highly unlikely to be physically harmful. Although logically they may know they're in a safe situation, that is not the way they feel. Some people who have to give a talk in public feel fear and even terror.

It's important to know that people with anxiety are not deliberately overreacting. The problem is that the brain has misread a safe situation as a life-threatening emergency. A person has no control over this. One important point is that *being safe* and *feeling safe* can be two very different things.

For a condition to be a mental illness, it needs to affect function. For example, feeling a bit nervous when flying in turbulence is not anxiety—that is really common—but being so nervous that you cannot get on the plane is anxiety.

When we talk about adult anxiety, we talk about the difference between genuine fear and anxiety. For example, if someone is terrified of bees because of a severe allergic reaction to a bee sting, that is not anxiety. That is a very rational fear, and the person should be afraid because bees could be life-threatening. Anxiety, on the other hand, is fearing something that won't kill you but your mind is telling you will.

There is a popular post that has been doing the rounds on social media that reads, "When you can't control what's happening, challenge yourself to control the way you respond to what's happening." While this sounds like good advice, it can be bad advice for someone with anxiety. In almost a hundredth of a second, the body activates the flight, fight, flock, freeze, or faint mechanism. This happens instantaneously before there is a chance to control it. Saying that you can control how you respond to a situation is often unhelpful to someone with anxiety. However, with the right help, sometimes medication or therapy, people can learn how to be less reactive.

Different Forms of Anxiety

Generalized Anxiety Disorder

There are quite a few different forms of anxiety. We call ongoing worry and fear *generalized anxiety disorder*, where there is no specific trigger; the person feels anxious all the time. When the person is out, they may worry about getting lost or being hit by a car; when they are at home, they may worry that the house will burn down.

Phobias

Specific fears are sometimes called phobias. This is when someone is very afraid of one thing, like spiders, speaking in public, or flying. They are fine until they see a spider or have to go on a plane.

Obsessive-Compulsive Disorder

Obsessive-compulsive disorder (OCD) is another form of anxiety in which a person repeats the same action a certain number of times. If your child has to switch the light on and off twenty times before they can leave the room, or check the door is locked ten times, they may have OCD.

Some people say they feel if they don't do this repetition, something bad will happen to them or their family. Some people refuse to go to the bathroom in public because of their fear of germs. Some people with a cleaning obsession are scared of germs, or cleaning the house is a form of cleaning themselves.

Panic Attacks

The most severe form of anxiety is what's called a *panic attack*. A panic attack occurs when a person may have sudden and uncontrollable feelings of absolute terror. A panic attack often mimics the symptoms of a heart attack in that people feel like they can't breathe. They feel like their chest is going to explode, their throat is in a death grip, and they're going to die. It is absolutely awful. If you are not sure if it is a heart attack or a panic attack, it is important to get it checked out by a medical professional.

If you are trying to help someone who is having a panic attack, you need to look at the person and say, "I know this is really scary; I think you are having a panic attack. I need you to try and take a deep breath." Someone who is panicking can find even taking small breaths difficult, so you will need to do this over and over again. It is helpful to commend the person even when you see a little progress. You could say, "I know this is really difficult, and you are doing really well. Okay, let's take another breath." If you take deep breaths too that can help; the person will probably mimic you. It can take ten or even twenty minutes to calm someone who is having a panic attack, so please know you will be there for a while.

Be aware that it is really distressing to see a child have a panic attack, but the calmer you are and the slower you speak, the better it can be.

Phone Anxiety

A relatively unknown type of anxiety is phone anxiety. Many people struggle to talk on the phone. They don't know what to say; they get nervous and want to hang up. Often at the end of media articles on mental illness there is a long list of helplines. For people with phone anxiety, this can restrict them from getting the help they need. We try to encourage articles to present a phone number, a text number, and an email address. It is really important that we try to make help as accessible to as many people as we possibly can.

Anxiety Changes the Way We See the World

Anxiety often makes the world a very scary place. People without anxiety may have an enjoyable walk around the neighborhood. But if you are someone with generalized anxiety (where you feel anxious all the time), it isn't at all enjoyable; you worry all through the walk. You might start to worry that you're going to drop your purse or wallet, your phone is going to run out of battery, you're not going to know how to get home, or maybe someone will attack you. Instead of seeing the world as being a happy place, anxiety turns it into a very scary place.

Often people with anxiety will overthink everything. After meeting a friend, they may stay up until 3 a.m. thinking over every little thing that was said and wondering if they said the wrong thing or offended anyone. People with anxiety often have difficulty sleeping because their mind is always active. When their mind is so active, they often become tired really easily.

Researchers have noticed that many people who have anxiety also have depression. If you are afraid all the time and think bad things will happen to you, it is not surprising that you start to feel down.

Out-of-Control Thoughts

Someone who has anxiety often has thoughts that get out of control. Let's say a person in school fails a test. The reality is that it can probably be made up for in another exam. The person with anxiety can start to think that because of this one failure, they will fail every other subject, and that means they will never get a job and will end up homeless.

Some people have anxiety about anxiety. Someone with anxiety who is about to go to a party may think, *I will have an anxiety attack there and embarrass myself.* So a person doesn't even need to be in the situation that causes them anxiety; they could just think about it and feel anxious.

Sometimes when people are anxious, they do some pretty dumb things that they regret later. A few years ago, in the United States, there was a man at a gas station. He had a terrible fear of spiders. He saw a spider on the fuel door on his car so he took out his lighter and lit the spider on fire—plus the gas and the gas pump.[3] Sitting here logically, we know that is a dumb thing to do, but he wasn't thinking logically. He was thinking in the moment. He was thinking, *I want to survive the here and now.* When people are really anxious, they don't make good decisions.

Is Anxiety Treatable?

The good news is that anxiety can be treated and managed, so all the problems associated with anxiety can be reduced or relieved entirely with the right help. Throughout this book, we look at lots of ways you can help someone who has anxiety.

Conclusion

In this chapter, we looked at how the human body responds when it is under threat and some of the key behaviors associated with anxiety. Hopefully, this knowledge will help you look differently at a number of troubling situations.

You may think after we have shown you all this information that you can now diagnose your friends and family (or yourself) with mental illnesses. Please don't—it can be more complicated. For example, often people with depression can feel tired, have memory problems, and get angry easily, but these can also be the symptoms of a brain injury. So it is really important to let a qualified health professional make a diagnosis.

Chapter Eighteen:
Children and Anxiety

"Children are our most valuable natural resource."
—*Herbert Hoover*

Anxiety in children seems to be rising at an alarming rate. In the chapter about understanding mental illness, we presented the Ngram showing that the terms *child anxiety* almost never appeared until the early 1990s, and then there was a sevenfold increase over the next thirty years.

In the previous chapter, we showed how anxiety can affect adults. But what do you think happens when children experience this? As you may recall from the chapter on child development, children's brains are not fully developed. Children do not have the same abilities as adults to recognize and express their emotions. What do you think would happen if you felt afraid, scared, depressed, or worried and didn't have a way to talk about or express it? This is what many children experience. If they can't talk about their feelings, those feelings often come out as behavior problems, such as tantrums, yelling, screaming, biting, kicking, headbutting, or running away.

We often assume that when a child displays behaviors such as kicking or screaming, they are being naughty. However, the child is usually not being naughty, but rather showing signs of being afraid. We gave the example of a child who thought brushing her teeth would make them fall out. The parents misinterpreted the tantrums and kicking as a sign of naughtiness, when really the child was afraid.

When we talk about adults having anxiety, we talk about them having irrational fears. For example, if an adult is afraid of flying, they often know, deep down, that it is not as dangerous as they think it is, but they still feel fear anyway. In children, it is debatable whether they know their fears are ungrounded; for example we know of a child who wouldn't go to the toilet because he thought his insides were going to fall out. It's unlikely he understood that this was not real. To him, the fear of his internal organs falling out when he sat on the toilet was a very real situation. It takes a long time to build a complex view of the world. So many of the fears that children have, in their minds, are not irrational fears—to them they are very real. As we have said, all behavior is communication, and we need to understand that many children are trying to communicate that they are afraid in the only ways they know how.

Let's go back through the five emergency responses again, but this time look at how children may display them.

Flee/Flight

We often think that children who run away are being naughty. We need to ask why they are doing this. Again, in most cases, children are not being naughty; they are just afraid. They do not want to be where they are. There is probably something in the environment that is making them so uncomfortable, they have to leave. Just because we cannot see it does not mean it is not there.

We worked with a young woman at 298 Youth Health who ran into walls at school. The teachers thought she was being silly. One day, she ran into a wall with so much force, she knocked herself out. She did not do this deliberately; she had terrible anxiety and was running away from what she thought was a threat.

Fight

A few years ago, Michael was called into a school. There was a young girl who, when she went up to other children on the playground, punched or kicked them for no obvious reason. Michael sat down with her and got to know her a little bit. Then he asked her, "Do you worry a lot?"

She said, "All the time."

Then he said, "When you go to sleep at night, do you find it easy to switch off?"

She said, "Oh no, I can't do that." She had terrible anxiety, which no one had noticed.

Someone with anxiety may think everyone around them is a threat or trying to hurt them. They may attack others thinking they are defending themselves. The fight response can come out in children as kicking, biting, scratching, beating their arms against an adult, throwing objects, and so on.

Flock

In some situations, the flight response in children is closely tied to the flocking response. Some children may try to run home or go to those they feel safest with.

Freeze and Faint

A few children will be so anxious, they will freeze or faint. Although fairly rare, it does happen.

Physical Responses

In the past, we used to think that a mental illness would only affect someone's mind while the rest of the body would be okay. But that's just not the way it works. Your brain is connected to the body via the spinal cord, which takes messages to the brain and back out again. So the brain and the body are connected. It was the philosopher Rene Descartes in the seventeenth century who said that the mind and the body are separate. It is only in the last thirty or forty years that medical science has started to understand just how wrong this assumption was.

We often think that if children say they have a sore tummy, they are making it up to get out of something they don't want to do; however, upset stomachs can be a by-product of mental illness. In addition to getting upset stomachs, anxious children may also wet or soil themselves, have diarrhea, or vomit.

What do all these things have in common? They are associated with the digestive system. When the sympathetic nervous system activates, it slows down the digestive system. One theory is that your body wants to put as much energy as it can into staying alive, so it slows unnecessary processes to conserve energy. If you are being attacked by a tiger, you don't need to digest food, so digestion gets slowed down. It's estimated that digestion uses 5 to 15 percent of our total energy.[1] When you're in danger, your body diverts that energy to processes that can save your life. So when people with anxiety experience real tummy pains, these are not imaginary or made up.

Another theory about why people have stomach upsets or wet themselves suggests the adrenaline that is released by fear is then balanced by other nerves that make the gut muscle relax. This relaxation empties the gut, causing nausea, vomiting, diarrhea, and increased urination—after all, you can run faster with an empty stomach, bowel, and bladder.

We sometimes think children who want to go to the toilet all the time are trying to avoid something. But if they have anxiety, they may genuinely need to go to the toilet. Making them stay in class because they have just been often makes them feel more anxious because they worry that they will wet their pants.

The image on the right shows how many organs are associated with digestion.

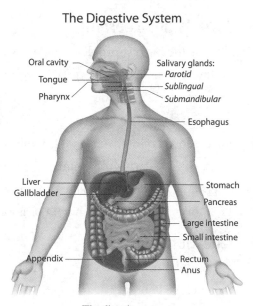

The digestive system.

Organs that involve digestion include the stomach, pancreas, liver, large and small intestines, bowel, rectum, bladder, and the gall bladder. The kidneys help process many of the after-products of digestion. If the processes of all these organs are slowed down, it can explain why anxiety can be so debilitating.

We talk a lot about eating well, but what about digesting well? A number of studies have found that children with mental illness are often malnourished.[2] We need to ask what could be behind this. If children are anxious all the time, they cannot digest their food well.

Sickness

We know that people who have anxiety have a lot more cortisol in their system because their body constantly thinks they are under threat. Scientists have found that when people have more cortisol in their system, they get sick more easily.

We do need to remember, though, that children naturally experience more sickness than adults. Most adults have one to four colds per year, whereas children have five or six, so we need to keep this in mind in the context of normal child development.[3]

Anxiety and Learning

One of the biggest problems with anxiety is that it interferes with our ability to remember things. When we are really anxious, our brain is not interested in trying to remember schoolwork or what your boss just said; it wants to focus on survival. This has significant implications for anxious children in school. Children who are extremely anxious often can't learn. Most countries spend large amounts of money on education; if we have anxious children who are unable to learn well, then this money is not being put to good use.

Questions

Some children with anxiety ask questions all the time. These questions include, "When are we going out? Who will be there? What should I wear? How many other people will be there? Is there anyone I know there?" They do this because they are worried about what will be happening next, and they ask lots of questions to make themselves feel secure.

Conclusion

More and more children are experiencing high levels of anxiety. We must make every effort to learn about how anxiety can affect children and how to respond appropriately. Hopefully, the things we have shown you in this chapter will give you more empathy and understanding toward some of the challenging behaviors anxious children may display. It is not just anxiety that can cause children to behave in problematic ways; in the next chapter, we look at how stress can affect a person.

Chapter Nineteen:
The Effects of Stress

"When you're overwhelmed by your emotion, you listen less and you judge more."
—*Tariq Ramadan*

We often use the words *stress* and *anxiety* interchangeably, but they aren't the same. Anxiety is caused when people are afraid of things, while stress occurs when people are overwhelmed. In the chapter about anxiety, we said that people with anxiety often can't eat because their digestive system shuts down. Stress is the opposite. People who are highly stressed tend to eat a lot of comfort food. It's important to know that stress and anxiety are not the same thing, although they can result in very similar behaviors.

When children (and adults) are stressed, they can behave aggressively and act out. When stressed, we are more likely to snap at people and less likely to respond calmly and rationally; sometimes people even become physically aggressive. An example is when we have the urge to throw a computer out the window when it doesn't work properly.

The word *stress* is not a medical or psychological term; it comes from engineering. Stress refers to the tension within a structure. Some stress is really good. If a building were made out of wet spaghetti, it would collapse, so some stress and tension keeps the building up. In winter, we see building roofs collapse when there is too much snow on them. This is when the stress has become excessive, and when the stress is excessive, objects start to break. This is a good analogy of how people react to stress. When we are under too much stress, things start to go very wrong indeed.

Physical Effects of Stress

We often think that all stress is bad; however, a moderate level of stress improves our health. The immune system is weakened by excessive stress, but moderate stress can actually improve it and make it stronger. Moderate stress has been shown to improve wound healing, slow infectious diseases, and prevent the growth of cancerous tumors.[1]

It is important to know that not all stress has the same effect on us. While moderate stress can be really positive, excessive stress can be very damaging.

- Moderate stress can come from playing a competitive sport you enjoy; many people feel alive and full of energy and feel a great sense of satisfaction afterward.
- Excessive stress could be having your rent due on Friday with no way to pay it or feed your family. Excessive stress can bring on the same symptoms as anxiety.
- Acute stress is more of an adrenaline response, getting your body ready for fight or flight; your heart rate increases, your breathing becomes faster, and your gut activity slows to empty your stomach, bowel, and bladder.
- Chronic stress is more of a cortisol response, suppressing the immune system and decreasing metabolism.

Any kind of constant stress can wear on a person. A great book by Gabor Maté, *When the Body Says No*, reviews the negative impact of long-term and excessive stress on the body. Maté talks about how conditions such as back pain, vision issues, and cancer can all be exacerbated or even caused by stress. He gives several examples of people who always pleased others and put themselves under high stress, often developing serious physical health problems in the process. This is their bodies' way of saying, "enough is enough! I can't take this anymore."

Added Pressure

In terms of children and stress, perhaps one of the reasons we have so many behavioral problems with children is because we put them under far too much pressure. In the early 1990s, it was unheard of to have academic learning in preschool. Now there has been a move around the world to include more and more academic learning at a younger and younger age.[2] In fact, a new term is *preschool ready*. This means that before children start preschool, they should already have some math skills and a large vocabulary.

We think that too much academic learning at an early age puts children under a lot of pressure. A great book that discusses these issues is called *Let the Children Play*, by Pasi Sahlberg and William Doyle. The book is backed by numerous studies showing that too much academic learning in preschool can have disastrous consequences, including many of the behaviors we mention in chapter one. The authors highlight the unbelievable pressure we're putting on some children, sometimes as young as two years old.

Social Stress

Social aspects of the modern world can make life very stressful. It's estimated that we view about four to ten thousand ads on social media each day,[3] and we can interact with more people during an average day than the average person in the middle ages did over their entire lifetime.[4] An interesting study found that one part of the brain that processes fear, the amygdala, shows more activation when we see new faces.[5] It sends a signal to our brain saying, *this new person is unknown—the person could be a threat*. We feel more fear when we see a new face.

What does this mean when we see thousands of new faces each day? On social media, we often see one new face after another, which could mean we are always stressed and anxious because we are always seeing new people.

Contagious Stress

In the chapter on smell, we mentioned stressful events can be contagious through smell. Previously we mentioned the study where a group of researchers asked people who were going to do their first skydive to put sweat pads under their arms. (For most people, their first skydive would be an extremely stressful and anxiety-inducing experience!) The sweat was then inhaled through a nebulizer by a group of volunteers who had *not* been in a stressful situation. The researchers scanned the brains of the people who inhaled the sweat and found that they showed activation in their amygdala and hippocampus, two parts of the brain involved with processing stress and fear.[6]

In other words, we do not need to experience a stressful event to become stressed; being around people who are stressed may be enough to cause us stress to us. We know that stress amongst adults has increased dramatically in the last twenty years,[7] and if adults are highly stressed, they could be passing that stress on to their children.

Stress Affects the Brain as Well as the Body

Generally speaking, when human beings are stressed, they take in far less information than they would if they were calm and well-rested. When we're stressed, our view of the world shrinks. We tend to focus only on the immediate problems in front of us. Our ability to understand complex information diminishes, and our ability to understand what other people are saying also often diminishes.

An interesting study conducted in 1973 called The Good Samaritan Experiment is an example of how stress causes the brain to miss things. Two groups who were training to be Catholic priests heard a lecture on the parable of the Good Samaritan from the Bible. The story is all about the importance of helping people in need. The lecturer concluded the first lecture slightly early. He said, "We've finished early; why don't you head on over to your next class?" In the second group, the lecturer finished late, and he said, "We've finished late; you need to go to your next class immediately." After the groups were dismissed, they passed a man (who was part of the study) lying on the ground pretending to be injured. The researchers found that when the students had some extra time, 63 percent of them helped; however, when they were running late, only 10 percent helped.[8]

The irony of the study is they had just spent an hour hearing a lecture about helping people in need. Sadly, when we are stressed, we don't see the full picture and we miss important things. We become focused on our own needs and ignore the needs of others.

Putting the Theory into Practice

It is important to note that what causes stress for one person may not cause stress for another. Both of us give talks to large audiences and don't feel nervous doing this, yet, we know there are many people who would find this immensely stressful.

Think about your child or children. What kinds of stress do they have—is it moderate or excessive? Remember that stress can be cumulative; if a child has twenty things that are a bit stressful, adding the stress from all those can be overwhelming.

It is important not to judge stress with an adult view of the world. We may think adults have the stress of paying a mortgage or rent and children don't have anything to be stressed about. Children can find things such as school, making friends, and sports practice as stressful as an adult paying a mortgage. If a child says they find something stressful, we need to believe them.

When a child is stressed, try to help them work through the difficulty. For example, if they get stressed about baking in class, you could spend some time at home going over some of the basics, such as how to measure ingredients. Often if children have practiced something, they feel more confident and become less stressed.

If working through the difficulty doesn't lessen the child's stress, it might be time to consider removing some stress from their life. Do they need tennis on Monday after school, ballet on Tuesday, self-defense on Wednesday, gymnastics on Thursday, and Highland dancing on Friday? We are not exaggerating; we know many primary school children who have scheduled activities five nights a week. Children should keep the ones they like the most, but they need some nights where they do nothing.

Chapter Twenty:
Trauma: Childhood Experiences and Lifelong Effects

"It is easier to build strong children than to repair broken adults."
—Frederick Douglass

Almost all parents hope their children will grow up in a loving environment, free from trauma. Sadly, we don't live in a perfect world and many children do experience trauma. When many people think of childhood trauma, they often think of sexual abuse, and yes, this is a significant kind of trauma, but a natural disaster, a serious illness, or bullying can also be traumatic. There are many explanations for the behaviors we mention in chapter one. While trauma can be a significant one, we do want to be clear—not all children who have behavioral problems have experienced trauma, but a significant number have.[1]

What Is PTSD and Why Can't Someone Just Get Over What Happened?

Some people who experience a significant trauma develop PTSD. Someone with PTSD does not experience memories of the trauma as something that happened in the past; rather, their mind forces them to relive the experience as if it is happening to them over and over again. Often the flashbacks are more than just visualizations; many people experience them through their body, as if they are being physically hurt again and again. Some children who were abused may experience thousands of traumatic events; they may not relive each event, but their body remembers and acts as if it is constantly under threat.

Sometimes adults say that even if they experienced a trauma fifty years ago, they remember it like it happened to them yesterday; the memories do not soften over time. This is why people can't "just get over it." It seems their bodies are stuck in a constant state of reminding them they are in danger. Even if people don't develop full PTSD, many people are far more alert and on edge after a traumatic event.

It is worth noting that many people who have experienced trauma develop a high sensitivity to noise, smells, light, or fast-moving images. If there is even the slightest reminder of a traumatic event, it can become a trigger.

We worked with a young woman who was traveling in a car with her brother. The car was involved in a serious accident and her brother was killed. After this, she developed PTSD and started to have lots of flashbacks. The woman thought they were random and had no explanation. A therapist got her to write down where she was when the flashbacks occurred. Eventually, they determined that she seemed to have them when she was around leather. They theorized that when the woman—who was in the back seat—was in the crash, her face was pushed into the leather seat in front of her. Somehow her brain now associates leather with danger. Leather is everywhere, from leather jackets to seats to purses, handbags, shoes, and belts. As you can imagine, this made life exceptionally difficult for her and she was afraid to leave the house. (We did get her some treatment using play therapy and this fear went away.)

Is It the Parents' Fault?

We often blame parents if their children display poor behavior, yet a 2017 study—involving over four thousand children with PTSD—found that just 5.3 percent of the behavior of children with PTSD can be attributed to parenting style.[2] In other words, what the parents did, whether they punished the child or set no boundaries, made little difference to the child's behavior if the child had PTSD.

Childhood Trauma

We must point out that trauma does not affect every child in the same way, and trauma at different ages can have different effects. It used to be thought that if a child experienced a traumatic event in their early years, it wouldn't have much impact on them and they would just forget about it and get over it.

But in the last thirty years, there has been a significant amount of research that strongly contradicts this. Scientists have found that childhood trauma, even if it is not consciously remembered, can have a lasting impact if it is not treated.

In his groundbreaking book *Trauma and Memory*, Peter Levine talks about the fascinating case of Baby Jack, a child who experienced a traumatic birth when his umbilical cord became wrapped around his head three times. Even though Baby Jack could not consciously remember this, the traumatic birth seems to have impacted his behavior. So even trauma that occurs before we can consciously remember it can have an impact on us.

Studies by Dr. Bruce Perry (an internationally recognized expert on trauma) suggest that trauma in the first two months of life is far more devastating than trauma at a later time.[3] In his book *What Happened To You?*, he writes, "Some of the children we studied had attentive and responsive care for only the first two months of life—and then their world imploded. Years of chaos, threat, instability, and trauma followed those first two positive months, yet they did much better than children who experienced initial trauma and neglect followed by years of attentive, supportive care."[4]

It is really important to know trauma can affect people in different ways: there can be a one-off trauma, such as a car crash, and there can be repeated trauma, such as daily physical abuse. In trauma research, it is often thought that prolonged abuse is worse than a one-off trauma. While this is generally true, it is not always the case. We worked with a young man who had experienced a pedophile stroke the inside of his leg; nothing else happened, but the impact on his life was devastating.

Trauma Affects Child Development

Trauma can have a significant effect on the brain. Trauma changes brain development; it can slow down, stop, or even speed up brain development (though not in a positive way).[5] Dr. Perry, along with Maia Szalavitz, wrote an amazing book called *The Boy Who Was Raised as a Dog*, which presents a number of case studies of children who have experienced unthinkable trauma and what helped them recover. Dr. Perry shows that trauma can often slow down a child's brain development; for example, Laura was a four-year-old girl who was severely underweight and not reaching her developmental milestones, such as walking and talking in sentences. The doctors were mystified by this until they realized that her mother was not caring for her.[6] It was as though trauma had paused her brain and body development.

Some children who experience trauma revert to previous behavior. For example, a nine-year-old may show good self-control, make friends, and do difficult schoolwork, but if they experience trauma, they may start soiling themselves, have trouble concentrating, and showing the emotional regulation of a two year old.

Lifelong Impact of Childhood Trauma

Our revolutionary understanding of trauma came from the Adverse Childhood Experiences Study. This study was conducted in collaboration with the Kaiser Permanente Center for Weight Loss. You might think that childhood trauma is an odd topic for a group to study that works with people who are overweight. They realized many of the people they worked with often had a history of untreated trauma before the age of eighteen. They conducted a very large study, involving 17,500 American adults.[7]

The researchers initially asked about ten different types of trauma. They asked about neglect and physical, sexual, and emotional abuse. In addition, they asked about substance abuse within the household and if there was any divorce or parental separation. The study also asked if there was domestic violence in the house, if a family member had been imprisoned, or if there was the loss of a parent. Subsequent studies have added other items to add other things, such as being in a disaster. Collectively, these factors are referred to as adverse childhood experiences, or ACEs.

The researchers matched a history of trauma with a history of mental and physical health outcomes. Unsurprisingly, they found that if someone had a history of childhood trauma, they were more likely to have a mental health problem, such as depression, anxiety, or PTSD. *Please note that even though the study found that traumatized people were more likely to have these problems, it did not mean that everyone who experienced childhood trauma has them.*

What really surprised the researchers was that not only did ACEs lead to an increase in the rate of mental illness, but they also led to an increase in the rate of physical health problems. People with a history of childhood trauma have a greater risk of developing obesity, cancer, heart attacks, and other serious health problems later in life, leading to early death. We do want to stress that these negative health effects are from *untreated* childhood trauma. If a person gets effective treatment, the negative outcomes can go away.

With this in mind, a 2021 study found that in large groups—such as a national population—ACEs do predict poor health outcomes; but at the individual level, this may not be true.[8] Again, a history of childhood trauma does not guarantee that you will have poorer health outcomes.

Heightened Stress Responses

When children experience trauma, their stress response can become ultra-sensitive and even very small things can trigger them. We worked with a thirteen-year-old girl at 298 Youth Health who, when anything went wrong in her life, burst into tears. One day, she was two minutes late for school and sobbed uncontrollably for almost an hour. The teachers thought she was a drama queen and just needed to get over it. We eventually found out that she had been physically abused by her father for years. When she made a small mistake, her father hit her. She developed an elevated stress response, and even small problems put her into a highly reactive state. If children have experienced childhood trauma, their tolerance for stress can go down and they can easily become hyper-aroused, meaning they are always on alert and can become angry.

Some people who have experienced a lot of trauma can develop the opposite of hyper-arousal. Hypo-arousal is when people feel less arousal than what is normal (*hyper* means "more than" and *hypo* means "less than"), or they experience no emotions or sensations. Sometimes people who have a history of trauma may touch a hot stove and say they feel no pain. They often describe this as "feeling dead inside." They may react to trauma by withdrawing, becoming less responsive to people, and sleeping all the time.

Cortisol in the Body

One reason why trauma can cause health problems is because when we are stressed or believe we are under attack, our bodies produce cortisol. As we have mentioned, cortisol is one of the survival chemicals. When you are under attack, your brain uses all the available resources to stay alive in the here and now. Cortisol is ideally supposed to be in your system for a short time, such as long enough to run away from a tiger. As far as we know, there are no negative outcomes if cortisol is in your system for a short time; however, scientists have found that if cortisol remains in your system for a long time, it compromises your immune system, slowing it down or even shutting it off. If your brain thinks you are being attacked, then the energy it puts into your immune system is better used elsewhere. Having cortisol in your system for a long time can weaken your immune system and place you at a greater risk of serious health problems later in life.

Professor Rachel Yehuda is a professor of psychiatry at Mount Sinai School of Medicine who discovered something unusual: while people with depression and anxiety often have higher levels of cortisol in their system, those with PTSD seem to have *lower* levels of cortisol.[9] This may seem to contradict what we previously said, but as well as maintaining the emergency response (fight or flight), cortisol also seems to shut it off. This fact may explain why people with PTSD struggle to control their emotions: they don't have the chemical that helps shut off their system.

Rates of Trauma

Another shocking finding from the ACE study is that the rates of childhood trauma were far beyond anything anyone had ever imagined. It was previously thought that childhood trauma was fairly rare, but the study found that a staggering 68 percent of the general population had one or more ACEs.[10]

Absence of Love

Professor Karlen Lyons-Ruth, from the Harvard School of Medicine, has conducted a number of groundbreaking studies on the impact of the absence of love. Previously, we had thought that trauma was an event that happened, such as abuse; however, Dr. Lyons-Ruth's work suggests that the people with the worst long-term outcomes are those who did not have a loving caregiver.[11] Perhaps the worst kind of trauma is an absence of love.

It has been found that infants in orphanages or institutions where they are provided with food and shelter—but not love—die. In the book *Touching* by Ashley Montagu, the author recounts the true story of an American institution in Philadelphia: "The mortality among infants under one year of age, when admitted to the institution and retained for any length of time, was 100%."[12]

Effects of Trauma

Scientists have found that trauma often changes the function of people's brains. Firstly, brain scans show that the thinking and control part of the brain—the prefrontal cortex—may not work so well in people who have experienced trauma.[13] This is one of the reasons why people who have experienced trauma can be very reactive. Their mood goes up and down within seconds and they find their mood and anger hard to control.

Scientists have also found that the parts of the brain associated with where we are in time and space (the parietal lobe) do not work.[14] One significant issue can be disassociation, which is when people zone out or forget they do things. The theory is that if someone is in a terrible situation, they block out the experience in their mind so they don't have to be present. While it may be helpful to go to another place when they experience abuse, they seem to have trouble turning this off.[15] This means that they can disassociate when they are in a super-market, even though they are not in danger. *Please note that it can be more common for children to daydream than adults; daydreaming and disassociation are very different.*

Because the response to trauma is a response to a threat, many people who have experienced trauma see the world differently. A study found that people who have post-traumatic stress often perceive an expressionless face as an angry face.[16] This may be one reason why some people who have experienced trauma sometimes have trouble forming stable relationships, because they think everyone is angry with them and is going to hurt them.

Difficulty Talking about Trauma

Scientists have found that a part of the brain called Broca's area does not work so well when people have experienced trauma.[17] This is one of the speech and language parts of the brain. The way we usually tell people to manage trauma is to talk about it, but if the speech and language part of the brain doesn't work so well, then a person who has experienced trauma can't always talk about it. We now have therapies that don't rely on people talking about their trauma, such as art and drama therapy. We talk about these in a later chapter.

Information Disruption

In his landmark book *The Body Keeps the Score*, Dr. Bessel van der Kolk, an international expert on trauma, shows that trauma can cause significant disruption to the information our bodies give us. An example of this is when he places an object, such as a key or a can opener, into the hands of a person who has experienced significant trauma. He then asks the patient to guess what it is without looking. Often his patients cannot tell him what the objects are; they have no connection with their bodies.[18]

Digestion Issues

We previously mentioned that anxiety can disrupt the way the digestive system works, but there are other ways trauma can disrupt the body. An interesting study found that bacteria in the gut can be altered by childhood trauma.[19] This means that trauma may play a significant role in how we absorb and process nourishment out of the food we eat.

Addiction to Trauma

One of the most challenging aspects of trauma is that some people become addicted to it.[20] The technical name for this is *repetition compulsion*. One might assume that if someone is in a domestic violence situation, they will leave it. Tragically, many people return to be with the abuser or they get into another violent relationship. It is thought that in times of high stress, people would rather be in a situation they know and understand than an unknown yet safer one.[21]

It is not just adults who repeat trauma; even children do this. A number of children and young people who saw the Christchurch mosque shooting video started watching real-life beheadings on the internet. When many adults heard about this, they immediately assumed the children who did this must be "sick and twisted." It's important to have compassion and understanding if you discover something like this. Many people who watched the shooting video did not go looking for it, it just came up on their social media. It is important to know that children can get stuck in this cycle of becoming addicted to the adrenaline and endorphins (chemicals that make you feel happy) created by a traumatic experience.

We will cover this more in the chapter on dangerous behavior, but there is significant research that links self-harm (the clinical term is *non-suicidal self-injury*) to childhood trauma. We often think that only teenagers do this, but we are seeing an increasing number of young children engaging in these behaviors. We must be aware that the children who have experienced trauma can act out and behave in very distressing ways. This is when expert help is required. Often parents are too embarrassed to tell helping professionals the full extent of the issues; this is why it is important to find a helping professional that you can be really open with. Experienced therapists in this field will probably be difficult to shock.

Self-Loathing

Perhaps the most serious injury that many people who have experienced trauma receive is that to their self-worth and identity. Often people who have experienced significant trauma say that they hate themselves. There have been many programs in recent years that aim to improve young people's self-esteem. If trauma is the real cause of much of this, then we need to look at ways to heal the trauma to restore a person's self-worth, rather than just telling everyone they are special.

Secondary Trauma

Many people think that someone will only be affected by a trauma that happens to them first-hand; however, scientists have found that there are other ways we can be affected by trauma. One of these is called *vicarious* or *secondary trauma*.

There was an interesting study conducted with people who were either present on the day of the Boston bombing and people who watched it repeatedly on TV. The researchers asked the subjects, "How do you feel?" Surprisingly, the people who watched it repeatedly on TV reported higher levels of distress than the people who were there.[22] Again, watching helplessly can be very distressing.

Also, if you watch something on TV, you can potentially see it from multiple angles. Many people in the midst of a disaster say, "I only saw a small part of it." But if you watch it on TV, you tend to see it from every single angle. We think this is particularly relevant for children with smartphones. What do you think happens if we have trauma blasted at us on our smartphones on a newsfeed every day? In the past, trauma may have been relatively contained to the news at 6 p.m., but now we're presented with trauma around the clock. We believe that this is one of the things that could have led to a rise in severe mental illness and behavioral problems in children and adults.

Regarding siblings, we used to think that if the sister is sexually abused, then the sister would experience worse mental health outcomes than the brother. Research suggests that it could be the brother who experiences the worse mental health outcomes.[23] If something happens to you first-hand (the sister is sexually abused), it is easier to process and work through. But what about the brother? What impact would it have on a child if he knew his sister was being abused and he was unable to help? It can be extremely traumatic for the brother.

Some people who watch helplessly on the sidelines develop full-blown PTSD even though they weren't directly affected. We must be clear: this will have a significant impact on the sister as well. Often when abuse is discovered, all the help and support goes to the person who was abused; in this case, the sister. We must look at the way the entire family is affected.

If one child in a family is sexually abused, it is really important to offer support to their siblings and parents. It is incredibly distressing for parents to discover a child they love dearly has been sexually abused.

Intergenerational Trauma

Another type of trauma that scientists are beginning to discover is called *intergenerational trauma*. Scientists have found that the genes for trauma can be turned on from one generation to the next. The clinical name for this field of study is *epigenetics*.[24]

Much of our understanding of intergenerational trauma comes from the work of Professor Rachel Yehuda. She originally did a lot of work with Holocaust survivors, but then she started to look at the effects of the Holocaust on the survivors' children. These children said, "We've got PTSD too." At first, she ignored this, but then she undertook some research and started to find that the children of Holocaust survivors also had high rates of PTSD.[25]

This was further illustrated in a very interesting study conducted on rats. The researchers took rats and gave them an electric shock and exposed them to the smell of cherry blossoms. They followed these rats for three generations. The middle generation was not exposed to the smell. When the researchers exposed the third generation of rats to the cherry blossom smell, they feared it.[26] This experiment shows how trauma can change our genes. It makes sense. If something killed or endangered your ancestors, you'd want it to be encoded in the DNA of their children. Of course, this biological memory can backfire, such as when descendants of Holocaust survivors today suffer as though they are living the horrors their ancestors experienced.

Brain Plasticity

The most important finding in all of neuroscience is neuroplasticity. This means that your brain is not fixed; it can change, develop, and grow. The bad news is that when children have experienced trauma, then their brains develop in the wrong way. They often live in constant fear and believe that everyone is going to hurt them.

But the exciting news is that the opposite can happen. Even if someone has had a really bad start to life, their brain can change and adapt for the better. This is the reason why helping professionals are able to make a difference. If our brains were fixed and there was nothing we could do to change adversity, then seeking help wouldn't work at all. The reason it does work is because we *can* change.

Conclusion

As bad as trauma is, we are now starting to find new ways in which people can heal from trauma. There is a video on the internet called *Child of Rage*, which features a young girl from an abusive home saying she wants to kill and hurt people. Many people assume this child has no hope and cannot recover. In the end, she does get some help and the story has a happy ending: she went on to become a nurse and never killed anyone.

We often talk about the negative effects of trauma. People might assume that if someone's been traumatized, they're going to end up as a heroin addict or even die by suicide. But both of us have worked with many people who have experienced significant trauma, and we have seen some incredible stories of recovery.

Chapter Twenty-One:
Trauma: Healing the Wounds

*"What we don't need in the midst of struggle
is shame for being human."*
—Brené Brown

In the previous chapter, we told you about many of the bad things involving trauma. The good news is, we are always discovering new and more effective ways to treat trauma.

Because many trauma treatments have been developed for adults, we must warn about the dangers of trying to use adult therapy on children. We have previously mentioned the importance of understanding child development. Especially when it comes to treating trauma, we must remember children's brains are not fully developed. Therefore, many adult therapies—which require complex, abstract thinking—do not work for children. The following treatments and therapies are available for children, but they must be carried out by therapists who understand child brain development.

Although many of the things we have talked about so far are things that can contribute to the causes of bad behavior in children, this chapter will talk about things that will help to counteract some of these causes and help calm your child. They may not help at the time of the tantrum, but they will help to decrease their frequency over time if you keep repeating them.

This chapter is specifically about healing trauma, although many of these treatments and therapies work for other challenges children may display.

Positive Childhood Experiences

We said earlier that 68 percent of the population has experienced one ACE, but 68 percent of the population are not heroin addicts. Researchers have found that although trauma is a risk factor for poorer life outcomes, having a stable and loving home is a protective factor. If children have protective factors when something bad happens to them, they greatly reduce the risk of severe negative outcomes. Researchers focus a lot on ACEs, but there are also positive childhood experiences (PCEs). A large study of over six thousand people found that having some or all of the following factors greatly increased one's likelihood of doing well in life even if bad things had happened to the person. These factors include when individuals—

- felt able to talk to their family about feelings,
- felt their family stood by them during difficult times,
- enjoyed participating in community traditions,
- felt a sense of belonging in high school (not including those who did not attend school or were home-schooled),
- felt supported by friends,
- had at least two non-parent adults who took genuine interest in them, and
- felt safe and protected by an adult in their home.

The researchers found adults who reported six or seven PCEs had a 72 percent lower chance of poor mental health, even if they had a number of ACEs. In their conclusion, the researchers say,

> Findings suggest that PCEs may have lifelong consequences for mental and relational health despite co-occurring adversities such as ACEs. In this way, they support application of the World Health Organization's definition of health emphasizing that health is more than the absence of disease or adversity. The World Health Organization's positive construct of health is aligned with the proactive promotion of positive experiences in childhood because they are foundational to optimal childhood development and adult flourishing. We must focus on trying to put positive experiences into children's lives.

If children have experienced trauma then there are things that can be done.[1]

If trauma has occurred, protective actions can be taken to help people recover. The first steps should always be to try and put protective factors in a child's life. One of the PCEs is to enjoy participating in community traditions. This could include being in a sports club, an art group, a walking group, or a cultural immersion group.

You can also create your own family traditions or continue those of your culture. One family's tradition was that the father brought home a bag of candy every Friday night. (The children weren't allowed to have candy any at other times.) As the children got older, the father decided he would stop doing this because he felt they were too old for such things. The oldest child—who was then 16—asked where the sweets were. "It's Friday night, isn't it, Dad?"

To help a child achieve the PCE of at least two non-parent adults taking genuine interest in them, you could enroll them in a youth group or Scouts. Such involvement in these organized groups may achieve this experience; otherwise, these non-parents could be a teacher, a coach, or an activity leader.

Encourage your child to talk to you about how they feel by telling them how you feel, especially positive feelings. Try to use lots of different words for feelings so they learn more words to use. There are also many children's books that help show children different words for feelings; reading these together would be a great way to open the discussion of personal feelings.

As you can see, some protective factors are surprisingly easy to put in place, yet they can have dramatic and positive results.

Different Therapies

Many people who have experienced trauma are told to "talk about it." We said earlier that Broca's area, the speech and language area, does not work well for people who have experienced trauma, so they often can't talk about it. Fortunately, there are many therapies that don't involve talking.

The following therapies need to be done with a trained therapist because they know how to help people process and work through their emotions in a safe way. *Please note: not all of these therapies work the same way for everyone.*

Play Therapy

Play therapy uses toys, puppets, and objects to allow a person to safely process an event. For example, a child who loses a brother may struggle with the concepts of death and eternity; using a toy to represent the brother and placing this in a box in the ground may help a child to work through these emotions. Or in the case of sexual abuse, a child may choose a dinosaur as the abuser and a toy kitten as themselves. It can be helpful to visually see the power imbalance. Often when people see this, they can start to address some of the self-blame that often follows abuse. When people discover the power imbalance, they can start to understand how they were manipulated into a situation.[2]

Art Therapy

Some people who struggle to talk about what they are experiencing might be able to express their emotions in a visual way, such as through art.

A simple exercise for a child is to use a black marker to scribble over a piece of paper to represent their inner turmoil. Having done this, they may then see what they are experiencing and can show it to the therapist. We call this *art therapy*.[3]

Drama Therapy

Some people are not allowed to express their emotions; maybe they come from a culture where they don't talk about their feelings. Drama therapy can offer a way for people to learn about and understand the emotions of others without having to experience them firsthand.[4] For example, let's imagine that someone has depression. They come from a home where it is not acceptable to express any form of sadness. They could take part in a small drama production where they play a depressed person. This allows them to understand the emotions in a socially acceptable way.

Music Therapy

One of the big problems with trauma is that talking about it just doesn't help many people. When a trauma happens, it happens to all of our being. But sometimes talking about trauma doesn't cover our whole being. Talking is processed in a fairly small part of the brain. Music, unlike talking, seems to be processed across the whole brain.[5]

There are many activities that can be part of music therapy. Many people may not be able to speak about their trauma, but they may be able to write a song or piece of instrumental music that can express what they are going through. Music therapy can work in other ways; for example, many people can't talk about their trauma, but they can sing about it!

If music is processed across the brain, this may make music therapy a particularly powerful way to heal many hurts that people can't overcome with talk therapy alone.[6] There is also good evidence that music therapy can aid recovery after a stroke or head injury.[7]

Movement to music is even more helpful as it involves the whole body. If your child is raging, sometimes putting on calm music and moving yourself in time to the music can invite them to gradually become still and even join in.

Animal-Assisted Therapy

One significant problem with trauma is it can be such a violation of trust that people struggle to trust anyone at all. Animal therapy can be a way to rebuild that trust by starting with a safe relationship with an animal. Many people who have lost faith in humanity like animals because animals can't betray a person.[8]

Neurofeedback Therapy

Neurofeedback is when a person is connected to an EEG (electroencephalogram) machine. This machine reads brain waves, which are then presented on a screen, often in the form of a game or a puzzle.

Often people who have been through trauma say they don't know what their body is doing; they are disconnected from the feelings and emotions within them. When they see what their brain is doing, they can learn to understand what the feelings mean. As we have mentioned, trauma disrupts many of the brain's normal connections. This process allows them to see what their brain is doing, giving them a chance to learn how to respond appropriately. It is often helpful for children (and adults) who have ADHD, brain injuries, or childhood trauma.[9]

Ecotherapy and Adventure Therapy

There's an interesting form of therapy called *ecotherapy*. The theory is that being around nature can dramatically reduce the symptoms of mental illness. In fact, there is more than just feeling good—walking in nature, as opposed to a city, produces natural killer cells (which are used to fight off diseases like cancer[10]) and can reduce a person's cortisol levels.[11]

A similar kind of therapy that builds on the power of ecotherapy is adventure therapy. This can involve completing obstacle courses (which you can even construct in the house for small children), camping, horse trekking, or learning how to sail a boat. There are a couple advantages to this; firstly, physical exercise can reduce stress and create "happy chemicals" in your brain.[12] Secondly, the idea of going out on an adventure or setting yourself a personal challenge can be really rewarding. Some people who have experienced a lot of trauma feel they can't do anything right, but being able to achieve a tangible goal can really help with their self-worth.

EMDR Therapy

There's a newer therapy called EMDR, which stands for Eye Movement Desensitization and Reprocessing. After years of being plagued by distressing memories, psychologist Francine Shapiro discovered that when she moved her eyes side to side, she felt calmer.

EMDR is based on our knowledge of the phases of sleep, namely the REM stage. REM sleep, or rapid eye movement sleep, is called REM because the eyes move rapidly, often left to right. Inside the brain, the shifting eye movements seem to allow the brain messages to shift from side to side. Scientists believe that somehow the moving from one side of the brain to the other (cross lateralization) in REM sleep is responsible for healing and pacifying our memories.

EMDR therapy involves getting you to shift the focus of your attention from one side of the brain to the other. This can be done by a therapist moving a finger in front of your face from left to right, but it can also be achieved by tapping on the left side of the body then the right. The theory is that EMDR somehow tricks your brain into thinking it is in REM sleep.

If someone experiences sexual abuse, they may be told many times that it is not their fault. Despite being told this over and over again, many people don't believe it. Often when people undergo EMDR, however, it helps them to finally accept what people have been telling them.

There are a number of people who think EMDR is fake science. We know a man who was sexually abused at age five; when we met him, he was fifty-five. He had nightmares every single night of his life. He had tried almost every known medication and therapy, but nothing seemed to work. He thought EMDR sounded like the dumbest form of therapy he had ever heard of, but he was eventually talked into going. After ten sessions, he reported he could sleep through the night without nightmares! *Please note: not everyone has such a powerful success story;*

there are some people who say it does nothing for them. It is also important to note that no therapy is perfect; a small percentage of people who try EMDR leave with stronger memories of the events; but overall, far more people find it helpful than harmful. A large study published in 2020 even found that some people may need additional sessions to maintain the effects of EMDR.[13]

Chronotherapy

Under normal circumstances, good sleep really helps people. Scientists have also found that immediately after a disaster or a trauma, if we can keep people awake for a long time, such as an entire twenty-four hours, then the memories of the trauma seem to pacify themselves. Staying awake for a long time can stop the memories from being strongly implanted in their brains.[14]

Trying Again

Sometimes a method of treatment that failed once for someone may work years later. We were recently approached by someone with PTSD who had tried EMDR a few years ago and said it did nothing. He had tried multiple forms of treatment, but nothing was working. He was desperate for something. We suggested trying EMDR again. This time it made a considerable difference; he was sleeping better and didn't get so angry and upset. *Please note: if a treatment is harmful in some way, it should not be tried again. For a child, some treatments may help better once they have developed more.*

Further Reading about Trauma and Healing

Bessel van der Kolk

One of our favorite authors is Bessel van der Kolk. He wrote an amazing book called *The Body Keeps the Score* that talks about the impact trauma has on the body and the neuroscience of it, and contains many forms of treatment. Some readers who have experienced trauma themselves may find this book helpful. He also has some free talks available online and a number of easy-to-read articles.

Peter Levine

Peter Levine, a world-leading expert on trauma, has developed a technique called *somatic processing*. *Somatic* just means "of the body." We now know that trauma does not just affect the mind but also the body. Peter Levine talks about healing trauma through the movement of the body.

He has written an excellent book called *In an Unspoken Voice: How the Body Releases Trauma and Restores Goodness*, which looks at how to use the body to heal the imprint of trauma.

Conclusion

We hope you are not feeling overwhelmed by so many suggestions. We have found that when it comes to trauma, the pathway to healing is not always straightforward. When people approach us wanting to know what will work, we suggest one of these techniques. We have found that there could be two people who have experienced almost identical traumas, yet they may respond to treatments in very different ways. This is why we must never put our faith in just one kind of treatment. If the first treatment does not work, then we move on to the next one, and so on. Neither of us have ever said to anyone, "There is nothing that can be done for you"; there is always something else to try. More often than not, treating trauma is a case of trial and error and a lot of persistence. Often it is the relationship with the person who is delivering the therapy, no matter what the therapy is, that is the most helpful part.

Chapter Twenty-Two:
The Dangers of Exposure Therapy

"Nothing dies harder than a bad idea."
—Julia Cameron

In this book, we do not critique every possible type of therapy and help out there. By and large, we have tried to show you lots of effective therapies and techniques to get help and improve the well-being of your child. However, we do want to look at exposure therapy because of its widespread use among clinicians, parents, and teachers. Exposure therapy has mainly been tested on adults with anxiety and PTSD; we strongly caution against assuming adult therapies will work the same way with children.

Attempting to Build Tolerance

There is a treatment method for anxiety called *exposure therapy*, or *prolonged exposure therapy*. Even if many people do not know the clinical name for it, people are familiar with the concept. Let's take, for example, someone who has a fear of going underground to catch a subway train. This person may know she needs to take it for work, however, she may find herself unable to go underground. She might fear all the crowds of people, fear the train shaking, or just dislike being underground. Not being able to go underground can become very disempowering and have a significant impact on her life.

In this case, the idea of exposure therapy is to gradually help the person get used to the idea of going on the subway. With the help of a trained therapist, the person might go to the entrance of the subway station and stop there. Maybe the next week she goes down the first step or two. Then she might imagine going a bit further, gently building up confidence. We call this advancement *tolerance* because the person learns to tolerate the thing they don't like.

In other words, exposure therapy slowly exposes them to the thing they fear. The idea is that eventually they build up more and more resilience until they can finally face the thing they're afraid of.

Exposure therapy is not a new idea. It was pioneered by Joseph Wolpe and others in the 1950s. In theory, it may sound like a good technique for children who are avoiding things, but we have considerable concerns about the way this has been used, especially on children. We are not the only ones: Bessel van der Kolk, Judith Herman, Joseph LaDoux, and Peter Levine all have reservations about its use for people who have experienced trauma, and Alicia Meuret found that many children who undergo exposure therapy have negative reactions. In *Trauma and Memory*, Peter Levine talks about a veteran (Ray) who started exposure therapy, but instead of improving, he started having more intense nightmares and became much worse. There are some people who may benefit from exposure therapy, but as we have said, there cannot be a one-size-fits-all approach.

We must understand that exposure therapy can backfire. Instead of creating a tolerance, forcing children to do things can create sensitivity. Many people know about the concept of tolerance where you slowly get used to the thing you fear. However, what many people don't realize is that the opposite can happen and you can build up sensitivity. A child who develops a sensitivity to school may start off with a small amount of distress, but as they go to school more and more, that distress may build. Some child therapists don't seem to realize that sensitivity is a possibility and, for some children, exposure creates the opposite of what is desired.

Avoidance

Many therapists now use the term *proactive avoidance* to describe situations when sometimes the best thing we can do is avoid something for our well-being. For example, if a solider returning from war gets overwhelmed by loud noises, sometimes the best thing to do is to proactively avoid things that trigger them. We do need to balance this with the arguments made by Greg Lukianoff and Jonathan Haidt in *The Coddling of the American Mind* that too much avoidance causes problems. Obviously too much avoidance is a bad thing, and if it is done too often, it can make things worse. It can be a tricky balancing act knowing when to encourage a child who is fearful and knowing when to stop something because it is causing distress.

Conclusion

Exposure therapy can be a useful tool, but it must be used carefully and correctly. We are concerned that many amateur and even professional therapists are using this but don't realize the harm it could cause with children. It really concerns us that a number of therapists seem to think exposure therapy is the only thing that will work. We're not saying that exposure therapy is a bad treatment, because in some cases it does work well. However, if it results in a deterioration of behavior and a child getting worse, then obviously it should be stopped immediately. With all the treatments that we discuss, we are very clear: if it is not working, then you should stop.

Chapter Twenty-Three:
Sensory Processing Issues

"We live in a world where there is more and more information,
and less and less meaning."
—*Jean Baudrillard*

Sensory processing issues (SPI)—also known as *sensory processing disorder*—are a significant problem for a lot of children. This occurs when a person experiences the world more softly or intensely than other people. At the time of writing, sensory processing disorder is not a recognized medical condition, but it undoubtedly exists. The debate about how it should be defined—whether it is a disease in itself or a symptom of other diseases—is well outside the scope of this book. Whatever the cause or where it fits in, we must recognize and respond to it in children.

What are SPIs?

People with SPIs experience life more strongly or quietly than other people. For example, if most people watch a TV program at a medium volume, they will hear it at a medium volume. Many people with an SPI would hear it at either an exceptionally loud or quiet volume. If someone is overly sensitive to sound, every small sound they hear can sound like someone banging a hammer on an anvil next to their ear. Almost no one would be able to stay calm and regulated if this was happening. Imagine a school hallway with linoleum flooring; someone with SPIs would find every footstep and squeak of rubber on the floor unbearable.

Sound sensitivities seem to be the most common, but it can occur with all the senses.

Going to an indoor pool is an activity that many children consider fun; however, it can be a nightmare for someone with SPIs. Indoor pools usually have bright lights; when they reflect and bounce off the walls, people with SPIs can feel like the lights are bombarding them. Most indoor pools have gritted tiles; this could feel like spikes to someone with SPIs. When most people get chlorine in their eyes, it stings a little, but to a child with SPIs, it can become unbearable. While pools tend to have warm water, to a child with SPIs, they may be very hot. When we consider all this, we can easily see how a trip to the pool would be overwhelming and, in some cases, traumatic for someone with SPIs.

SPIs can also be present in other ways, such as in children who often complain about scratchy, itchy, or rough clothing. A lot of people with SPIs find clothing labels very distressing; these people sometimes describe labels as a knife digging into their skin. Sometimes they find the inside seams of socks or mittens very distressing; to them, it could feel like a saw grating against their skin. Rather than just thinking that children are being difficult, we need to listen more to see what could really be going on.

At the same time, it is important to distinguish between not liking something and being sent into a state of dysregulation. Many people do not like the sound of a balloon popping; for most people, it is unpleasant, but after it pops, we can regain our composure quickly. If someone is affected by an SPI, their nervous system goes into a state of hyperarousal and they enter survival mode, where they cannot think or behave rationally. Some people can stay in this affected state for hours.

What Causes This?

People without an SPI are usually able to filter out the information they don't need. For example, in a busy café, most of us can filter out all the other conversations and listen to the person we are talking to. We think people with SPIs struggle to filter out irrelevant information, so their brain presents them with everything or nothing. In the following section, we look at a number of conditions that can include SPIs.

Autism

We cover autism in the next chapter, but most people on the autistic spectrum have SPIs. In the book *The Autistic Brain* by Richard Panek and Temple Grandin, Grandin says that one of the most debilitating parts of autism is the sensory overload, yet until recently, this idea received almost no attention.

Brain Injuries

Many people who have brain injuries develop some form of SPI. They frequently have a constant ringing in their ears and find lights overpowering. As a result, quite a few people with brain injuries wear caps while they're indoors to block out some of the light from overhead lights or wear dark glasses in places where there is strong outdoor lighting.

PTSD

Adults who develop PTSD often become highly sensitive to loud sound in the way children with SPIs do. For example, some people with PTSD become very distressed by loud noises, such as fireworks or a car backfiring. Perhaps some SPIs are a trauma response that aren't at the level of a full diagnosis of PTSD.

Isolation

It seems that many people in the modern world are more isolated than ever before. A fascinating study looking at prisoners in solitary confinement may shed some light on how this affects sensory processing. One of the most surprising effects is that people in solitary confinement develop a strong sensitivity to even quiet sounds.[1] *Please note: Solitary confinement does not usually include silence. Often people in solitary confinement are still in noisy prisons. It is not the lack of sound that causes this, but rather the lack of social contact.*

People with Sensory Issues Don't Know They Have Them

You might assume that if people are affected by sensory overload, they would realize what is happening, but that is often not the case. One young person we work with said he hated sports at school. Interestingly, he didn't fully understand why he disliked sports until we suggested that the whistle was affecting him.

We also know a family who had severe behavioral problems with a son who had autism. He had multiple tantrums a day, sometimes thirty to forty. They eventually put noise-canceling headphones on him, and his behavior changed immediately. The family said it was as though he was a different person. The family had struggled with this for years and neither the son nor the family had understood what had caused his behavior.

Over-Responsive

When people have SPIs, they can get overwhelmed by all the information coming at them. An article on the website The Mighty listed responses to the question, "What is it like to experience sensory processing disorder?" One of the responses reads, "It was a bit like the film *Bruce Almighty*."[2] If you haven't seen the film, it's about a man who has the powers of God. One night, he gets inundated with millions of prayer requests coming at him all at once. He becomes overwhelmed. It's too intense and immensely stressful. Likewise, people with SPIs are bombarded with input from all over and do not know how to process it.

Here is another way someone else in the article describes the effects of SPIs: "It's like when your computer freezes because there are too many tasks open or a task is stuck. And your brain hits 'Ctrl-Alt-Del' automatically. In my case, this means sudden fatigue, balance problems, speaking problems, disorientation."

Under-Responsive

Not all people with sensory issues experience everything intensely; some experience life at a much lower intensity than others. This may lead to children not hearing instructions or not seeing objects on a computer screen. If a child does not respond when a parent gives an instruction, they may assume a child is being disobedient. It is possible that the child did not hear the parent.

Under-responsive touch can be particularly dangerous. For example, if a child who is under-responsive to touch places a hand on a hot stove, they may burn it and feel little to no pain. Our bodies are usually very sensitive to pain to prevent further damage. Some under-responsive people with SPIs won't get the signals that they are in pain.

Often children who are under-responsive are "clumsy." They often don't have agile movement. In order to move effectively, we rely on being able to understand where we are in space and how our weight and balance is distributed. For example, if you are balancing on a beam, you need to know how much of your weight is on one side. If children don't receive this information, they become clumsy. They can fall over a lot and could injure themselves.

Children can also break things because they don't understand how much pressure needs to be applied. For example, they may not hold a cup tightly enough, which means it falls through their fingers. They may spill drinks often because they don't realize they are not holding a cup level. These are things an occupational therapist may be able to help with.

Please note: Under-responsive SPIs are not the result of damage to the body. For example, if someone has a damaged eardrum, they may have hearing loss, but this is not what causes under-sensitive SPIs. Physical hearing loss is a separate issue, although it could co-occur with SPIs.

Having now talked about over- and under-responsiveness, some children may have both; for example, they may be overly sensitive to smells but have difficulty catching a ball because they are under-sensitive to touch.

How Common Are SPIs?

While there do not seem to be many recent studies that look at rates for the general population, we found one from 2004 that suggests 1 in every 6.25 children has an SPI![3] Interestingly, the rate in adults is about 1 in 20!

Factors that Make SPIs Worse

Many people who find sensory issues moderately annoying, find them overwhelming if they are sleep deprived or stressed. For example, Ashley has been sleeping well for the past week. When she listens to a concert, she often finds the music quite intense, but she can listen all the way through a two-hour concert.

One day Ashley goes to a concert after she has been sleeping poorly for the past week. Before the music starts, the people talking and moving to their seats gives her a migraine. As soon as the music starts, she feels that her head is about to explode, feels the walls are closing in on her, and wants to violently throw up. Within twenty seconds of the concert starting, she needs to leave.

Learning and SPIs

SPIs can significantly impact a child's ability to learn. Sometimes students are misdiagnosed with learning disabilities or a low IQ because they can't seem to read. One reason can be that some people with an SPI can't read text on white paper because the white is too intense for them—it would be like trying to read off a bright spotlight for people without an SPI. If you change the paper to light brown or maybe light blue, the person can often read well. Tinted glasses may also be able to help with this issue.

Also, some people with an SPI may have issues with similar sounding words, such as *cat*, *hat*, and *bat*. They fail to process the consonants differently in their head, so they hear it as the same sounds. In the film *Rain Man*, the character played by Tom Cruise has a brother named Raymond, but he hears it as "Rain Man."

Alarms

One significant issue for children with SPIs can be the school bell: it's often a loud, high-pitched tone. For some children with SPIs, every time they hear the bell, it sets off their brain's emergency response.[4]

As we mentioned in the chapter on child development, children naturally hear higher sound frequencies than adults. If we look at this in the context of SPIs, we can see how this can be terrifying for some students. We have encouraged many of the schools we work with to replace the school bell with quieter music. The schools that have taken this advice have all said what a difference it makes.

We once worked with a girl who had an SPI with a severe sensitivity to noise. Her school had a fire drill where they set off a high-pitched fire alarm. Because of the sound, she went into a freeze response, huddled up in a ball on the ground, and burst into tears, unable to move. If that had been a real fire, she could have died.

There are smoke alarms that can replace the high-pitched squeal with a human voice. Researchers suggest that the sound of a mother's voice is three times more effective at waking children than a traditional alarm.[5] If you have a child who has sensory issues and finds alarms distressing, it is worth thinking about what other types of alarms are available.

At the time of writing this book, we are trying to work with the New Zealand Police to change the sound of their siren. We have had significant issues with a number of young drivers who flee police and end up accidentally killing themselves or others because they are so distressed and are unable to think about the consequences of the actions.[6] We believe the very design of the police siren is the problem: the quickly oscillating and high-pitched siren puts many people into the fight-or-flight mode rather than the safely-stop mode. We are trying to find an "alerting sound" that is not dysregulating. (We are grateful to Dr. Porges for his assistance with this.)

Addressing SPIs

People often become distressed or anxious because the natural rhythms of their body are out of alignment. Dr. Stephen Porges has developed a treatment for helping people called the Safe and Sound Protocol

(SSP), which involves a person listening to special sounds for, say, an hour a day for five days. The sounds help to calm and regulate the vagus nerve. A lot of people on the autistic spectrum have received this treatment. Before treatment, many people reported a severe sensitivity to many sounds in the environment. After treatment, they found noises in their environment less invasive and distressing.[7] The SSP can also help with the effects of trauma, such as feeling anxious, not being able to sleep, and inability to focus. We know several people whose sensitivities to sound and touch improved after they went through the SSP.

Making the World Quieter

Many supermarkets now offer a low-sensory hour, when they have dimmed lights and no music. A number of other organizations—such as swimming pools, cafés, and even some churches—are trying to offer accomodations that cater to people with SPIs. If you live in an area where this is not available, you could talk to a manager to see if they would be willing to try this.

Noise-canceling headphones can also be really helpful. Traditional earmuffs muffle and block the sound but usually don't cut out the sounds completely. Noise-canceling headphones listen to the sounds in the environment and produce sounds that are the opposite of what is in the environment. This cancels out the noises people hear. Most people with sound sensitivities prefer noise-canceling headphones to earmuffs.

Alternatively, Flare Audio has developed a product called Calmer Life that is like earplugs but still allows you to hear. They cut out the high frequencies, which many people with SPIs find very helpful. These devices can be especially helpful for people with SPIs to get to sleep.[8]

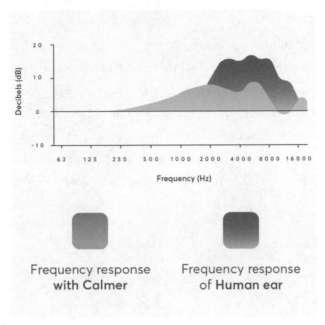

Frequency response without and with Calmer Life.

Putting the Theory into Practice

We were once approached by a family with a teenage daughter who often cut herself and had made several suicide attempts. For over two years, the family had tried many forms of therapy, including cognitive behavioral therapy (CBT), EMDR, art therapy, and several medications. Nothing made a difference.

We were talking to her mother one day when we asked, "Does your daughter have a sensitivity to sound?" Her mother said yes; no one yet had recognized the significant of this. We explained how a lot of the self-harm and suicidal behavior was probably caused by sensory issues. The family started to address this by buying her noise-canceling headphones, limiting loud noises she was around (such as from the vacuum cleaner), and getting the school to stop using the bell. They got her to go through the SSP, and within a few weeks, her symptoms of mental illness, self harm, and suicide went away.

Conclusion

SPIs are a substantial cause of angry, aggressive, or even violent behavior in children. Part of the problem is that many children don't know they have it, so they seem to have unexplained, explosive outbursts. It can be a complex subject because everyone with SPIs can find different things upsetting and overwhelming. When parents start to understand SPIs, they can start to change the environment around their children and take proactive steps to address or even treat them.

Chapter Twenty-Four:
Neurodevelopmental Challenges: ASD, ADHD, and FASD

"When a flower doesn't bloom, you fix the environment in which it grows, not the flower."
—*Alexander Den Heijer*

As we've illustrated with SPIs, the brains of some people do not work the same way other people's brains do. Some children have what we call *neurodevelopmental challenges*. There are a significant number of these; however, we don't have enough space to cover all of them. Three common challenges that play a significant role in dysregulated children are autistic spectrum disorder (ASD), attention deficient hyperactivity disorder (ADHD), and fetal alcohol spectrum disorder (FASD). The names are a bit of a mouthful, but we will explain them simply.

ASD

Autism is defined by having difficulty with social interactions. We use the term *autistic spectrum* because some people have a mild form of autism while others have a stronger form. For example, at one end of the spectrum, some people may find it difficult to pick up social cues but be very intelligent and articulate, able to build strong relationships, and able to gain a meaningful job, such as a computer programmer.

At the other end of the autistic spectrum, some people may be non-verbal, meaning they cannot speak and have great difficulty in the world. People at this end of the spectrum may have trouble controlling their movements and may do things such as flap their hands a lot. They often have great difficulty controlling their emotions.

Professor Stephen Shore is an expert on autism and has said, "If you've met one individual with autism, you've met one individual with autism."[1] This means that everyone with autism is unique; no two people with autism are alike.

Temple Grandin, a prominent biologist who has autism herself, has done a good job of explaining what her experiences of autism are like. One of her books, *The Autistic Brain: Thinking Across the Spectrum*, co-written with Richard Panek, looks at the strengths of someone with autism. Grandin also has a number of good videos about autism on YouTube.

Often people with autism have difficulty with fine motor skills. Brain imaging studies have found that autistic people have a smaller cerebellum (as much as 20 percent smaller) than non-autistic people.[2] The cerebellum is associated with movement; if people with autism have a smaller cerebellum, then this may explain why they seem to be clumsy.

We like to think that the brains of people with ASD have an ineffective filtering system, meaning they are overwhelmed by sensory information more easily than people who don't have ASD. This overwhelming sensation could be made worse by the fact that our world is speeding up and becoming more intense.[3]

People with autism often get overwhelmed by too much information. The term *intense world syndrome* has been coined to described what many people with autism experience. Many people with autism are overwhelmed by everything in their environment, so they may withdraw into their own world.

Tito Rajarshi Mukhopadhyay has a different experience of autism. He is nonverbal, yet he is a highly intelligent poet. In his book *How Can I Talk If My Lips Don't Move? Inside My Autistic Mind*, he discusses some of the ways his autism affects him. He says he finds live human faces overwhelming because they move and change too quickly, but he is alright looking at a still photo of a face because it doesn't change. The book offers fascinating insights into how someone with autism may think and act.

Changes

Sometimes people with autism find small changes difficult. One young person Michael worked with always had to have five balls of Blu Tack with him; if he had four or six, he went into a tantrum that could last hours. One of the patterns that he needed in order to feel safe was the five balls of Blu Tack.

It may seem like a really small thing to us to have the right number of balls made from Blu Tack, but the autistic brain may not think like this. Having order is essential. Often someone with autism may become distressed if they start school at 9 a.m. most days and then 9:05 the next day. Even small changes can overwhelm some people with autism.

In *How Can I Talk If My Lips Don't Move?*, Tito writes that when he saw birds sitting in a tree, he also saw someone walk past. Therefore, in his mind, he always assumed the two things happened together. If he saw the birds without someone walking past, he would become extremely distressed. To many people, this may be a small change, but to someone with autism, it could be like saying to a non-autistic person, "We want you to start work tomorrow in your new office on the other side of the world in a country where you don't speak the language or know any of the culture." That would overwhelm most people.

Often people on the autistic spectrum see small changes as significant changes. We live in a world where systems are changing regularly. For example, just about every computer program has regular updates. We may think that a small change in an icon is insignificant, but to someone with autism, it can be very distressing.

Multi-Step Problems

People with autism often struggle if they have to complete something that involves multiple steps. If you ask most people to pour some flour into a bowl, then some sugar, then some eggs (three steps), most people can do this. But someone on the autistic spectrum may get overwhelmed and get lost after just one step. Instructions need to be given one step at a time.

Difficulty Understanding Emotions

An interesting study first asked children with and without autism to identify emotions of a TV character, such as sadness and joy.[4] They were all able to do this. But when the children with autism were asked to identify a mismatch in emotions, they struggled. For example, if someone smiles after another person spills hot coffee on them, they are not really happy about this at all—the smile means they are just being polite. Often the emotion we display on our faces does not reflect how we truly feel. Children without autism mostly understand this concept, but children with autism seem to struggle with it.

Communication

Many people with autism take things literally. The organization Autism New Zealand talks about a child with autism who was told by a teacher to go and wash their hands in the toilet. The child took this literally and washed their hands in the toilet bowl! This occurs because people with autism follow instructions exactly as they are said. The English language is filled with metaphors and analogies, and many autistic people find these very difficult to understand.

If we change our communication, we can help people with autism to understand the world better. If someone is angry and they say, "I feel like I'm going to explode," this is a very confusing statement to someone on the autistic spectrum (they may think the person is literally going to blow up). A better way to word this would be, "I am feeling angry." Another example is if you ask someone with autism to do a task "soon;" that could mean in five minutes, an hour, or a few days. You need to be precise in what you say.

A book by Temple Grandin and Sean Barron, *The Unwritten Rules of Social Relationships*, has plenty of great information to help people on the autistic spectrum, but it's also for parents and teachers to know how to better communicate and form social relationships with people on the autistic spectrum.

Finding Help

Until quite recently, it was thought that autism was unmanageable and untreatable; however, now we are starting to find ways to manage autism. There are many groups and societies around the world and online that specialize in helping people with autism, as well as their families, employers, and teachers. One such group in the United States is The Autism Society. In New Zealand, there is Autism New Zealand. They offer educational programs about autism and how to best work and communicate with autistic people.

Groups that support people with autism can often help them find meaningful work and suitable jobs; for example, jobs that involve constant change and needing to quickly learn lots of new information are often not well-suited to someone on the autistic spectrum. Jobs that have less change are better suited to someone on the autistic spectrum.

The lives of people with autism can be greatly improved with understanding and the right help and support.

ADHD

ADHD occurs when people have great difficulty concentrating and showing self-control because the circuitry in their brains is not working well. For example, they may find it exceptionally difficult to sit through an hour-long math class, get distracted very easily, have trouble finishing projects, and not be able to resist saying inappropriate things out loud. It is a condition that has a great many misunderstandings.

Some people think ADHD is about kids who want to run around too much; however, the technical name for this action is called "childhood." It is indeed a mark that society has lost its way when it tries to make natural childhood fun into a disease. However, genuine

ADHD can have serious consequences for someone's life. A 2015 study found that having unmanaged ADHD doubles the risk of early death due to acting without thinking of the consequences (e.g., running out in front of a car).[5]

Gabor Maté, a world-renowned doctor, wrote a great book on ADHD called *Scattered Minds*. He wrote the book because he has ADHD himself. He attributes his ADHD largely to his upbringing. He was born in Hungary in 1944; his father was put into forced labor and his grandparents were killed at the hands of the Nazis. He believes this trauma played a large role in how he developed ADHD. The possibility of trauma as a source of similar symptoms is important to consider.

Misconceptions about ADHD

ADHD is really misunderstood. Some people think all children are hyperactive, so it is not real. Yes, children are usually more energetic than many adults, but some children have significantly more diffi-culty with self-control than others. Brain scans of people with genuine ADHD reveal something interesting:[6]

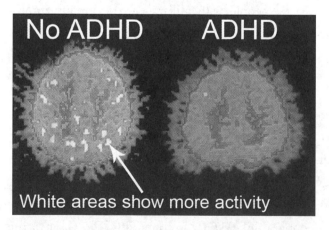

Scans of a brain without ADHD and a brain with ADHD.

The non-ADHD brain, on the left, shows a lot more activity than the ADHD brain. Does it seem as though these are the wrong way around? Shouldn't the ADHD brain be firing in all directions and show lots of activity?

When researchers first saw this, it didn't seem to make any sense. When they looked closer, they found that one of the parts of the brain most affected by ADHD is the prefrontal cortex, which helps us control our emotions and focus our attention. If the part of the brain that helps us control ourselves doesn't work so well for someone with ADHD, then it makes sense that people with ADHD have difficulty controlling their emotions and concentrating, and thus have an under-active brain.

We used to think that children had ADHD and then grew out of it. This was because researchers asked the adults with ADHD if they still had the symptoms, and many said no. When the subjects' friends and family were asked, they said the symptoms continued into adulthood. ADHD can persist for life unless it is managed.[7]

Another myth is that people with ADHD can't concentrate at all. Gabor Maté managed to make it through medical school and has written several complex books. So, it is not impossible for people with ADHD to achieve great things, but it can be more difficult.

Be Aware of Different Needs

People with ADHD may say inappropriate things. We know of someone with ADHD who was unable to get a job for about two years. Finally, someone gave him a chance. As soon as he walked into the workplace, he saw a female co-worker with large breasts. He loudly said, "She's got big boobs." Needless to say, he was not employed for long.

Often children with ADHD feel they are worthless because they feel they can't do anything right. Sooner or later we all think of inappropriate things, but most of us can control what we say. Often people with ADHD don't have the control part of their brain working so well. The person above was sorry for what he'd said, and he immediately regretted it. He wasn't trying to be offensive; he just didn't have the same self-control many of us have. ADHD can make it hard to get and keep jobs, so it is important to address it.

Help and Diagnosis

We want to be clear: Many children without ADHD are misdiagnosed with it. There are other factors that can lead to similar behavior, and in other chapters we demonstrate that trauma, poor sleep, and a lack of free play can all cause symptoms similar to ADHD. ADHD is supposed to be a diagnosis by exclusion; in other words, a clinician needs to rule out all other possible explanations before they come to a diagnosis of ADHD. Too often, it is the first diagnosis they go with.

There are a lot of controversies regarding a diagnosis of ADHD. Sometimes it can be managed with medication, but other times, we need to adapt the world to the way their brain works. For example, someone with ADHD may only be able to manage a fifteen-minute science class rather than a full hour.

In the chapter on treatments for trauma, we mentioned that neurofeedback can be helpful for trauma, but it can also be helpful for ADHD. A large study found that neurofeedback makes a big difference in impulsivity and inattention and helped somewhat with hyperactivity.[8]

A fairly new line of treatment involves the administration of micro-nutrients. A 2020 review found that when used correctly, this can be as—if not more—effective than traditional ADHD medication.[9]

There are lots of ways to manage the behavior associated with ADHD if we understand its true causes. When parents and teachers start to understand what is happening, they can take appropriate steps to get a child the needed help.

FASD

FASD is a permanent brain injury that is caused when a child within the womb is exposed to alcohol. (We should also mention that children

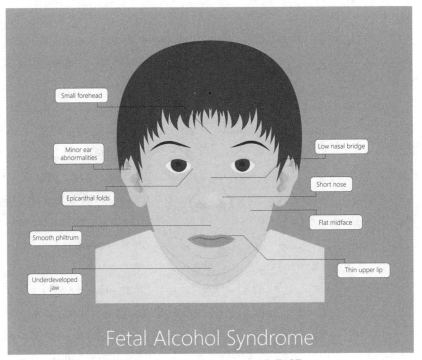

Small forehead

Minor ear abnormalities

Low nasal bridge

Short nose

Epicanthal folds

Flat midface

Smooth philtrum

Underdeveloped jaw

Thin upper lip

Fetal Alcohol Syndrome

Distinctive face of someone with FASD.

exposed to other drugs, such as methamphetamine and heroin, in the womb can also cause challenges in their life.)

You may think FASD is a new discovery, but during the British Gin Epidemic (between 1720 and 1750), the College of Physicians in London warned the British House of Commons that alcohol is "too often the cause of weak and feeble, distempered children."[10]

There are many parts of the brain that are affected by FASD. One significant challenge is that the corpus callosum does not work well.[11] The brain is made up of two parts, or hemispheres. The corpus callosum—located at the base of your brain—sends signals back and forward from one side of the brain to the other. If someone's corpus callosum does not work well, we can start to understand how FASD impacts them.

We still don't fully understand how much alcohol it takes to cause FASD. It used to be thought that a woman could have quite a few drinks before a child would develop FASD, but researchers have recently started to question this. The advice now is that there is no known safe quantity of alcohol that women can consume while pregnant and breastfeeding.

It can take some time for a woman to know that she is pregnant; in the meantime, she may have inadvertently had a few drinks. There can be a tremendous amount of fear and guilt that she "ruined" her child for life; however, the academic journal article "Alcohol Syndrome: The Origins of a Moral Panic," by Elizabeth Armstrong and Ernest Able, suggests there can be good outcomes for a child with FASD who gets the right help. If people with FASD get help and support early, then they have much better outcomes in life.[12]

When we think of FASD, we often think that people will have a low IQ and a distinctive face, with an upturned nose, thinner upper lips, and a flat nasal bridge. The distinctive face can be part of FASD, although only 10 percent of people with FASD have those facial features.

Understanding Social Interactions

People with FASD have trouble reading and understanding social cues and facial expressions. So much of what we say is not in the words we use, but in our tone and facial expressions. If a person does not understand this, it can make the world a confusing place. For example, if we hit another person, we will hopefully read on their face that we have upset them and we should stop. People with FASD are often not able to read the expressions on faces, so they may keep doing something that upsets someone and not realize they are upsetting them. If you explain to them how a certain action makes you feel, they will often understand it. Because of this, people with FASD may not learn from their mistakes as easily as other people do.

There Is Hope

We have both worked with a number of young people with FASD who were pretty much written off as a hopeless cases. Some people said, "They have FASD, so they're never going to amount to much." But we've seen some amazing success stories of people with FASD who have gone on to lead very successful lives. It's about finding something that they can do well.

Putting the Theory into Practice

We once worked with the mother of a fifteen-year-old boy. We quickly picked up that her son had a mild case of autism. His life had been difficult: he had been expelled from two schools for emotional outbursts, often punched holes in walls, was often bullied, and had trouble making friends.

We asked him to leave the room and talked to the mother about the possibility of autism. She had always suspected something wasn't quite right, and she had wondered about a diagnosis of autism. She was reluctant; she thought the label of "autism" would ruin her son's life, and she struggled to come to terms with it.

Eventually we talked her into getting an assessment for her son. She told us she cried when it came back showing her son had autism; it was very difficult for her to accept. After a while, she was able to join a support group for parents, and now that the school understood what was causing the emotional outbursts, they were able to manage this much better. There were still a few struggles, but the diagnosis did make a big difference and greatly improved many of the challenges the family had.

Eventually, the mother wished she'd gotten the diagnosis sooner. Sometimes diagnoses can be scary, but they often mean that better and more specialized help will be available.

Conclusion

ASD, ADHD, and FASD are complex issues and require specialist help. There is a significant amount of additional information on these issues that we have not presented; this is only a brief overview. We hope we have given you enough information to know a little about this and have pointed you in the right direction to find more help if you need it.

Even if your children don't have these conditions, it is really important to try and get them to interact with children who do. In the past, people with these conditions were isolated in special schools; now they are rightly finding a place in more mainstream schooling.

Chapter Twenty-Five:
Technology: The Good and the Bad

"Technology is just a tool. In terms of getting the kids working together and motivating them, the teacher is the most important."
—*Bill Gates*

One of the most difficult challenges many parents face today is the new world of technology. In this chapter, we look at some of the positives and negatives of technology.

When we give seminars and ask the audience what has led to today's rise in mental illness, the first thing almost every audience says is, "screens." People use the term *screens* to mean a number of things, including TVs, smart phones, social media, smart watches, tablets, and laptops. We will use the term *screens* to encompass all of them, with some special mentions of social media.

There seems to be a general belief that screens are responsible for the high rates of mental illness we have today.[1] We previously mentioned a study which suggests that rates of mental illness in US high school students have climbed sharply since the year 2010.[2] The first iPhone was released in 2007. So, the rise in mental illness does seem to coincide with the release of smart phones.§

In fact, mental illness began to rise long before smart phones. Results from the Minnesota Multiphasic Personality Inventory show that the percentage of young people who were worried about developing "madness" increased from 4.1 percent to 23.4 percent between 1948

---

§ In science, we say "correlation does not mean causation." This means that just because two things are related does not mean that they cause one another; for example, when ice cream sales increase, the murder rate increases. This does not mean that ice cream sales cause murders—there is another factor: hot weather. More people buy ice cream on hot days, and more people are murdered on hot days.

and 1986. That was a time before people had smart phones, so things were going wrong before smart phones were around. There is no one cause of the rise in mental illness we have today.

Many people (wrongly) make social media out to be the single villain that has caused the rise in mental illness. In this book, we suggest that trauma, fewer social connections, poor sleep, and the lack of free play are significant causes of the rise in mental illness. Social media may not help, but it is not the sole cause of things going wrong. There are also many positive aspects of screens.

The Positive Aspects of Screens

Screens are tools, and when they are used wisely, they can make a positive difference to children and young people. For example, we know a young man who developed an eating disorder. He couldn't find another male to connect with in his area who was going through the same challenges, but he was able to form positive friendships online that were able to help him. When used correctly, the internet can be an amazing place to make friends and connections that are not otherwise available. (Michael met his wife on the internet—she was living in the United States at the time!)

A 2019 study from Oxford University found that teenagers who spend one or two hours online for personal use each day report better emotional well-being and connectedness. It is important to note, though, that when there was more than two hours of screen time, teenagers' emotional well-being started to decline.[3]

In the past, there were many remote and isolated areas where it was difficult to access help. Researchers have found that technology allows people in remote or isolated areas to access much-needed help. A 2015 study found that therapy delivered online by trained professionals can be very effective.[4]

The internet is more than just cat videos; it is an incredible source of information. In the past, if you wanted to find information, you were limited to what your local library or bookstore had. Now there is almost unlimited information at our fingertips. This can be a great way for children to learn a language, master DIY projects, learn to cook, become an origami guru, or broaden their minds.

Challenges with Screens

We have just shown you some of the positives of screens; now we look at some of the ways in which they can be problematic.

Sitting Time

One of the biggest negative effects that screens have is not on mental health, but rather physical health. A study found that the more time adolescents (fourteen- to eighteen-year-olds) spend in front of screens, the more likely they are to be overweight or obese.[5]

In a report titled, "Guidelines on Physical Activity, Sedentary Behavior and Sleep," the World Health Organization (WHO) suggests limiting screen time for children under five to less than one hour a day, with no screen time for infants under the age of one.[6] One of the main reasons behind their suggestion is to try and reduce the chances of obesity in children by making them more active.

Comprehension

Another thing to consider is that students may have better comprehension and understand things better when they read on paper rather than screens.[7] One reason may be that when many people read something on a screen, they just skim it, whereas on paper, people are likely to read it more thoroughly.

Wasted Time

One aspect of screen and social media use that often does not get a lot of attention is wasted time. Screens can be a fantastic way to learn new and valuable information and improve your life, but they become problematic when people waste large amounts of time using them.

It is quite okay to take a break and watch a few mindless videos, or "like" or "follow" a few funny pages on social media. But when people spend hours and hours doing this, it becomes problematic. We all have limited time on this earth, and we must try and to use the limited time we have to the best of our ability.

Social Media

A 2020 study found that regular social media use only leads to a small increase in depressive symptoms. Social media may not help reduce depression, but it is not the single villain responsible for the rapid rise in mental illness.[8]

Social media can also make some people feel like everyone is doing better than them. Many people are selective about what they post online, only posting or exaggerating the good things in their lives. This can lead many people to feel like they are failing in life when, in reality, they are doing well.

To illustrate this, we had a client at 298 Youth Health who thought she didn't have enough friends—she had ten good friends. We thought that was quite a few, but she thought everyone else on social media seemed to have a lot more friends. Social media distorted her perception of how well she was doing in life.

Screen Addiction

A lot of young people like playing games and being on screens; however, some people seem to develop a genuine addiction where they cannot stop themselves using screens or games. Some of these people are on screens for hours and hours at night, which disrupts their sleep.

Some parents have been told the best thing to do if this occurs is to take away the phone or modem, but if a child has developed a genuine addiction, they can have a chemical dependence in their brain for the thing they are using. We have tragically heard of addicted children who assaulted their parents or tore apart locked cupboards looking for a modem. If your child has reached this point, they will need specialized help. Fortunately, there are more and more professionals who specialize in gaming addiction.

Cyber Bullying

We used to think that everyone was bullied in school; it happened to everyone and they just got over it eventually. Researchers are now finding that bullying can have devastating and long-lasting consequences, including depression, anxiety, self-harm, and even suicide. Many children who have been bullied display the kinds of behavioral problems we address in this book. Many adults report that, decades later, the bullying they experienced at school still affects them.

Bullying is never acceptable and should always be stopped as soon as possible. All parents and teachers should be working toward helping young people live without bullying. A new form of bullying is cyber bullying.

Cyber bullying includes sending abusive messages online, publicly belittling people, and posting private content on a public forum. For example, if a woman was pregnant and didn't want others to know, posting this online would be a form of cyber bullying.

Cyber bullying is often much more pervasive than traditional bullying, and children who experience cyber bullying may be more likely to become suicidal than those who experience traditional bullying.[9] Technology means a child can now be bullied in their home, twenty-four hours a day, seven days a week. There is no break. Some children face a constant barrage of abusive messages.

Some people believe cyber bullying may be worse than traditional bullying because the audience can seem greater. If someone posts something unpleasant on a child's social media profile, it can seem like everyone that child knows and loves has seen it; they have been humiliated in front of their whole world.

Research suggests that both victims and perpetrators of bullying, including cyber bulling, experience poor outcomes in life and higher rates of anxiety and depression.[10]

We will discuss how to address cyber bullying after we mention online predators and dangerous content because the solution is the same for all these topics.

Dangerous Content

The internet can give people access to the greatest parts of humanity, but it can also give them access to the entirety of human evil. When the mosque shooting occurred in Christchurch in 2019, the gunman livestreamed it. Tragically, a lot of young children saw this. Many of them did not go looking for it—it just came up on their Facebook feed. Quite a few of the people who saw it did not realize what it was before they saw some very disturbing content.

We have heard countless stories of children finding videos of real beheadings, rapes, and other gruesome images on the internet. We encourage parents and teachers to talk about what is safe and unsafe on the internet. This must be done carefully; if you say to a child, "Don't go looking for beheading videos," they probably will become curious and go look for them. A better approach is to say, "If you see anything that you find disturbing, please come and talk to me."

It can be immensely shocking for parents and teachers to discover that innocent children have seen these things. Some parents and teachers may need help themselves to manage this.

Open Conversations

Many people say the best way to stop young people accessing content is to put filters on devices and to limit access. The problem with this is a lot of children know how to get past filters or their friends share devices with them.

A better approach is to try and form an open and positive relationship with your child. We encourage you to say, "If ever you find something disturbing or if someone embarrasses you or hurts you, please come and talk to us as soon as possible. Even if you have made a mistake, we want you to come to us as soon as possible." Even if you feel like shouting at them if they do tell you that they have been hurt or done something wrong online, it is really important to respond well and say, "I am so glad you told me that."

After the mosque shooting, some schools suspended or expelled students who saw the video. Doing this makes it less likely children will speak up and seek help.

Punishing mistakes drives the harm caused underground, while an open relationship allows healing to take place as soon as possible.

Conclusion

Some people believe the impact of technology on young people is always negative. While there are many negative effects, we have shown in this chapter that there can also be a lot of positives and benefits from technology use. Technology is a tool that can be a positive or a negative.

Part Two:

Helping Your Child

Chapter Twenty-Six:
Finding the Right Help

"We need to help young people and their parents understand that it's not a sign of weakness to ask for help."
—Kate Middleton, Duchess of Cambridge

When some parents read behavioral management or self-help books, they feel like failures. We think the very idea of self-help books could be the problem. Many of these books suggest you can manage these challenging situations on your own. Many books propose that their solution is the answer to everything. The behaviors we describe in chapter one are so difficult to manage, they are not behaviors that any one person can manage on their own. We disagree that self-help books alone will make everything okay. Families should never have to go through difficult situations alone. They need help, and often from multiple people.

The Multidisciplinary Approach

There is a traditional African saying: "It takes a village to raise a child." This means that raising a child is a big responsibility and one person cannot do it on his or her own. The same may apply to seeking help. The situations and behaviors we described in chapter one are immensely challenging. No one person has it within themselves to solve these alone. One must start to work collaboratively by involving helping professionals.

In the past, parents would have a meeting with a child's teacher and get one piece of advice. Then they would go to a doctor and often get an entirely different piece of advice. Then they would go to a social service and get advice that contradicts the first two pieces of advice. It was frustrating for all involved.

In 1995, Sue helped establish 198 Youth Health, New Zealand's first Youth One Stop Shop, or YOSS for short. The idea of a YOSS is that a multidisciplinary team of medical doctors, nurses, counselors, youth workers, social workers, and many other helping professionals all work together in one location.

198 Youth Health was eventually redeveloped to become 298 Youth Health, which is now one of fourteen Youth One Stop Shops throughout New Zealand.

298 Youth Health does not just work collaboratively with its internal staff, but it tries to get to know as many other service providers within the city as it can and network with them. The staff also often has other social service providers come to staff meetings to share what they offer. This can be time-consuming, but it means that when someone needs help, we often know exactly where to send them.

Some professionals feel that they don't have time to work with others, but we have found that a multidisciplinary team saves significant amounts of time because we don't work against other professionals. Using this approach, the people who need help are usually sent to the right place the first time, rather than spending one or two hours with one professional before discovering they were not right, and so on, and so on.

This is one reason why a professional may seek your permission to share your information with other professionals. They know that sharing information with other professionals will be much more beneficial to you.

Solving the Actual Problems

When Michael worked at 298 Youth Health, he was hired to work with people between the ages of ten and twenty-five. Some organizations would say, "You are *only* to work with people aged ten to twenty-five. You're not allowed to work with their families" or, "You're not allowed to do anything outside of your job description." Sue allowed Michael the freedom to see what the real problems were and to actually solve them.

For example, Michael once worked with a young man who was highly stressed because his grandmother was dying. The family was poor, and the mother had no money to travel across New Zealand to see the dying grandmother. This caused huge stress in the household. Michael approached a local church, asking them to fund some gasoline so the mother could travel. This was well outside his job description, but by addressing the real problem, he was able to help the young man.

Help for the Whole Family

We recommend that parents get some help and support for themselves. In New Zealand, we have a great organization called Yellow Brick Road, previously called Supporting Families with Mental Illness. We often think that mental illness just affects one person, but this is not the case at all. If a child is really struggling, it will disrupt the whole family. If a parent goes to work after having an emotional time trying to get a child to have breakfast, brush his teeth, and get to school, their work will not be perfect. This is why we need to encourage other people affected by a child's disruptive behavior to get some help and support for themselves.

Finding the Right Helping Professional

One of the big questions is, "How do you choose the right helping professionals?" Unfortunately, not all helping professionals are helpful.

We worked with a fifteen-year-old who had been given twelve different diagnoses in his lifetime. He was given a diagnoses of ADHD, generalized anxiety disorder, bi-polar disorder, borderline personality disorder, conduct disorder, oppositional defiance disorder, intermittent explosive disorder, and antisocial personality disorder, including some others that we can't remember. Incredibly, none of the previous people asked about a history of trauma. (It turned out he had a significant history of both physical and sexual abuse.)

Each professional was more interested in diagnosing a new illness rather than helping him. The tragic thing is none of these professionals realized the harm they were causing. Each new diagnosis just left the family more confused and frustrated. It is important to explain to a therapist what it is that you want. If you feel that a therapist is just interested in giving a label rather than actually helping, we suggest you look for someone else.

Here are some other key things to look for when choosing a helping professional:

- Is this person someone who you and your child get along well with?
- Does the person seem interested in genuinely helping or just diagnosing mental illness?
- Does the person show compassion and understanding or show blame and criticism?
- Does the person know what he or she is doing or is the person out of his or her depth?
- Does the person look at the whole client, family relationships, and home and school environment, or does the person have a narrow view?
- Is the person part of a professional body? For example, in New Zealand, counselors should be part of an organization such as the New Zealand Association of Counsellors.

It can be a good idea to ask trusted family members or friends if they know someone who has been helpful in the past. Although, someone who was helpful for a friend or family member may not be right for your situation, so this is not a guarantee.

Next we will look at what some of the different helping professionals do. These are a very loose descriptions, and many of these professionals can do different things, but there can be a lot of crossover.

Nurse

Many schools have public health nurses; if your child's school has one, this can be a great place to start. Nurses can be great people to talk to about what is going on and can perform a number of important health checks for children. They can usually give you a solid direction for the kinds of help you may need. Often, they are really good at linking people with the right services and supports in the area.

General Practitioner or Family Doctor

You can go to any general practitioner (GP) or family doctor with concerns about mental illness or mental well-being. They can be good gatekeepers because they probably know many local services you can access. They can look into what might be going on and, in some cases, prescribe medication.

Counselor

A counselor is someone a child can talk to and who should be able to teach some age-appropriate strategies to help the child overcome some of their difficulties. For example, if a child has trouble fitting in and making friends, a good counselor should be able to help them learn new ways to talk to people and make friends. When choosing a counselor, it is important to try and find the right fit; for example, many counselors have a specialty area, such as children or eating disorders.

Psychotherapist

A psychotherapist is quite similar to a counselor; however, this professional focuses on what triggers the issues in the first place. Often, a psychotherapist will go back to someone's childhood to look at where their distress came from. Given what we know about the impact of childhood trauma, this can be especially helpful.

Psychiatrist

A psychiatrist is a medical doctor who specializes in mental illness. A psychiatrist can help with more complex and challenging mental illnesses, as opposed to mild to moderate problems and behaviors. Sometimes psychiatrists have a much broader range of options to try than other professionals, and so may be able to help with very complex problems.

If you're not sure whether you need a GP or a psychiatrist, then you should go to your GP first and they will tell you if you need a psychiatrist. Private psychiatrists are often quite expensive, and those in the public system who are free may have long waiting lists.

Psychologist

Psychologists are often more suited to complex forms of mental illness or distress. Unlike a doctor or psychiatrist, they cannot prescribe medication. Many psychologists have a specialty area, such as eating disorders or children's therapy.

Peer Supporter

This is often someone who has personal experience with the challenges they are helping with. It can be really helpful to talk to somebody who has been through what you are experiencing. If you have a child who has behavioral difficulties, it can be really helpful to have another parent who has faced similar issues be there to support you.

Social Worker

A social worker is somebody who helps with practical needs, such as finding housing or helping someone find a job. We have focused a lot on children who struggle, but sometimes social workers may be able to help support the whole family. Social workers can also be really good to talk to and help point people in the right direction to find other help.

Youth Worker or Mentor

Youth workers or mentors tend not to offer therapy, but they might do something with the child once a week, such as play sports, create an art project, or maybe just go for a walk. This can give the parents a break and the young person something fun to do. We recommend that if you decide to do this, where possible, involve the young person when choosing someone.

There is some really good evidence that building a positive relationship with a youth worker or a mentor can be immensely helpful.[1] Teenage girls who had mentors were four times less likely to bully others, and boys with mentors were three times less likely to feel anxious.[2]

We do stress that if you involve youth workers, you should fully explain the situation and what you want the youth worker or mentor to do. If little Johnny likes to run in front of cars, telling the youth worker that the child is an angel does not benefit anyone.

Finding the Right Person

When choosing a helping professional, some people ask, "Should I choose the most qualified person?" Qualifications can be a helpful guide, but we have come to realize that it is the relationship between client and therapist that is most important.[3]

Michael hosts a local radio show on mental illness. He has interviewed hundreds of adult guests with personal experience of mental illness. He asked many of them, "If you had one piece of advice for someone going through this, what would it be?" Person after person has said to him, "I wish I had known I could change counselors or doctors, and you should too."

If you think a professional is not helping, you can stop seeing them and find someone else. In an earlier chapter, we mentioned the importance of understanding child development when we're trying to manage behavioral issues in children. Sadly, there are a lot of therapists who don't seem to understand this, especially when it comes to children and teenagers. They try to use advanced forms of therapy, that even many adults would struggle with, on children and young people.

Taking a Child to Therapy

Trying to get an anxious child into therapy can be an immense challenge. There is no hard-and-fast rule about what works best for all children. For some children, telling them a week in advance that you have booked the appointment, taking them to see the building beforehand, showing them an online picture of the therapists, and sitting down and going through step-by-step what the therapy will involve can really help. For other children, though, giving them time to worry will make their anxiety worse—sometimes it's just best to take them there with little warning.

A fascinating study found that the more control therapy clients are given, such as how bright or dark the room is, the better their recovery.[4] Most trauma is about some form of loss of control, so we must try to empower people seeking help rather than making them more helpless. When possible, try to give a child the option to be in control, such as by asking them, "Would you like me to stay with you or leave the room?"

We know many children throw such a violent tantrum that their parents cannot get them to a therapy session. If you can't get your child to therapy sessions, it is really important to keep trying. If someone missed an appointment at 298 Youth Health, we would send them a message saying, "We are sorry you missed your appointment; would you like to book another one?" Many people who'd desperately needed help said they were so thankful for the message because they'd thought if they missed an appointment, they would not be seen again.

If an attempt at getting help does not work, you must keep trying.

Confidentiality

Some parents are not sure how much information they should provide to a therapist. It is a difficult balancing act between protecting privacy and making sure children have the best care. We recommend telling the helping professionals as much as possible; the more information they have, the easier it is to help. For example, the knowledge that a child was beaten by a family member could allow the helping professional to make better choices about the right kind of help your child needs.

Most countries have something like the New Zealand Privacy Code. It says that in most situations, you should keep confidential information private. Under this code, Rule 11 says that if you need to break confidentiality to protect someone from injury (physical or mental) or to save someone's life, then you have a legal right to do so.[5] For example, if someone told you a child is being sexually abused, you must tell someone who can stop it. You should always remember that safety and human life are always more important than confidentiality and privacy.

Where to Start

The world of help-seeking can be confusing. There are so many different options for help. How do you think someone would react if you asked them the following: "Would you like to see a psychiatrist? Would you like to see a psychologist? A counselor? A social worker? Or maybe a psychotherapist? Would you like a CBT counselor? A dialectical behavioral therapy (DBT) counselor? A gestalt therapist? A solutions-focused therapist? Or a person-centered therapist? Which would you like?"

If we give too many options, it can be overwhelming. We have begun telling people, "If you or your child are overwhelmed and you don't know where to start, go to your GP." A good GP shouldn't automatically prescribe medication, but they should be able to help you find more help in your area—and they may even know how to access this for free.

When to Start

Some people ask, "Do I need to wait until my child is really bad before I get help?" Some services will only see people who are critical, but it is important to know that not all services do this. Often it is much easier to help someone when things are starting to go wrong rather than leaving it until conditions are really bad.

Barriers to Getting Help

One of the problems with seeking help is that it can be expensive. When Sue established 198 Youth Health, she established it as a free health center for young people because she knew that those who needed it most were not be able to afford it.

There are many charities that offer help for free; doing an internet search for free counseling or social services in your area can be a good start. If this is not available, you may be able to approach an organization, such as a local church or charity, to see what other options are available.

Some people live in isolated areas where there is no help. Many helping professionals now offer help via phone or through online video apps, so even people in isolated areas can access help.

No matter where you are or how much money you have, someone will be able to help.

Making a Complaint about a Professional

If you do need to make a professional complaint about someone you are working with, here are some things to consider. We encourage you not to complain about every little thing that might go wrong. Therapists do make mistakes, and they are human. If you are unhappy about a small thing a professional does, we encourage you to openly talk to them and try to see what can be changed. Most people can only improve if they are aware of what they have done wrong.

What we do suggest you make a complaint about is a substantial breach of trust or professional practice.

Every helping professional should be part of a registered association or body that upholds standards of practice. As a registered member, each professional should have done the appropriate training and abide by clear rules of conduct. If you contact the professional's association, they can often help you make a complaint.

Conclusion

The world of seeking help is often quite confusing and difficult. If you are not sure where to start, we suggest choosing one thing you want to address; maybe it is your child's sleep, the sensory issues, or their anger. Once you have chosen that one thing, start looking for professionals who can help with that. *Please remember: seeking help for children with challenging behavior is likely to be a long process; please don't expect significant results within a few sessions.*

Chapter Twenty-Seven:
Challenges with Many Current Approaches

"It isn't that they cannot find the solution. It is that they cannot see the problem."
—*G.K. Chesterton*

There are many books, seminars, online videos, and blog posts about behavioral management that are less than helpful. They offer solutions that just cannot work. We believe one of the big causes of this is that a number of books and online blogs suggest that for severe behavioral problems, you just do X, Y, and Z and you'll have the perfect child.

In this chapter, we look at some of the reasons why many of the current approaches to behavioral management don't work. These flawed approaches tend to fall into three broad categories: 1) the rules approach, 2) the one-problem model, and 3) the one-size-fits-all solution.

The Rules Approach

The first major approach to child and behavioral management is the rules approach.

The rules approach assumes children who display the behaviors we talk about in chapter one are naughty, disobedient, or malicious. The proponents of the rules approach believe that the reason children are so disobedient is not enough rules or boundaries.

One-Problem Model

The next type of problematic parenting and behavioral management advice falls under the category of the one-problem model. It assumes that the reason children misbehave is because there's one problem. If you can fix or change this, then you'll solve their behavioral problems.

Examples of the one-problem model include screens, lack of exercise, social media, video games, rap music, deadbeat dads, toxic masculinity, and racism. What this model fails to realize is that behavioral problems are usually caused by a combination of factors. To generalize that all behavioral problems narrow down to one factor does not consider individual circumstances.

Take sugar, for example. It certainly does add to some children's behavioral difficulties; however, for children who don't have much sugar, there must be other explanations as to why they're showing behavioral problems.

Take a moment to think how parents feel when they hear the one-problem model. Many of them have limited their children's screen time, stopped their children listening to rap music, and have reduced their children's sugar intake. Despite doing all these things, their children still show behavioral problems and the parents are still being blamed for it. Blaming parents like this only makes them feel worse and makes them less likely to seek help.

One-Size-Fits-All Model

The next broad category is the one-size-fits-all model.

We are concerned about the explosion of literature in the child discipline and behavioral management field that says there is one technique for solving all behavioral problems. These books say, "Use this technique the author has devised—no matter who the child is, no matter what the situation is—and it will fix the behavior." This is naive. No one book, no one treatment, and no one form of therapy is going to work for everyone.

Many people think mindfulness (focusing on your breathing) is a magic cure that will treat children with all forms of anxiety. While mindfulness can be really helpful for some people, a study published in 2019 found that 25.6 percent of adults who tried mindfulness had unpleasant experiences with it.[1]

Throughout this book, one of our guiding principles is that there is no one-size-fits-all solution. We must cater to individual differences. This also applies to families with more than one child; what may have worked for one of the children may not work for other members of the family.

We include about fifty books in the reference section that you can read to learn more about specific issues. We do this because we are certain we do not have all the answers.

Punishments

Many people assume the best way to modify a child's behavior is to punish them when they do something bad. For punishments to work, a child needs to have chosen to do the wrong thing. Often when children have an explosive outburst, they get upset and act without thinking. Punishments don't modify this behavior because a child is not necessarily choosing the wrong thing; when they have an explosive outburst, it could be because they are tired, anxious, upset by sensory issues, etc. They are often not deliberately doing the wrong thing.

The following are some additional issues with using punishments to modify a child's behavior.

See Needs

Many behavioral management approaches punish children for distress. This just adds to their pain and suffering. Imagine being a child, trying to communicate with adults, and trying to say, "I'm distressed. I don't feel safe. I'm in pain"—only for an adult to punish you. This experience would show you that when you ask for help, you are not given the help you need. We can only imagine the long-term consequences of this.

If a child came into the hospital with a burst appendix, we wouldn't punish the child and say, "Now sit in the corner and have a time out."

We would see that the child gets the needed help. The important thing is to see the need underlying the behavior and try to get help for that rather than immediately reaching for a punishment.

Making Things Worse

Punishments tend to exacerbate rather than deescalate the problem. Some people suggest that when a child misbehaves, you should take away their stickers from a sticker chart, if they have one. However, we often find that if you say, "Right, that's it. You've lost your stickers now," the child becomes more aggressive, distressed, and upset. Punishments usually increase the problematic behavior rather than solve it.

Numbness from Trauma

Many children who have experienced trauma, numb themselves. When it comes to punishment, people assume that children will become fearful of that punishment, but children who have numbed themselves often don't feel the fear of the punishment, so, this strategy does not work.

Importance of Regulative Factors

Punishments should never remove things that help regulate a child. In the book *Let the Children Play*, the authors say that schools take away break times (recess) as a punishment. We must see that break times are not a reward, but rather a chance to let off steam and de-stress. Taking away this option multiplies the problems rather than solves them. Children who don't get breaks tend to act out more.

We have to be very careful that when we look at punishment, we don't take away ways to manage stress or opportunities for social connection. For example, stopping a child from seeing beloved grand-parents should not be a punishment for bad behavior.

Are Children Ever Naughty?

Are we saying that children never need boundaries or rules? Of course not. They do need to have some limitations. However, it is important to know that, by and large, the problems we're referring to are not problems of naughtiness.

But Rewards Are Okay, Right?

The reward method assumes children can calmly choose the right thing to do, but when children become distraught, they don't think about future consequences. As with the punishment method, using rewards to change a child's behavior will not work.

We use rewards all the time to try and change behavior, but believe it or not, there is very little evidence that they work, and considerable evidence that they backfire. In a classic 1973 study, researchers asked groups of children to draw pictures. For their pictures, one group would receive a certificate with a gold seal and a ribbon on it, while the other group would draw for the sheer enjoyment. They found the children who knew they would receive the rewards drew half as many pictures, which were judged to be far less creative than those who did it for enjoyment.[2]

In the book *Punished by Rewards*, Alfie Kohn offers strong evidence from many other studies that rewards are not a good idea. He suggests that rewards demotivate us and we start to only do things because of a reward. Kohn suggests that rewards for reading, such as giving vouchers for pizza, also don't work. If you were to be given a voucher for reading twenty books, would you read challenging books to test yourself or would you read the simplest and easiest ones you could find to get through as many as you could? Rewards also suggest that the task you are doing is not enjoyable, so you need to be rewarded to do it. For example, being given pizza vouchers for reading implies that reading is a chore and not something that is enjoyable for its own sake.

Conclusion

Many parents feel like they are a failure when they read behavioral management books and discover they can't make the techniques work for their child. Often this is not because the parents are doing them incorrectly; it is because the techniques simply don't work for their child. That is why we look at a wide variety of techniques, strategies, and therapies, and there can be no one-size-fits-all approach.

Chapter Twenty-Eight:
Removing a Child from School

"Part of the happiness of life consists not in fighting battles, but in avoiding them. A masterly retreat is in itself a victory."
—*Norman Vincent Peale*

Many parents believe it is not possible to take a child out of school on a permanent or even temporary basis. We seem to have this idea that children are biologically dependent upon school. We emphasize many times throughout this book that there can be no one-size-fits-all solution for children. Unfortunately, the standard schooling system assumes one size does fit all and we should make every child go to school.

But not every child in the world *does* go to school. For example, if a child has a severe allergy to grass, then they may be allowed an exception from in-person schooling. We need to understand that there are many other children who find school very upsetting. In particular, we are concerned about forcing children with SPIs to go to school. Yes, some children with these issues may manage reasonably well, but it is important to know that some are overwhelmed by almost everything in the environment. We believe that forcing these children to go to school when it obviously causes immense distress is just cruel.

Children with SPIs find schools where hundreds of children are running around and making noise very distressing. We need to understand individual differences.

Education or Health?

Some people ask, "What about the child's education?" Well, their education is not going to happen if they are very anxious. As we have previously mentioned, it is biologically impossible for a child to learn if they are immensely distressed. If you are stuck in survival mode, your brain switches off the memory part of the brain and devotes resources to the survival parts. An anxious child can't do the very thing we send them to school for.

There are several specialized schools that are designed for children with SPIs. So while a large school may not be the right environment for your child, there may be a smaller one that is more suitable.

Michael once worked with a young boy who had severe anxiety. He was so anxious, his hair was falling out and he often vomited both before school and during class. Michael sat down with the teachers and the parents. They eventually came to the conclusion that school was not the right environment for this child and he should instead be homeschooled. After eighteen months, the parents decided this was one of the best decisions they had ever made. The boy was a lot calmer, learned a lot at home, and was excelling at life.

Some children may need to be taken out of school on a permanent basis, but in other situations, it may be a temporary measure, such as a week or two away. Maybe the break could occur while the child is getting some of the treatments we talk about in this book.

Conclusion

For many children, school is a fun and enjoyable place where they meet new friends, gain new experiences, and enjoy learning. Even if children don't always enjoy school, many need to go because of the benefits it brings; however, there are some children who do not manage well in school. The number of these students is rare, but they do exist. For some children, going to school becomes highly traumatic. For these children, we must put their well-being above education.

Chapter Twenty-Nine:
Building Connections

"I have friends in overalls whose friendship I would not swap for the
favor of the kings of the world."
—*Thomas A. Edison*

I n the last thirty years, there has been a significant emphasis on health
and well-being. We are bombarded with messages about eating the
right food, getting enough exercise, and avoiding toxic chemicals. Unfortunately, this focus on well-being often neglects the most important
part of being healthy and living a long life: strong social connections.
One of the largest studies on longevity (living a long life) found that
strong social connections reduce chances of early death by up to 50
percent.[1]

We previously mentioned the PCEs study. One of its key findings is
that even when children had experience traumatic events, if they had
multiple PCEs, they are 70 percent less likely to develop mental illness
than those who don't have them.[2] All PCEs involve connections.

If we want our children to do well in life, we must start teaching
them how to build and maintain connections and friendships. If a
child does not know how to hold a conversation, the world becomes a
very scary place.

We have already mentioned that anxiety in children can present
as behavioral problems. If children know how to talk to those around
them, they may feel less anxious.

Isolation and Loneliness

At a time when we are discovering the importance of social connections, we are having fewer meaningful connections, which are necessary
to help us to feel like we belong, and we are becoming more and more

isolated from each other. In the 1500s, there were roughly twenty people in a family household to which people felt they belonged; in 1860, that number decreased to ten; today, it is about three or four people.[3]

Previously we mentioned the polyvagal theory, which states that there is a part of your brain, the vagus nerve, that can help to regulate your nervous system and help you feel safe. When we feel safe, it helps our heart beat at a nice steady pace and helps us form connections with those around us. When we feel threatened, the vagus nerve puts us into an emergency response. When a child goes into survival mode and becomes dysregulated, meaningful connections aren't able to form because the child is focused on survival. Before people can form meaningful connections, they must feel safe.

Being alone and being lonely are two very different things. A person who has many friendships and connections may go for a walk by themselves or read a book on their own. When they do this, they probably won't feel lonely. Another person may walk in a crowded street or have hundreds of friends on Facebook but feel lonely because they have no one to talk to about the significant parts of their life. Saint Mother Teresa said, "The most terrible poverty is loneliness," and we think she is right.

Social Skills

As we previously mentioned, a lack of free play in childhood has led to a significant decline in social skills. When a child who is allowed to go to the park alone wants to play on the swings or the seesaw, then learning to talk to a child already using the equipment is necessary. When the child always has an adult who does all the talking, the child never learns these vital life skills.

The lack of social skills in childhood is starting to have real-world consequences in the workplace. Many employers observe that when an employee has a problem with a colleague, rather than talking to someone about it, the employee just quits, not knowing how to solve the problem or what to do about it. Many companies today are looking for employees with collaboration and people management skills.[4] People management often involves being able to manage conflict and get teams to work together when there are considerable differences.

A child won't learn people management by sitting in a classroom learning emotional intelligence from a textbook. They will learn it by interacting with people and figuring out how to talk to those around them.

What Is a Connection or a Friend?

The most important factor in longevity is the depth of your connections. You might think that to live a long life, all you need to do is add a few random people on Facebook. But it's not as simple as that. It's not just the number of friendships that's important; it's the depth of friendship. Saying that someone is your friend on Facebook is not the same as having a genuine friendship in real life.

A genuine friendship is with someone who you can share your joys and struggles. Tragically, many people today say they don't have a single friend. Maybe they have acquaintances, but there's no depth of connection.

We believe one of the reasons why mental illness has skyrocketed in the last few years is because we are becoming less and less socially connected. We desperately need to reverse this trend, and we can only do it if people know how to talk to those around them.

Are Strangers Dangerous?

Tragically, society upholds this idea that other people are dangerous. We often tell children, "Don't talk to strangers." This can backfire, as the only way to make new friendships is by talking to people we don't know. Instead of telling them, "Don't talk to strangers," we need to say, "We encourage you to talk to people you don't know, but if the relationship deteriorates, or they make you feel uncomfortable, then you need to end that friendship."

Who Can We Make Friends With?

Some people think they can only make friends with people who are very similar to themselves, but that's not true at all. In fact, some of the best friendships we have are with those who are different from us. The idea that you can only have friendships with people who like exactly the same things we do is nonsense. In fact, a great way to build a friendship is by learning about things we don't know about. If someone has a hobby or an interest that we don't have, we can ask them to tell us about it.

Starting a Conversation

A lot of children have said that when they meet someone for the first time, they don't know what to say. They say the person's name, the person says their name, and then they don't know what to say after that. They get nervous, they look at their phones, or they awkwardly walk away.

We have taught young people some basic questions they can ask new people, such as, "What do you like doing in your free time?" "Who's in your family?" "Do you follow any sports teams?" "Are you interested in music, movies, or TV?"¶

Sometimes children get nervous and forget what to say. Rather than trying to memorize a lot of questions, help your child memorize just a few of the basics, such as, "What have you done so far this week?" "Is there anything you're looking forward to later in the year?"

Often when someone does say something to them, many children don't listen to what that person has said. They spend their time thinking, *What is the next thing I'm going to say?*

An important aspect of friendship is listening to what a person has

---

¶ Check out *The Complete Book of Questions: 1001 Conversation Starters* by Garry Poole for more questions to ask in this type of situation.

to say. If we can teach children to improve their listening skills, they can become better friends.

The next step in helping children build better friendships is teaching them how to give good answers. If we ask a lot of people a question, such as what movies they like, and they say, "I don't know," this often means they are too embarrassed to say what they like. Sometimes giving two options can be a good way to avoid this. For example, if you say, "What sort of movies do you like? I like comedy and romance," that usually gives people something they can build on.

Brené Brown, a respected author and researcher, has done a lot of work around vulnerability. In order to have a true friendship, we have to make ourselves a little bit vulnerable to let other people know a little bit about us. She suggests we not tell people our deepest, darkest secrets when we first meet them, but we might say what our hobbies and interests are.

A good way to help children build conversation skills is to get young people to go to a retirement home and talk to some of the residents. Unfortunately, many residents at retirement homes are often very lonely. They'll be thrilled to see anyone who wants to come and talk to them. This can be a great way to build some conversation skills.

Common Problems

Quite a few challenges can arise when trying to build friendships. The following are a few suggestions about how to address the common ones.

Awkward Silences

One thing a lot of children worry about is awkward silences. They think that for a conversation to go well, they have to be able to talk all the time. But in genuine conversations, it's natural to have some pauses. These are not awkward moments; they are times to think.

If we allow a pause, it means that people are thinking, and they often come up with something meaningful; whereas when people blurt out the first thing that's on their mind, they often say the dumbest thing that's on their mind. It's all right to have awkward silences.

It Doesn't Have to Be Perfect

The other thing about conversation is it doesn't have to be perfect! It's okay if children get tongue-tied. It's okay if they get a bit stuck. We've found that a lot of young people see conversations that happen on TV and assuming that is what happens in real life. In TV and movies, we see characters having great conversations that flow naturally. The problem is that they aren't real.

One day, Michael was presenting a seminar about ADHD, FASD, and ASD. Usually, he can effortlessly rattle these off when he presents, but on this day, he got so tongue-tied saying all the acronyms that he asked the group to take a five-minute break while he composed himself. The group was really understanding.

Ending a Conversation

Many children worry about how to end a conversation. To end a conversation, they can say, "Thank you, I've really enjoyed talking to you. I now need to go and talk to this person," or, "I now need to go do this."

The Next Step

A lot of children struggle with turning a single conversation into a friendship. If they've had a good conversation with someone, they could say something like, "A group of us are going to the movies later in the week; would you like to join us?" Sometimes it's easy to invite people to a group event rather than a one-on-one event.

Controversial Conversations

Many schools now ban students from discussing controversial topics at school. There has been a strong push in society to ban speakers and material that some people find upsetting. Over the long term, this causes harm. Young people need to know how to have difficult and awkward conversations. They don't learn that by discussing the weather.

The attempt to keep people emotionally safe has led to an epidemic of anxiety. Too often if someone posts something on social media we don't like, we unfriend or unfollow them. This means we get trapped more and more in our little bubble. We are now starting to see people who won't have friends who don't follow the same political party they do! Schools and parents must encourage students to have challenging conversations about real topics. Life is full of difficult people and situations; if we are to get through life, we need to know how to manage them.

A significant problem today is outrage culture. It occurs when someone posts a poorly thought-out tweet or post on social media or says something stupid. Then people attack them on social media. Often people lose perspective. We recently had people in New Zealand who were outraged by a cartoon about measles in Samoa. Yes, the cartoon was offensive and poorly thought out, but did we need people protesting in the streets?

We need to choose our battles. The fact that the pedophile Jimmy Saville was allowed to continue abusing children for years is a reason to get out into the streets and march. Or the fact that insulin in the United States went from $1 in 1923 ($15 in today's money) to $450 today—that is a reason to march in protest. A stupid tweet or social media post is not. Outrage culture is a symptom of a society that does not know how to calmly discuss things that upset us. Jon Ronson discusses this in his book, *So You've Been Publicly Shamed*.

Conclusion

Connections and friendships are what give life meaning, and to give children the best chances of happiness, they must know how to build connections and make positive friendships.

If you want some more ideas about how to build better friendship skills, there is a great book called *The Fine Art of Small Talk* by Debra Fine. This book has lots of ways to help you get to know someone and build better connections. Friendship is not a quality that just a few rare people have. It is something that can be taught and anyone can learn.

Chapter Thirty:
Dangerous Behaviors

*"Remember: everyone in the classroom has a story
that leads to misbehavior or defiance.
Nine times out of ten, the story behind the misbehavior
won't make you angry. It will break your heart."*
—*Annette Breaux*

In our chapter about child development, we talk about the fact that children have less self-control than many adults and can act in problematic ways. In this chapter, we look at some dangerous behaviors young children may display. We first explore these issues first and then suggest ways to manage them. We use the word *children* here to refer to people who have not yet reached puberty, but these behaviors can occur in teenagers and adults as well.

Head Banging

Many children who are extremely distressed often bang their head repeatedly on walls or desks. These are not gentle taps; these children often force their heads onto objects with all their energy. This can be quite common in with children who have SIPs.

Some parents have suggested that putting pads down on a desk or a wall where a child bangs their head is a good way to manage this behavior; however, one of the things that can cause a long-term brain injury is the repeated shaking of the child's brain within their skull. So pads do not necessarily protect against this, although they may lessen the likelihood of bruising.

Often children who do this say they want "it" to stop. When asked what "it" is, they often don't know. In some cases, we think they want to stop being alive because they are in so much pain, or maybe they just want the emotional pain to stop.

Self-Harm

We have become aware that a number of young children are cutting themselves or self-harming in other ways. The clinical name for this is *non-suicidal self-injury*. We have been shocked to see that some very young children are trying this to get rid of emotional pain. We strongly encourage you not to put adult ideas onto why children do this. For example, sometimes we say that teenagers or adults self harm because they're trying to present a physical manifestation of an invisible pain. By and large, we think that children do not self-harm for reasons like this; they are simply overwhelmed and are trying to stop the overwhelming feelings.

Physical Assault

Many children with behavioral difficulties can be violent. We are hearing more and more that this is not a gentle slap, but rather substantial punches and kicks. When there is this kind of violence, it is important to consider the impact it has on other children, especially younger siblings, because they can bear the brunt of a child's anger.

Using Weapons

We have discovered that a number of anxious young people have been able to buy real swords or large knives on the internet using saved credit card information. Some children may want these as "cool toys," but other children may plan on using them for harmful purposes. If you discover your child has obtained a weapon, it is important to understand why they did so.

Suicide

We have mentioned that suicides in ten- to fourteen-year-olds tripled between 2007 and 2017.[1] For every one death by suicide, there are many suicide attempts. When children express suicidal intentions, they may be at their breaking point. Adults may think these behaviors are just seeking attention, but children who do this may be desperately seeking help.

Some parents will suggest that all children these days say, "I want to kill myself." For some children, it has become part of a common language. In a number of cases, they may not understand what this means; we encourage you to take the situation seriously and gently talk to your children to see whether it is a phrase they heard or if they really are in great distress.

Unintentional Harm

We also want to be very clear: in many cases, children who self-harm don't understand how their biology works, so they may not understand how much harm they could cause and the fact it can lead to a long-term injury.

Harmful Sexual Behavior

A number of children with behavioral problems perform sexual acts on other children. This has been recognized as a significant problem and there are now many groups around the world who work with children who do this. Sadly, many of these services are seeing very young children displaying this behavior. Many parents who discover this are often so embarrassed they don't reach out for help. There are many groups who will understand and have also, unfortunately, seen this kind of behavior many times.[2]

Addressing the Issues

All the behaviors we have mentioned can be extreme and often life-threatening. They must be taken with the utmost seriousness. We have worked with children who'd shown significant head banging, self-harm, or suicidal behaviors and often asked them, "Why did you do it?" Sometimes they were able to tell us, but many times they said they "just don't know" or "just can't think." What they often mean by this is that the emotional pain they are experiencing has gotten to a breaking point, they are not thinking clearly, and they want that pain to stop. When it comes to self-harm, head banging, and suicide, we believe that in the overwhelming majority of situations, a child is saying, "I am overwhelmed. I'm so distressed. I don't have any options. I just want this to stop." This can be especially true for children on the autistic spectrum.

If you are seeing any of these dangerous behaviors, they are not something you can handle yourself. This is something that you need to get expert and competent professional help. Having previously mentioned problematic professionals, we insist that if you go to a healthcare professional who says something like, "Oh, just ignore it," "All children say they want to kill themselves these days," or "It's just normal," you need to find someone else. It is vital that you and any helping professionals take these behaviors seriously.

Extreme Measures

Throughout this book, we suggest many non-harmful techniques for managing disruptive behavior. We strongly recommend that you try these techniques before anything more drastic.

However, we are aware that sometimes a child's behavior becomes so severe that extraordinary measures are required. In most situations, we would never recommend physically holding your child down. If a child draws on walls or throws toys, that would not be a reason to hold the child down, but if the child's physical safety, someone else's safety, or, worse, people's lives are in danger, then drastic action may be needed. Similarly, we usually don't cut off people's limbs, but if someone develops gangrene, then we may cut off a part of the body in order to save the rest. Holding a child down should only be done as a last resort to prevent serious physical harm or death.

There are some courses parents can take in safe child restraint, which are often are offered by groups supporting children with autism. Although the courses are often run by groups supporting children with autism, the techniques provided often work for children who are not on the spectrum.

We are also aware that in extreme cases, parents have had to call the police on their children. If the behaviors we have talked about are life-threatening or the child is likely to seriously injure himself, we do understand that you don't have many options and that is all you can do.

Conclusion

It can be incredibly distressing as a parent to realize that the child you brought into the world and love dearly is displaying some shocking behavior. We have previously mentioned the importance of getting help for the entire family. Many families often suffer in silence. We encourage you to reach out and get support for yourselves. This can be an immensely distressing topic and we don't want anyone to have to go through this alone. There are people who can support you.

Many parents think that if a child displays any of these dangerous behaviors, it means the child is going to end up in the criminal justice system or die by suicide. Both of us have worked with many children who had displayed these dangerous behaviors and were able to get them some good help, many going on to lead successful lives. Children and young people can recover, but they must get the right help, and the sooner the better.

Part Three:

Mistakes and Learning

Chapter Thirty-One:
Mistakes and Parenting

"Anyone who has never made a mistake has never tried anything new."
—*Albert Einstein*

There are many parenting gurus who imply that if you make one mistake, your child's life will be completely ruined. Tragically, many parents are living in fear that their child will become a heroin addict or spend a lifetime in prison from just one simple parenting mistake.

Some parenting gurus take this to the extreme. They claim that if your child is not in bed by a specific time, they will grow up as a defiant, disobedient child. It is one thing to have a routine and quite another to think that not sticking to it will ruin a child's life.

In the thousands of years that human beings have been on this planet, people have overcome all kinds of obstacles. Take a moment to think about how human beings have grown up in the past. In ancient times, people were often faced with real danger. Many tribes in Africa had to live with the constant fear of being attacked by wild animals. If people were as fragile as many of these parenting gurus make out, humankind would never have made it this far and would have died out a long time ago. We believe that, by and large, human beings are naturally resilient.

Even serious mistakes don't automatically mean your child's life is ruined. Many people assume that if children and teenagers get in trouble with the law, they are headed for a life of crime. In his book *Age of Opportunity*, Laurence Steinberg, an international expert on teenagers, talks about some very hopeful research he has done. His research suggests that 90 percent of young people who get in trouble with the law do not go on to become career criminals. So teenagers can make mistakes and recover.

Overcoming Adversity

The city we live in is Christchurch. In the last decade, we have experienced numerous earthquakes, the mosque terrorist attacks, and a series of significant fires on the Port Hills. Certainly, there are a number of children who have really struggled with these. But we are also amazed to see that quite a large portion of children, all things considered, have managed to cope remarkably well.

Sometimes we forget just how resilient children can be. Is it any wonder we have a generation of anxious children if some of these parenting gurus are filling parents' heads with information about how fragile children are? We have worked with children who have experienced severe sexual, physical, or emotional abuse. Some have been in terrible car crashes; some have been attacked by vicious dogs. While a few of these children do go down a very dark path, we're always amazed to see significant numbers of children who have been through these experiences come out positively on the other side. Many of these children have gone on to have meaningful relationships, meaningful jobs, and a sense of purpose in life. Obviously, what happened to them was dreadful, and we would not wish those events upon anyone, but one of the amazing things about the human spirit is, by and large, it has the incredible power to overcome great adversity.

Conclusion

In the past, many children survived being chased by lions, so stop worrying that you will irreparably screw up a child if the bedtime routine isn't perfect or your child can't read a chapter book by age five. It's called childhood: it can be messy, but it is never perfect.

Chapter Thirty-Two

If You Have Made Mistakes

*"Making amends is not only saying the words but also
being willing to listen to how your behavior caused another's pain,
and then the really hard part . . . changing behavior."*
—David W. Earle

When parents read this book, they may become aware that they have made some mistakes. If you become aware that you have done something to make your child fearful or really upset, then talk to them about it. Maybe explain how you felt when the child misbehaved and then ask, "How did you feel?" If you have made a mistake, don't be afraid to apologize.

Sometimes parenting gurus imply that you should hold on to all the power and if you show any sign of weakness then that will give the child a license to run wild. But really, the opposite is true. It can be healthy to reflect on how you have been interacting with your child. If you have made mistakes, gently examine them and consider how you might be able to improve next time.

Some parents may feel a lot of guilt for the mistakes they have made. If you are one of them, just know: every parent will make many mistakes.

Showing that you can apologize and admit when you make mistakes is a great way to teach children valuable skills that they will need in life. Apology and admission can help you form a deeper connection with your child and will increase honesty and openness.

Learning to Manage Conflict

A book by Edward Tronick and Claudia Gold, *The Power of Discord*, states that healthy relationships include 30 percent discord. Part of good, solid relationships is knowing what to do when things go wrong.

One of the reasons we suspect many children have difficulty in relationships is that they don't know what to do if they've made a mistake or offended someone. A generation of parents saying they will never argue in front of their children means children don't learn how to manage conflict. If you have made mistakes, this can be a great chance to teach your children how to make amends.

We hear of many young people in romantic relationships who break up because one of them makes one mistake or they do one thing to offend someone. They break up rather than talk to their partner and discuss how they feel. Often the relationship could be saved if people were better at talking about what makes them unhappy.

Breaking Point

We understand that having a child with behavioral problems can be immensely draining and stressful. Some parents will lose their tempers with their children; some may scream at their children with uncontrolled rage. While we never condone this behavior, we do understand that some parents reach their breaking point.

Some parents become so overwhelmed when an infant won't stop crying, they shake the child to get them to stop, which can cause lasting brain damage. In prenatal classes, we teach new parents that if they are overwhelmed to the point they are going to do something like this, it is okay to walk away.

An anonymous author said, "An escalated adult cannot de-escalate an escalated child." Before you try to engage a child who is distressed, you do need to stop and think, *Am I in a good space to do this?* If you are not, then walking away can be a necessary step.

If you ever feel that you are at your breaking point, we encourage you to reach out to an experienced and trusted friend. You could also reach out to your doctor; if the doctor doesn't listen or understand, then find another. You do not need to work with a child with behavioral management issues on your own; there is help and support for you too.

Conclusion

In short, if you have made mistakes, it can be really helpful to talk to the child about it. Admit that you got it wrong, ask them what they want, and work on a positive way forward.

Chapter Thirty-Three:
Unhelpful Advice

"The problem with unsolicited advice; it often says much more about the
giver than the recipient."
—*Shannon Ashley*

One of the most frustrating aspects of being a parent is all the advice people give you, even when you don't ask for it. Some people will say, "Did you know that breastfeeding is really bad? A child will become dependent on you." Then others give the opposite advice: "Do you know that breastfeeding is essential to having a strong bond with a child?" Most of this advice is contradictory and poorly thought out.

Alexander Pope said, "A little learning is a dangerous thing." Unfortunately, a lot of people know just enough about some topics to be really dangerous and, frankly, annoying.

Advice Based on Science

Our professions of medicine and psychology are sciences. When we say sleep is important to our well-being, we didn't just dream it up. We read numerous studies that were conducted by carefully trained scientists. Rather than just going on a hunch or on intuition, scientists test their ideas. For example, to learn how sleep may affect someone, we gather two groups and ask one group to have good rest and another to be sleep deprived. Then we test them, such as putting them in a driving simulator, to see how they perform. We don't report data that are good guesses—we report data that have been carefully studied.

This is important because many parenting gurus say they tried one technique on their children and it worked. While it may have worked for their children, it may not work for everyone. This is why scientists repeat studies again and again with lots of people, so random chance and coincidence are ruled out.

Generally speaking, the best scientific studies are those that include many participants. The best kind of study you can read is a meta-analysis, which takes a lot of studies with many participants and comes up with an overall result. The advantage of this type of study is that it usually has a large number of participants, which greatly increases the reliability of its results.

Conclusion

We all need to rediscover the virtue of humility, which means not always thinking of ourselves as experts, and instead always be open to learning. This quality is something everyone will need in life. And it's particularly important for those who seem preoccupied with giving unwanted advice to parents. We realize how frustrating that can be.

When parents run into this type of advice giver, we encourage them to gently reply, "I really appreciate your advice; however, I am getting help from a qualified doctor." If it gets worse and the advice giver continually gives unwanted information, sometimes the parents may have to draw firm boundaries and say, "I am really sorry, but this is offending me. I do not want your advice. I need you to stop this now."

Too many advice givers are certain that their advice is "the right answer." We have been exceptionally careful in this book to offer a wide range of techniques and solutions. Few advice givers understand that their solutions may not work for everyone.

Chapter Thirty-Four:
Continual Learning

"The noblest pleasure is the joy of understanding."
—*Leonardo da Vinci*

We live in a world where exciting discoveries are always being made about how to help children with behavioral problems cope better in life; unfortunately, many of these techniques are not used because people don't know about them. An example of this is the SSP, which has changed the lives of many children with severe behavioral problems. Sadly, we have found that not many people have heard of this. In other words, there are millions of parents pulling their hair out because they think there is nothing that can be done, when a solution may already exist. This is why ongoing learning is so important.

One of the big problems today is that we tend to have a narrow view of education. It greatly frustrates us that many parents stick to one area. For example, the parents interested in sleep research often don't look at trauma or free play research.

We greatly admire the work of Dr. Stephen Porges. He made some of his remarkable discoveries because he combined two areas of study: psychology (the study of the mind) and physiology (the study of the body).

Unfortunately, a number of people get stuck in a very narrow bubble of techniques to help a child with behavioral problems. We really encourage you to try and be naturally curious, to try and learn about topics that may not seem relevant, because you never know what it might lead to.

How Do You Learn More?

There are many courses, both online and in person, that can teach parents about different techniques and books that can be helpful. It is important to remember to balance all the new ideas against your own values and check the reliability of the authors.

When Michael attended university, he was taught that the gold standard treatment for mental illness is CBT. No other therapies were mentioned. While he was working at 298 Youth Health, he had a client who had seen several CBT therapists but was not getting better. Michael Googled evidence-based alternatives to CBT and learned about art and nature therapies. Learning includes sometimes asking if there could be alternatives. Of course, not all the results he found were helpful, and some were just terrible ideas.

Thinking Critically about New Ideas

Critical thinking involves considering a problem from multiple angles and perspectives. Often it involves thinking about a problem, going away, and then thinking some more. Non-critical thinking asks if the idea is good or bad; critical thinking asks what its strengths and weaknesses are of this idea.

Some good questions to ask include:

- Who said this? Are they a reliable source?
- Why was this written?
- Does this advice sound right and make sense?
- Are there any potential problems with it?

When you go hunting for new ideas, you will be presented with some good ones and some bad ones. It is important that you are able to think critically about the information you receive. Accepting multiple answers does not mean that everything is right. Our chapter featuring exposure therapy, we showed you that some ideas, like this one, can be really harmful when used incorrectly. This is why we want more people to use critical thinking skills. Some people dismiss ideas too quickly; for example, someone who jumps to conclusions may think EMDR sounds like a waste of time, but a person with some ability to think critically will take time to evaluate it and understand the research behind it.

Expand Your Learning

Between the two of us, we have spent almost fifty years in our respective fields; however, neither of us would in any way claim we know it all, and we are continually learning. It's okay to be wrong and say you thought something was a good idea but now you know it isn't. Continual learning, in fact, encourages you to be wrong and say, "I got this wrong yesterday, but I can know more tomorrow." There is a remarkable book by Adam Grant called *Think Again*, which encourages us to think that we may not always be right and that sometimes self-doubt actually leads to better ideas. Being open to new ideas does not mean you should accept all ideas. One sign of a strong mind is that you can reject bad ideas.

The internet is an amazing resource, and believe it or not, YouTube is not just cat videos! If you search YouTube and search for techniques to overcome anxiety, a lot of two- or three-minute videos come up that just talk about mindfulness. However, if you look a bit deeper and search for something like *anxiety lecture*, you will find many universities around the world have put free lectures online. This can be a great way to learn a little bit more than short videos offer that often come up as the first search results.

TED talks are short fifteen- to twenty-minute talks about a given topic. These can be a really good introduction to the topic, but if you have found a good TED talk by someone, we encourage you to Google the presenter's name. Has the person done a longer talk, or written a book?

In this book, we strive to present research in a clear and easy-to-read and understand format. We carefully selected the best research and ideas. Both of us had many false starts. Both of us chose books that we thought would be great. We read them and found they're terrible. So, you don't always find the right answer straight away. For every book that we mentioned, we probably read at least five that we decided were not worth including.

In addition, we often read science articles and think, *I didn't understand a word of that. Let's try again.* Learning is a challenge, and we don't always get things the first time; sometimes we have to read about them several times to understand them. Talking about an article, paper, or book with someone else can also help us understand.

Learning Takes Time

If you are not good at reading, that's okay. Even if you're a slow reader and you can just read a few minutes a day, that is a huge effort. If you do that every day, by the end of the year, you probably will have read several books.

Conclusion

Knowledge is power. The more you can understand what is causing your child's behavioral problems, the more you can help them. We encourage you to love learning for its own sake and to continually keep learning.

Part Four:

Wider Family and Friends

Chapter Thirty-Five:

The Impact on Friendships and Families

"Friendship is born at that moment when one person says to another:
'What! You too? I thought I was the only one.'"
—*C.S. Lewis*

As mentioned in chapter one, often the parents of children with behavioral difficulties are reluctant to go out in case their children have a tantrum. They may order all their shopping to be delivered. They often don't attend events they've been invited to because they are embarrassed about their child's behavior.

On the rare occasion the parents do go out, many children with behavioral problems don't like being left with a babysitter, so the parents often stop going out and then feel trapped in their own homes. Sometimes the situation becomes so severe that they are reluctant to even have their friends over. So many families with children who have behavioral problems become isolated.

When someone sees a counselor for grief, the counselor will encourage the person to speak up and ask for what they need from their friends and family. For example, if you need someone to mow your lawn because you are so drained by what happens every day, then ask for that. If you need someone to pick something up from a shop for you, ask somebody. Sometimes you might need something as simple as making a meal. A good friend will be there for you in times of need.

The Need for Honesty

We talked before about the dangers of mind reading in romantic relationships, and we should remember to not mind read in our friendships either. It's important to tell your friends what is happening and what you need. We know it can be hard to ask for help, but it is important to realize that you are experiencing a challenging situation and can't do this alone.

We encourage you to be open and honest with your friends and explain the situation you're going through. Explain to them that your child is going through a difficult stage at the moment. Say, "I don't need advice. I don't need someone to ask me, 'Have you tried this?' or, 'Have you done that?' I am doing my best and I'm getting help for it. I want to keep you as a friend. At the moment, it is very difficult for me." Then you can explain what to do if things go wrong: "I do want you to come over, but you have to be aware that my child might have a meltdown."

In case a tantrum does happen, explain what you want your friend to do and how you want your friend to respond. Parents should say what helps or what doesn't help. For example, if a child is scared around new people, then please tell your friends or family what to expect.

We need to be accepting of children who show difficult behavior. One family that Michael knows was too embarrassed to invite Michael and his wife over for dinner, saying, "Our children only eat chicken nuggets." They thought we would judge them for it. We said, "Chicken nuggets are fine. We're happy to eat those; we like chicken nuggets." A good friend won't judge; they will help and support your family.

If you are reading this and are the friend of someone in this situation, we encourage you not to go over there and say, "Well, your children should be eating their vegetables." Understand that the parents of children with behavioral difficulties are really struggling. They have most likely tried to get their children to eat different things, which has probably resulted in violent tantrums. They don't need your judgment or advice. They just need you to be there.

We wish we could say that everyone will be understanding when you tell them how to help your children with behavioral problems. Sadly, there are just some people who don't get it and make your life worse. If you are reading this book, you may feel let down by several family members or friends. The fact that some people may have let you down does not mean that everyone will.

Sometimes when you ask for help, you can feel needy or like you should be able to cope on your own. If you have a child with behavioral problems, you must know this would be a massive challenge for anyone in your situation. You are not weak; you are overwhelmed.

Parenting a child with behavioral challenges may look easy from the outside, but it is not. If you ask for help, it is not because you are weak; it is because you have a huge challenge in front of you.

Conclusion

Sadly, parents of children with behavioral problems often lose some friendships because of the challenges associated with their children, but it doesn't have to be this way. We really encourage you to be honest with the people you know. If you ask for the help that you need, state what you'd like to see, and communicate how you want others to act around your children. It can help you overcome some of these difficulties and maintain your friendships.

Chapter Thirty-Six:
Acknowledging Grief

*"So it's true, when all is said and done, grief is the price we pay for
love."*

—*E.A. Bucchianeri*

Having a child with behavioral problems can feel immensely stressful, but many parents also feel grief. We want to acknowledge that many parents feel they have a different kind of grief from those experiencing a death. A death has a clear end to someone's life, but often the grief of a child with behavioral problems is ongoing, so the grief keeps changing and evolving. A term for this is *chronic sorrow*.

You may feel several types of grief. You may feel grief that the happy family you imagined is not what you have. You may feel grief that you cannot spend as much time with your partner as you want. You may feel grief that you have lost friendships and aren't able to go out much and do the things you want. Perhaps you feel you should be a "better" parent who can "cope better," or maybe you are grieving the identity you'd wanted. Maybe you have not been able to go on vacation for a number of years and you miss that. So, it's really important to acknowledge that you are grieving.

A significant amount of grief can be associated with children who have behavioral difficulties. When we are grieving, we can experience an overwhelming emotion that crashes over us. Grief can also be a subtle emotion that hides in the background. Grief makes it very difficult to think clearly, and many people describe it as a sudden wave towering over them. No matter how you are affected by grief, it can be a very scary emotion to feel; C. S Lewis in *A Grief Observed* writes, "No one ever told me that grief felt so like fear."

Grief in the Body

Grief can be physical; people can feel it in their heart, chest, and gut. Grief can be so severe, it can cause physical heart problems, namely the condition known as *takotsubo cardiomyopathy*. Takotsubo cardiomyopathy occurs when the left ventricle of the heart is weakened, so it can cause serious health problems or even death. It is possible Debbie Reynolds experienced this after the death of her daughter, Carrie Fisher.

It's important to know that when people are in a state of shock, they do not make good decisions and can behave in seemingly strange and unusual ways. Sometimes people who are grieving can go shopping for food and—because they are in such a listless, mindless state—come home and put away the items they bought in the washing machine.

Working Through Grief

Many parents seek counseling to work through the grief of a child with behavioral issues. In many situations this can be helpful; however, research from grief counseling shows that it can be harmful. A large study found that 38 percent of people who received grief counseling may have been better off not having counseling.[1] The reason for this is that shock and grief are natural reactions. If you immediately sit down with a counselor and unpack how you feel, you can go deeper into these feelings rather than let them pass. So, in most situations, a counselor is not required, but debriefing and unloading in a supportive environment can be very helpful. Sometimes people do get stuck in this grief, and that is when more help is required and when going to a grief counselor may be helpful.

One technique that helps work through grief is expressive writing. We mention this in the sleep chapter, but it can also be useful for grieving adults. The idea of expressive writing is to take fifteen or twenty minutes to write down whatever is on your mind, whatever thoughts or feelings you have. This can be a cathartic process for some people. It gets all the difficult and terrible emotions out of their heads and turns them into something positive.

Support for Those Who Are Grieving

Megan Devine says that when someone is grieving, we tend to gloss over the pain or try to make it all better. We may say, "There are so many people worse off than you."

But when someone is grieving, if we are to truly support them, we need to acknowledge the pain the person is in. It is when we start to acknowledge the pain that the other person feels validated. If you feel that your friends and family are trying to make it all better for you, you can tell them that what you want is acknowledgement of the pain and difficulty you are going through.

Conclusion

Most books are written about grief look at grief after someone has died, but it's important to acknowledge that grief can take other forms. If you have a child who has behavioral difficulties, you can love the child dearly but still grieve the difficulty and the loss of the life you had imagined. You are not selfish if you do this—you are human.

When every child is born, parents inevitably have dreams and goals for their children. Discovering you have a child with behavioral problems may mean those dreams are put on hold or may not happen. Acknowledging this and working through the grief will make the process of raising a child with behavioral problems a little easier.

Chapter Thirty-Seven:
Grandparents Raising Grandchildren

*"Grandparents, like heroes, are as necessary to
a child's growth as vitamins."*

—*Joyce Allston*

So far, we have mainly talked about parents raising children, but we are also aware that there is a growing number of grandparents who are raising their grandchildren. Two terms have been widely used for this situation: *grandparents raising grandkids (or grandchildren)* and *grandparents as parents*. Many grandparents we know who are raising grandchildren look after grandchildren who have moderate to severe behavioral issues.

Many grandparents grew up in a time when children did not display many of the behavioral problems we see today. When they grew up, children didn't swear at adults or self-harm or throw chairs through windows. It can be a significant challenge for many grandparents to understand the issues many children are facing today.

It is estimated, at the time of writing, that almost 10 percent of grandparents in most Western countries are raising grandchildren, and in the United States alone, there could be between two-and-a-half and four-and-a-half million grandparents raising grandchildren. Sometimes the grandparents will have a joint care arrangement in which they are providing considerable help for the parents. Other times, the grandparents are mostly or completely left on their own.

In some Maori, African, and Asian communities, grandparents raising grandchildren can be far more common and even may be culturally mandated. In Maori culture, there is the concept of hapū, which means the extended tribe or family. It is normal for grandparents to have a much greater role in raising children. This makes sense because it allows parents to earn the money for the whole family.[1]

Kenneth J. Doka, a professor and international expert on grief, says that many grandparents are "wounded healers."[2] The reason they are probably raising their grandchildren is because something has gone wrong in the lives of their own children, who could have severe mental illness, be incarcerated, have a severe physical sickness, or be dead. In other situations, the child may have been placed with grandparents to be protected. For example, a child may end up living with the grandparents to avoid being harmed by a violent or sexually abusive family member.

Grandparents are often grieving themselves when they are thrust into raising thier grandchildren. Sometimes they are given a very short time to decide if they want to raise them, and often these decisions are made in the midst of profound grief. It is important to note that one reason grandparents may be raising grandchildren is because of a trauma (such as the parents having been killed in a car crash), which may cause considerable behavioral problems in the grandchildren, adding to the challenges.

While many grandparents are happy to take on this responsibility, there can also be some considerable struggles. Firstly, there can be a significant financial cost to this. Almost two-thirds of grandparents who are raising grandchildren end up living below the poverty line. Many grandparents aren't working and rely on a benefit or a pension. Many countries have financial help available for people in this situation.[3]

Secondly, grandparents don't have the same health or physical energy that they did twenty or thirty years ago. Raising any child, but particularly one with behavioral problems, tends to drain a lot of energy. Even many young parents feel utterly exhausted after one day of trying to manage a child with behavioral problems. We can only imagine how much more difficult this can be for someone who starts off with less energy.

Thirdly, there can be heart-breaking legal battles against their own children. We have seen tragic court battles where grandparents had to fight for the custody of their grandchildren to get them away from abusive or unsuitable homes. This is a massive source of grief. If you are in this situation, there may be community lawyers that offer services free of charge.

Technology

We don't want to assume that grandparents are technology illiterate. Michael's grandmother, at the age of eighty-seven, bought a new computer, so we are aware that many grandparents do have access to the internet. However, we are also aware that others don't. We found during the COVID-19 lockdown that the technology gap between generations and socioeconomic levels became very apparent. Many things were only advertised online and not everyone has access to the internet or a smartphone. It can be especially important to ensure that services for grandparents are advertised through posters, newspapers, or TV, rather than online ads. We need to make help as accessible through other means as we possibly can.

Finding Help

We've found that grandparents often don't know what help is available. It is worthwhile trying to find out if there's a support group in your area. Many grandparents have never needed help from a social service in their lives, and they're sometimes reluctant to ask for help or are not sure how to do it. We really encourage them to reach out and seek help.

There can be several ways of finding more help; your local doctor, medical center, or charity (such as the Salvation Army) may know of what support is available. If you are able to do an internet search for "grandparents raising grandchildren" in your local area, you may find some resources. If you do not have access to the internet, a local library may also be able to help find the information you need.

There are many websites and books to help people in this situation. In New Zealand, there is www.grg.org.nz. The acronym stands for Grandparents Raising Grandchildren, a national organization that offer support all over the country, even to people in small areas.

Your local library may have some books on the topic. We recommend *So, You're Raising Your Grandkids! Tested Tips, Research & Real Life Stories to Make Your Life Easier* by Harriet Hodgson.

Conclusion

This chapter has offered a brief overview of some of the struggles that many grandparents raising grandchildren face. This is a growing issue and yet there are comparatively few resources that address this. We want to raise more awareness about this so grandparents can realize that they are not alone and learn what supports exist.

Part Five:

Immediate Techniques and Strategies

Chapter Thirty-Nine:
Putting It All Together

"He didn't accomplish a miracle. He just put the pieces back together."
—*Martin Brodeur*

Throughout this book, we have looked at things you can do to help calm children who show tantrums and explosive behavior. Now we will show you how you can put together everything you have learned.

Let's look at three girls; they are all nine years old and very similar. Their names are Ella, Emma, and Eleanor. All of them get upset very easily, often kick adults, have severe tantrums before school, and frequently break down crying. Although they may seem similar in terms of their behavior, we will show you how different strategies and techniques are needed to address challenging behavior.

Ella

Everything seemed to be going well for Ella until a year ago. She was doing well in school and had a good group of friends. Now everything is a battle and her parents and teachers are at their wits' end. The parents and her teacher talk and conclude that Ella seems to have quite severe anxiety.

Her mother hears that mindfulness could really help. She finds some guided mindfulness exercises on the internet that she gives Ella to listen to. They do this together. The exercises encourage Ella to take in a deep breath for ten seconds, hold it in for five, then slowly breathe out.

It takes about ten days before Ella shows some improvement. Slowly she becomes calmer and has fewer and fewer explosive outbursts, but there is more to do.

Ella still gets quite nervous at school, so her mother buys her a soft toy made from memory foam. Ella keeps the toy with her throughout the day; if she starts to get worried, she slowly presses on it and watches it reform.

Her mother also buys Ella a weighted blanket, which Ella loves to hold at night. Before this, Ella often laid awake for a number of hours because she was afraid of the dark. Now with her blanket, she feels much safer. However, she still often lies awake and cannot sleep.

The family takes Ella to a doctor who prescribes melatonin. Within a day of taking it, Ella gets much better sleep. Eventually the family realizes that Ella's anxiety mostly came from a lack of good sleep. After a few weeks with some of these new treatments, her family says that Ella seems like a new person.

Things to note:

1. **Not all anxious children need therapy.** Ella was able to get better without the help of a therapist.

2. **Sometimes more than one technique is needed to help a child.** Ella's family relied on four techniques to help Ella's behavior: mindfulness, the foam toy, the weighted blanket, and melatonin. It was both the weighted blanket and the melatonin that helped improve her sleep problems. If the family had stopped at the weighted blanket, Ella would still be sleeping poorly.

Emma

Emma's parents heard about the success with Ella, so they try to get their daughter to do some mindfulness exercises. To their surprise, they find it doesn't work; in fact, they make Emma's behavior worse. They take her to a therapist. The therapist tells the family that Emma has oppositional defiant disorder; "The tantrums are an attempt to manipulate you; you must not stand for this."

The parents don't think this sounds right, so they find a different therapist. This one tells them their daughter has serious signs of narcissism; if something is not done immediately, then Emma's life will turn out very badly—she will get pregnant before she is fourteen and may well end up in jail. The therapist says the family must enroll in a $10,000 course if they have any hope to save their daughter. The parents politely reject this offer.

The parents are exhausted and feeling hopeless, but they decide to try again. They meet a much better therapist; he acknowledges how difficult and upsetting it must be to have a child who shows such challenging behavior. He doesn't blame the parents and offers them support. He spends lots of time getting to know the family and Emma's background. Emma comes from a very loving family. The therapist asks if Emma gets overwhelmed with loud noises and busy events. The therapist discovers that Emma has quite severe sensory issues. To address this, the therapist suggests buying Emma noise-canceling headphones and offers SSP. These do help quite a bit, but there is still more to be done. The therapist suggests that when Emma gets overwhelmed, she should have a bottle with cold water to drink and, if she can, she should go to the bathroom and splash her face with cold water. This helps as well.

Both of Emma's parents want to make sure she gets into a good college and insist she spends many hours at night doing homework. The therapist discusses the importance of free play. The parents encourage Emma to take up art for fun in her free time. Within three months, they notice Emma has far fewer tantrums and does not become overwhelmed so easily.

Things to note:

3. **A technique that works for one child may not work for another.** Emma's parents heard that mindfulness worked for Ella, so they tried it with Emma but found it did not work.

4. **There is no guaranteed timeframe for a technique to work.** Ella showed an improvement after ten days, but it is unrealistic to expect Emma's situation to improve in the same timeframe.

5. **Not all therapists will be a good fit.** Emma's parents had to try a few therapists before they found one that fit well.

Eleanor

Eleanor is being raised by her grandmother because her parents died in a car crash a few years ago. Her grandmother sits down with and asks Eleanor why she gets upset all the time. Eleanor doesn't know.

From Eleanor's behavior, the grandmother eventually realizes that her granddaughter has PTSD from the loss of her parents. The grandmother does not have the money to afford therapy for Eleanor, so she approaches several charities and one agrees to help.

With this help, she finds a therapist who offers EMDR. The full course of EMDR treatments takes twenty sessions and eventually starts to really help Eleanor work through her trauma.

The therapist also suggests putting the scent of roses in Emma's bedroom at night. This seems to make quite a difference in her behavior; the grandmother notices that Eleanor sleeps better.

The therapist sits down with the grandmother and asks what kind of support system she has and how her finances are; the grandmother eventually admits that she is struggling. The therapist tells the grandmother about a group of grandparents raising grandchildren that meet in her area. The grandmother didn't know they existed. She starts attending the group's meeting and discovers that there is a lot more help available than she'd realized, and she really appreciates talking to others who are also experiencing what she is going through.

The group also helps the grandmother in another way: it was her son and daughter-in-law who were killed in the car crash. She didn't have time to grieve for them; within five hours of the crash, she was given full and sole custody of Eleanor. The group she joined help her to start processing her grief.

Things to note:

6. **It's not unusual for a child to be unaware of what causes their behavior.** When the grandmother asked Eleanor what was causing her behavior, she didn't know.

7. **It's not always just the child who needs help.** In order to really help Eleanor, the grandmother also needed help.

8. **Sometimes addressing a seemingly unrelated thing helps to get to the root of the behavioral issues.** Addressing her sleep issues was a large part of Eleanor's journey to recovery.

Conclusion

It is important to note that in all these examples, there was not just one technique that worked. It took multiple techniques before an improvement was seen. So, if you try one technique and it doesn't work, we recommend you try others and add others.

Chapter Forty:
Final Thoughts

"Everything will be alright in the end. If it's not alright, it's not the end."
—*Fernando Sabino*

We want to leave you with a few final thoughts. What do you think the long-term outcomes were for a child who'd had violent tantrums and used to throw things at his sister and had even thrown a chair at a teacher?

Many of us assume he must have become a psychopath and ended up in jail. We may assume that he never became anything. The name of the man in this example is Albert Einstein,[1] one of the most influential scientists to have ever walked the earth.

We are aware that many parents get very upset with themselves if children show tantrums; they feel they must be doing something wrong or their child will grow up to be a career criminal. This is not the case at all. Often tantrums are caused in part because children do not have a fully developed brain. Often when their brain matures, many of these problematic behaviors go away on their own. This does not mean that you are powerless to do anything. In this book, we have shown you a wide variety of techniques and strategies to effectively address challenging behavior.

As we conclude this book, we wish you the very best on your parenting journey. Being a parent or caring for children should be a wonderful journey. There will always be tough times, but we believe there should be far more moments of wonder and joy than negative ones. We know the majority of our readers will not be in that place. We wrote this book to change things for the better. In this book, we have hopefully given you a Swiss army knife full of tools and strategies to help you work through these difficult and challenging situations.

Books for Further Reference

Autism
The Autistic Brain: Thinking Across the Spectrum by Richard Panek and Temple Grandin

How Can I Talk If My Lips Don't Move? Inside My Autistic Mind by Tito Rajarshi Mukhopadhyay

The Unwritten Rules of Social Relationships by Temple Grandin and Sean Barron

FASD
Damaged Angels: A Mother Discovers the Terrible Cost of Alcohol in Pregnancy by Bonnie Buxton

When Rain Hurts: An Adoptive Mother's Journey with Fetal Alcohol Syndrome by Mary Evelyn Greene

Grief
A Grief Observed by C. S. Lewis

It's OK That You're Not OK: Meeting Grief and Loss in a Culture That Doesn't Understand by Megan Devine

Please Be Patient, I'm Grieving: How to Care For and Support the Grieving Heart by Gary Roe

Healing Power of Nature
Blue Mind: The Surprising Science That Shows How Being Near, In, On, or Under Water Can Make You Happier, Healthier, More Connected, and Better at What You Do by Wallace Nichols

Chasing the Sun: The New Science of Sunlight and How it Shapes Our Bodies and Minds by Linda Geddes

The Nature Fix: Why Nature Makes Us Happier, Healthier, and More Creative by Florence Williams

Play
Free to Learn: Why Unleashing the Instinct to Play Will Make Our Children Happier, More Self-Reliant, and Better Students for Life by Peter Gray

Let the Children Play: How More Play Will Save Our Schools and Help Children Thrive by Pasi Sahlberg and William Doyle

Playful Parenting: An Exciting New Approach to Raising Children That Will Help You Nurture Close Connections, Solve Behavior Problems, and Encourage Confidence by Lawrence J. Cohen

Play: How It Shapes the Brain, Opens the Imagination, and Invigorates the Soul by Stuart Brown, M.D., with Christopher Vaughan

Sleep

The Nocturnal Brain: Nightmares, Neuroscience, and the Secret World of Sleep by Guy Leschziner

The Sleep Revolution: Transforming Your Life, One Night at a Time by Arianna Huffington

Why We Sleep: Unlocking the Power of Sleep and Dreams by Matthew Walker

Smell

The Smell of Fresh Rain: The Unexpected Pleasures of Our Most Elusive Sense by Barney Shaw

What the Nose Knows: The Science of Scent in Everyday Life by Avery Gilbert

Trauma

The Body Keeps the Score: Brain, Mind, and Body in the Healing of Trauma by Bessel van der Kolk

Born for Love: Why Empathy Is Essential—and Endangered by Bruce D. Perry and Maia Szalavitz

The Boy Who Was Raised as a Dog: And Other Stories from a Child Psychiatrist's Notebook—What Traumatized Children Can Teach Us About Loss, Love, and Healing by Bruce D. Perry and Maia Szalavitz

Healing the Fragmented Selves of Trauma Survivors: Overcoming Internal Self-Alienation by Janina Fisher

In an Unspoken Voice: How the Body Releases Trauma and Restores Goodness by Peter Levine

It Didn't Start with You: How Inherited Family Trauma Shapes Who We Are and How to End the Cycle by Mark Wolynn

The Pocket Guide to the Polyvagal Theory: The Transformative Power of Feeling Safe by Stephen W. Porges

The Polyvagal Theory: Neurophysiological Foundations of Emotions, Attachment, Communication, and Self-Regulation by Stephen W. Porges

Trauma and Memory: Brain and Body in a Search for the Living Past: A Practical Guide for Understanding and Working with Traumatic Memory by Peter A. Levine

Trauma and Recovery: The Aftermath of Violence—from Domestic Abuse to Political Terror by Judith Herman

When the Body Says No: Understanding the Stress-Disease Connection by Gabor Maté

Other Topics

Age of Opportunity: Lessons from the New Science of Adolescence by Laurence Steinberg

Anxious: Using the Brain to Understand and Treat Fear and Anxiety by Joseph LaDoux

The Case Against Homework: How Homework Is Hurting Children and What Parents Can Do About It by Nancy Kalish and Sara Bennett

The Coddling of the American Mind: How Good Intentions and Bad Ideas Are Setting Up a Generation for Failure by Greg Lukianoff and Jonathan Haidt

The Complete Book of Questions: 1001 Conversation Starters by Garry Poole

The Double Helix: A Personal Account of the Discovery of the Structure of DNA by James D. Watson

The Fine Art of Small Talk by Debra Fine

A First-Rate Madness: Uncovering the Links Between Leadership and Mental Illness by Nassir Ghaemi

Flow: The Psychology of Optimal Experience by Mihaly Csikszentmihalyi

Homework Myth: Why Our Kids Get Too Much of a Bad Thing by Alfie Kohn

How to Stop Worrying and Start Living: Time-Tested Methods for Conquering Worry by Dale Carnegie

I Thought It Was Just Me (But It Isn't): Making the Journey from "What Will People Think?" to "I Am Enough" by Brené Brown

Insight: The Surprising Truth About How Others See Us, How We See Ourselves, and Why the Answers Matter More Than We Think by Tasha Eurich

Learned Optimism: How to Change Your Mind and Your Life by Martin Seligman

Lincoln's Melancholy: How Depression Challenged a President and Fueled His Greatness by Joshua Wolf Shenk

The Organized Mind: Thinking Straight in the Age of Information Overload by Daniel J. Levitin

Punished by Rewards: The Trouble with Gold Stars, Incentive Plans, A's, Praise, and Other Bribes by Alfie Kohn

Scattered Minds: The Origins and Healing of Attention Deficit Disorder by Gabor Maté

So You've Been Publicly Shamed by Jon Ronson

So, You're Raising Your Grandkids: Tested Tips, Research, & Real-Life Stories to Make Your Life Easier by Harriet Hodgson

Social: Why Our Brains Are Wired to Connect by Matthew Lieberman

Think Again: The Power of Knowing What You Don't Know by Adam Grant

Touching by Ashley Montagu

A Whack on the Side of the Head: How You Can Be More Creative by Roger von Oech

Endnotes

Chapter 2

1. Jonas Grinevičius and Ilona Baliūnaitė. "30 People Share How They Used To Believe In Something That Turned Out To Be An Embarrassing Misunderstanding." Bored Panda. 2020. https://www.boredpanda.com/embarrasing-misunderstanding-stories.

Chapter 3

1. Mariam Arain, Maliha Haque, Lina Johal, Puja Mathur, Wynand Nel, Afsha Rais, Ranbir Sandhu, and Sushil Sharma. "Maturation of the adolescent brain." *Neuropsychiatric Disease and Treatment* 9 (2013): 449. doi:10.2147/NDT.S39776.
2. Timothy J. Layton, Michael L. Barnett, Tanner R. Hicks, and Anupam B. Jena. "Attention Deficit–Hyperactivity Disorder and Month of School Enrollment." *New England Journal of Medicine* 379 (2018): 2122–30. doi:10.1056/NEJMoa1806828.
3. Charles Fernyhough. "The voices within: The power of talking to yourself." *New Scientist.* May 29, 2013. https://www.newscientist.com/article/mg21829192-300-the-voices-within-the-power-of-talking-to-yourself/.
4. Martin Hughes and Robert Grieve. "On asking children bizarre questions." *First Language* 1, no. 2 (June 1980): 149–60. Doi:10.1177/014272378000100205.
5. Sue Shellenbarger. "The Best Language for Math: Confusing English Number Words Are Linked to Weaker Skills." *Wall Street Journal.* Updated September 15, 2014. https://www.wsj.com/articles/the-best-language-for-math-1410304008.
6. Harold W. Stevenson. "Learning from Asian Schools." *Scientific American* 267, no. 6 (1992): 70–77. http://www.jstor.org/stable/24939332.
7. Judy S. Deloache. "Mindful of Symbols." *Scientific American.* June 1, 2007. https://www.scientificamerican.com/article/mindful-of-symbols-2007-06/#.

Chapter 4

1. Helen Wilkinson, Richard Whittington, Lorraine Perry, and Catrin Eames. "Examining the relationship between burnout and empathy in healthcare professionals: A systematic review." *Burnout Research* 6 (2017): 18–29. doi:10.1016/j.burn.2017.06.003.

2. David Rakel, Bruce Barrett, Zhengjun Zhang, Theresa Hoeft, Betty Chewning, Lucille Marchand, and Jo Scheder. "Perception of empathy in the therapeutic encounter: effects on the common cold." *Patient Education and Counseling* 85, no. 3 (2011): 390–97. doi:10.1016/j.pec.2011.01.009. Also see,

   Stewart W. Mercer, Maria Higgins, Annemieke M. Bikker, Bridie Fitzpatrick, Alex McConnachie, Suzanne M. Lloyd, Paul Little, and Graham C. M. Watt. "General Practitioners' Empathy and Health Outcomes: A Prospective Observational Study of Consultations in Areas of High and Low Deprivation." *Annals of Family Medicine* 14, no. 2 (2016): 117–24. doi:10.1370/afm.1910.

Chapter 5

1. Daniela Rabellino, Paul A. Frewen, Margaret C. McKinnon, and Ruth A. Lanius. "Peripersonal Space and Bodily Self-Consciousness: Implications for Psychological Trauma-Related Disorders." *Frontiers in Neuroscience* 14, no. 586605 (December 2020): 1256. doi:10.3389/fnins.2020.586605.

Chapter 7

1. James W. Prescott. "Body Pleasure and the Origins of Violence." *Bulletin of the Atomic Scientists* 31, no. 9 (1975): 10–20. doi:10.1080/00963402.1975.11458292.

2. Ashley Montagu. *Touching: The Human Significance of the Skin*. William Morrow Paperbacks, 1986.

3. Chi-Yuang Yu, Yao-Wen Hsu, and Chih-Yong Chen. "Determination of hand surface area as a percentage of body surface area by 3D anthropometry." *Burns: Journal of the International Society for Burn Injuries* 34, no. 8 (2008): 1183–89. doi:10.1016/j.burns.2008.03.010.

4. Christoffer Van Tullaken, Michael Tipton, Heather Massey, and C. Mark Harper. "Open water swimming as a treatment for major depressive disorder." *BMJ Case Reports* 2018, no. bcr2018225007 (August 2018). doi:10.1136/bcr-2018-225007.

5. "Weighted Blankets—Avoid a Tragic Mistake." Children's MD. February 2, 2015. https://childrensmd.org/browse-by-age-group/newborn-infants/weighted-blankets-tragic-mistake/. Also see,

   Sean Gordon. "Blanket suffocates autistic boy in Quebec." *Toronto Star*. June 20, 2008. https://www.thestar.com/news/canada/2008/06/20/blanket_suffocates_autistic_boy_in_quebec.html.

Chapter 8

1. Kathleen Liberty, Michael Tarren-Sweeney, Sonja Macfarlane, Arindam Basu, and James Reid. "Behavior Problems and Post-Traumatic Stress Symptoms in Children Beginning School: A Comparison of Pre- and Post-Earthquake Groups." *PLoS Currents* 8, no. ecurrents. dis.2821c82fbc27d0c2aa9e00cff532b402 (June 2016). doi:10.1371/currents.dis.2821c82fbc27d0c2aa9e00cff532b402.

2. Dimitri A. Christakis. "The Effects of Fast-Paced Cartoons." *Pediatrics* 128, no. 4 (2011): 772–74. doi: https://doi.org/10.1542/peds.2011-2071.

3. Qing Li. *Shinrin-Yoku: The Art and Science of Forest Bathing.* New York: Penguin Random House, 2018.

4. Charles C. Branas, Eugenia South, Michelle C. Kondo, Bernadette C. Hohl, Philippe Bourgois, Douglas J. Wiebe, and John M. MacDonald. "Citywide cluster randomized trial to restore blighted vacant land and its effects on violence, crime, and fear." *Proceedings of the National Academy of Sciences of the United States of America* 115, no. 12 (2018): 2946–51. doi:10.1073/pnas.1718503115.

5. Dorthe Varning Poulsen. "Nature-based therapy as a treatment for veterans with PTSD: what do we know?" *Journal of Public Mental Health* 16, no. 1 (March 2017): 15–20. Doi:10.1108/JPMH-08-2016-0039.

6. Tetsuya Matsubayashi, Yasuyuki Sawada, and Michiko Ueda. "Does the installation of blue lights on train platforms prevent suicide? A before-and-after observational study from Japan." *Journal of affective disorders* 147, no. 1–3 (2013): 385–88. doi:10.1016/j.jad.2012.08.018.

7. Hägerhäll, Caroline Madeleine, Laike, Thorbjörn, Küller, M., Marcheschi, Elizabeth, Boydston, C., and Taylor, Richard. "Human physiological benefits of viewing nature: EEG responses to exact and statistical fractal patterns." Nonlinear Dynamics, Psychology, and Life Sciences 19, no. 1 (2015); 1–12.

8. Florence Williams and Aeon. "Why Fractals Are So Soothing." *The Atlantic.* January 26, 2017. https://www.theatlantic.com/science/archive/2017/01/why-fractals-are-so-soothing/514520/.

Chapter 9

1. Amanda Macmillan. "The Sound of 'Pink Noise' Improves Sleep and Memory." *Time.* March 8, 2017. https://time.com/4694555/pink-noise-deep-sleep-improve-memory/.

2. Marco Schlosser, Terje Sparby, Sebastjan Vörös, Rebecca Jones, and Natalie L. Marchant. "Unpleasant meditation-related experiences in regular meditators: Prevalence, predictors, and conceptual considerations." *PLoS One* 14, no. 5 (May 2019): e0216643. doi:10.1371/journal.pone.0216643.

Chapter 10

1. Kathleen Liberty. *Reducing stress in schools: Information for principals, teachers and parents about stressed children in disaster-struck communities and how to help them in difficult times.* Christchurch: Kathleen Liberty, 2017.

Chapter 11

1. Lizzie Thompson. "The Top Nostalgic Scents That Take Us Back to Childhood—Including Bolognese and Crayons." Metro. December 16, 2021. https://metro.co.uk/2021/12/16/these-are-the-top-nostalgic-scents-that-take-us-back-to-childhood-15781512/.

1. Lilianne R. Mujica-Parodi, Helmut H. Strey, Blaise Frederick, Robert Savoy, David Cox, Yevgeny Botanov, Denis Tolkunov, Denis Rubin, and Jochen Weber. "Chemosensory Cues to Conspecific Emotional Stress Activate Amygdala in Humans." Plos One, 4, no. 7 (2009): e6415. https://doi.org/10.1371/journal.pone.0006415.

2. G. Sharvit, E. Lin, P. Vuilleumier, and C. Corradi-Dell'Acqua. "Does inappropriate behavior hurt or stink? The interplay between neural representations of somatic experiences and moral decisions." *Science Advances* 6, no. 42 (October 2020): eaat4390. doi:10.1126/sciadv.aat4390.

3. Olga A. Sergeeva, Olaf Kletke, Andrea Kragler, Anja Poppek, Wiebke Fleischer, Stephan R. Schubring, Boris Görg, Helmut L. Haas, Xin-Ran Zhu, Hermann Lübbert, Günter Gisselmann, and Hanns Hatt. "Fragrant Dioxane Derivatives Identify β1-Subunit-Containing GAB-A$_A$ Receptors." *Journal of Biological Chemistry* 285, no. 31 (July 2010): 23985-23993. doi:10.1074/jbc.M110.103309.

4. Laura Schäfer, Julia Schellong, Antje Hähner, Kerstin Weidner, Karl-Bernd Hüttenbrink, Sebastian Trautmann, Thomas Hummel, and Ilona Croy. "Nocturnal Olfactory Stimulation for Improvement of Sleep Quality in Patients With Posttraumatic Stress Disorder: A Randomized Exploratory Intervention Trial." *Journal of Traumatic Stress* 32, no. 1 (2019): 130–40. doi:10.1002/jts.22359.

5. "Stitching tighter connections between preemies and parents." Rush University. October 25, 2018. https://www.rushu.rush.edu/news/stitching-tighter-connections-between-preemies-and-parents.

Chapter 12

1. Lori Lee Fankhauser. "How Adults with PTSD Described the Effects of Their Emotional Support Animals: A Qualitative Descriptive Study." Doctoral dissertation, Grand Canyon University, 2021. ProQuest Dissertations Publishing (28412557). https://www.proquest.com/openview/b750e0effe654511863d7a0cb360d658/1?pq-origsite=gscholar&cbl=18750&diss=y.

Chapter 14

1. Faith S. Luyster, Patrick J. Strollo Jr., Phyllis C. Zee, and James K. Walsh. "Sleep: A Health Imperative." *Sleep* 35, no. 6 (June 1, 2012): 727–34. doi:10.5665/sleep.1846.

2. Flavie Waters, Vivian Chiu, Amanda Atkinson, and Jan Dirk Blom. "Severe Sleep Deprivation Causes Hallucinations and a Gradual Progression Toward Psychosis With Increasing Time Awake." *Frontiers in Psychiatry* 9 (July 10, 2018): 303. doi:10.3389/fpsyt.2018.00303.

3. Adam J. Krause, Eti Ben Simon, Bryce A. Mander, Stephanie M. Greer, Jared M. Saletin, Andrea N. Goldstein-Piekarski, and Matthew P. Walker. "The sleep-deprived human brain." *Nature Reviews Neuroscience* 18, no. 7 (2017): 404. doi.org/10.1038/nrn.2017.55.

4. Matthew P. Walker, Tiffany Brakefield, Alexandra Morgan, J. Allan Hobson, and Robert Stickgold. "Practice with sleep makes perfect: sleep-dependent motor skill learning." *Neuron* 35, no. 1 (2002): 205–11. doi:10.1016/s0896-6273(02)00746-8.

5. Michelle E. Stepan, Erik M. Altmann, and Kimberly M. Fenn. "Effects of total sleep deprivation on procedural placekeeping: More than just lapses of attention." *Journal of Experimental Psychology: General* 149, no. 4 (2020): 800–06. doi:10.1037/xge0000717.

6. Devon A. Hansen, Matthew E. Layton, Samantha M. Riedy, and Hans Pa Van Dongen. "Psychomotor Vigilance Impairment During Total Sleep Deprivation Is Exacerbated in Sleep-Onset Insomnia." *Nature and Science of Sleep* 11 (December 2019): 401. doi:10.2147/NSS.S224641.

7. Rebecca A. Bernert, Melanie A. Hom, Naomi G. Iwata, and Thomas E. Joiner. "Objectively Assessed Sleep Variability as an Acute Warning Sign of Suicidal Ideation in a Longitudinal Evaluation of Young Adults at High Suicide Risk." *The Journal of Clinical Psychiatry* 78, no. 6 (2017): e678–e687. doi:10.4088/JCP.16m11193.

8. Patrick H. Finan, Phillip J. Quartana, and Michael T. Smith. "The Effects of Sleep Continuity Disruption on Positive Mood and Sleep Architecture in Healthy Adults." *Sleep* 38, no. 11 (November 2015): 1735–42. doi:10.5665/sleep.5154.

9. Katharina Wulff, Silvia Gatti, Joseph G. Wettstein, and Russell G. Foster. "Sleep and circadian rhythm disruption in psychiatric and neurodegenerative disease." *Nature Reviews Neuroscience* 11, no. 8 (July 2010): 589–99. doi:10.1038/nrn2868.

10. June J. Pilcher, Christina Callan, and J. Laura Posey. "Sleep deprivation affects reactivity to positive but not negative stimuli." *Journal of Psychosomatic Research* 79, no. 6 (2015): 657–62. doi:10.1016/j.jpsychores.2015.05.003. Also see,

   Peter Hu, Melinda Stylos-Allan, and Matthew P. Walker. "Sleep facilitates consolidation of emotional declarative memories." *Psychological Science* 17, no. 10 (2006): 891–98. doi:10.1111/j.1467-9280.2006.01799.x.

11. Seung-Schik Yoo, Ninad Gujar, Peter Hu, Ferenc A. Jolesz, and Matthew P. Walker. "The human emotional brain without sleep—a prefrontal amygdala disconnect." *Current Biology: CB* 17, no. 20 (2007): R877–R878. doi:10.1016/j.cub.2007.08.007.

12. Céline Vetter, Shun-Chiao Chang, Elizabeth E. Devore, Florian Rohrer, Olivia I. Okereke, and Eva S. Schernhammer. "Prospective study of chronotype and incident depression among middle-and older-aged women in the Nurses' Health Study II." *Journal of Psychiatric Research* 103 (2018): 156–60. doi:10.1016/j.jpsychires.2018.05.022.

13. Stoyan Dimitrov, Tanja Lange, Cécile Gouttefangeas, Anja T.R. Jensen, Michael Szczepanski, Jannik Lehnnolz, Surjo Soekadar, Hans-Georg Rammensee, Jan Born, and Luciana Besedovsky. "$G\alpha_s$-coupled receptor signaling and sleep regulate integrin activation of human antigen-specific T cells." *Journal of Experimental Medicine* 216, no. 3 (February 2019): 517–26. doi:10.1084/jem.20181169.

14. Patrick H. Finan, Burel R. Goodin, and Michael T. Smith. "The association of sleep and pain: an update and a path forward." *The Journal of Pain* 14, no. 12 (2013): 1539–52. doi:10.1016/j.jpain.2013.08.007.

15. Shahrad Taheri, Ling Lin, Diane Austin, Terry Young, and Emmanuel Mignot. "Short sleep duration is associated with reduced leptin, elevated ghrelin, and increased body mass index." *PLoS Medicine* 1, no. 3 (2004): e62. doi:10.1371/journal.pmed.0010062.

16. Ninad Gujar, Seung-Schik Yoo, Peter Hu, and Matthew P. Walker. "Sleep deprivation amplifies reactivity of brain reward networks, biasing the appraisal of positive emotional experiences." *The Journal of Neuroscience: The Official Journal of the Society for Neuroscience* 31, no. 12 (2011): 4466–74. doi:10.1523/JNEUROSCI.3220-10.2011. Also see,

   Stephanie M. Greer, Andrea N. Goldstein, and Matthew P. Walker. "The impact of sleep deprivation on food desire in the human brain." *Nature Communications* 4 (2013): 2259. doi:10.1038/ncomms3259.

17. M.H. Hagenauer, J.I. Perryman, T.M. Lee, and M.A. Carskadon. "Adolescent changes in the homeostatic and circadian regulation of sleep." *Developmental Neuroscience* 31, no. 4 (2009): 276–84. doi:10.1159/000216538.

18. Marco Hafner, Martin Stepanek, and Wendy M. Troxel. "Later School Start Times in the U.S.: An Economic Analysis." RAND Corporation. 2017. https://www.rand.org/pubs/research_reports/RR2109.html.

19. Angela Gomez Fonseca and Lisa Genzel. "Sleep and academic performance: considering amount, quality and timing." *Current Opinion in Behavioral Sciences* 33 (June 2020): 65–71. doi:10.1016/j.cobeha.2019.12.008.

20. Ted Abel, Robbert Havekes, Jared M. Saletin, and Matthew P. Walker. "Sleep, plasticity and memory from molecules to whole-brain networks." *Current Biology: CB* 23, no. 17 (2013): R774–R788. doi:10.1016/j.cub.2013.07.025.

21. Rebecca G. Astill, Giovanni Piantoni, Roy J.E.M. Raymann, Jose C. Vis, Joris E. Coppens, Matthew P. Walker, Robert Stickgold, Ysbrand D. Van Der Werf, and Eus J.W. Van Someren. "Sleep spindle and slow wave frequency reflect motor skill performance in primary school-age children." *Frontiers in Human Neuroscience* 8 (November 2014): 910. doi:10.3389/fnhum.2014.00910.

22. Wei Cheng, Edmund Rolls, Weikang Gong, Jingnan Du, Jie Zhang, Xiao-Yong Zhang, Fei Li, and Jianfeng Feng. "Sleep duration, brain structure, and psychiatric and cognitive problems in children." *Molecular Psychiatry* (February 2020): 1–12. doi:10.1038/s41380-020-0663-2.

23. Judith A. Owens. "The ADHD and sleep conundrum: a review." *Journal of Developmental and Behavioral Pediatrics* 26, no. 4 (2005): 312–22. doi:10.1097/00004703-200508000-00011.

24. Charles E. Cunningham, Cailin Mapp, Heather Rimas, Lesley Cunningham, Stephanie Mielko, Tracy Vaillancourt, and Madalyn Marcus. "What Limits the Effectiveness of Antibullying Programs? A Thematic Analysis of the Perspective of Students." *Psychology of Violence* 6, no. 4 (2016): 596. doi:10.1037/a0039984.

25. Louise M. O'Brien, Neali H. Lucas, Barbara T. Felt, Timothy F. Hoban, Deborah L. Ruzicka, Ruth Jordan, Kenneth Guire, and Ronald D. Chervin. "Aggressive behavior, bullying, snoring, and sleepiness in schoolchildren." *Sleep Medicine* 12, no. 7 (2011): 652–58. doi:10.1016/j.sleep.2010.11.012.

26. American Academy of Sleep Medicine. "Study finds that sleep restriction amplifies anger." EurekAlert! August 28, 2020. https://www.eurekalert.org/news-releases/825249.

27.	Eti Ben Simon, Noga Oren, Haggai Sharon, Adi Kirschner, Noam Goldway, Hadas Okon-Singer, Rivi Tauman, Menton M. Deweese, Andreas Keil, and Talma Hendler. "Losing Neutrality: The Neural Basis of Impaired Emotional Control without Sleep." *The Journal of Neuroscience* 35, no. 38 (September 2015): 13194–205. doi:10.1523/JNEUROSCI.1314-15.2015.

28.	Donna A. Ruch, Arielle H. Sheftall, Paige Schlagbaum, Joseph Rausch, John V. Campo, and Jeffrey A. Bridge. "Trends in Suicide Among Youth Aged 10 to 19 Years in the United States, 1975 to 2016." *JAMA Network Open* 2, no. 5 e193886 (May 2019). doi:10.1001/jamanetworkopen.2019.3886.

Michael Perlis, N.S. Chaudhary, Michael Grandner, M. Basner, Subhajit Chakravorty, and G.K. Brown. "When accounting for wakefulness, completed suicides exhibit an increased likelihood during circadian night (Oral presentation)." *Sleep*. January 2014. https://www.researchgate.net/publication/304498989_When_accounting_for_wakefulness_completed_suicides_exhibit_an_increased_likelihood_during_circadian_night_Oral_presentation. Also see,

Andrew S. Tubbs, Michael L. Perlis, Mathias Basner, Subhajit Chakravorty, Waliuddin Khader, Fabian Fernandez, and Michael A. Grandner. "Relationship of Nocturnal Wakefulness to Suicide Risk Across Months and Methods of Suicide." *The Journal of Clinical Psychiatry* 81, no. 2 (February 2020): 19m12964. doi:10.4088/JCP.19m12964. Also see,

Andrew S. Tubbs, Patricia Harrison-Monroe, Fabian-Xosé Fernandez, Michael L. Perlis, and Michael A. Grandner. "When reason sleeps: attempted suicide during the circadian night." *Journal of Clinical Sleep Medicine* 16, no. 10 (2020): 1809–10. doi:10.5664/jcsm.8662.

29.	Niu Tian, Matthew Zack, Katherine A. Fowler, and Dale C. Hesdorffor. "Suicide Timing in 18 States of the United States from 2003–2014." *Archives of Suicide Research: Official Journal of the International Academy for Suicide Research* 23, no. 2 (2019): 261–272. doi:10.1080/13811118.2018.1472689.

30.	Katia Fredriksen, Jean Rhodes, Ranjini Reddy, and Niobe Way. "Sleepless in Chicago: tracking the effects of adolescent sleep loss during the middle school years." *Child Development* 75, no. 1 (2004): 84–95. doi:10.1111/j.1467-8624.2004.00655.x.

31.	Eti Ben Simon and Matthew P. Walker. "Sleep loss causes social withdrawal and loneliness." *Nature Communications* 9, no. 1 (2018): 1–9. doi:10.1038/s41467-018-05377-0.

32. James Chan, Jennifer C. Edman, and Peter J. Koltai. "Obstructive Sleep Apnea in Children." *American Family Physician* 69, no. 5 (March 2004): 1147–54. PMID: 15023015.

33. Jennifer Chung and Michael Crossley. "4 Academic Achievement in Finland." *International Guide to Student Achievement*. Routledge, 2012.

34. Christopher Drake, Timothy Roehrs, John Shambroom, and Thomas Roth. "Caffeine effects on sleep taken 0, 3, or 6 hours before going to bed." *Journal of Clinical Sleep Medicine: JCSM: Official Publication of the American Academy of Sleep Medicine* 9, no. 11 (November 2013): 1195–200. doi:10.5664/jcsm.3170.

35. Joshua W. Mouland, Franck Martial, Alex Watson, Robert J. Lucas, and Timothy M. Brown. "Cones Support Alignment to an Inconsistent World by Suppressing Mouse Circadian Responses to the Blue Colors Associated with Twilight." *Current Biology* 29, no. 24 (December 2019): 4260. doi:10.1016/j.cub.2019.10.028.

36. Patrick H. Finan, Phillip J. Quartana, and Michael T. Smith. "The Effects of Sleep Continuity Disruption on Positive Mood and Sleep Architecture in Healthy Adults." *Sleep* 38, no. 11 (November 2015): 1735–42. doi:10.5665/sleep.5154.

37. "Reading 'can help reduce stress.'" *The Telegraph*. March 30, 2009. https://www.telegraph.co.uk/news/health/news/5070874/Reading-can-help-reduce-stress.html.

38. David J. Kennaway. "Melatonin rich foods in our diet: food for thought or wishful thinking?" *Food & Function* 11, no. 11 (2020): 9359–69. doi:10.1039/d0fo02563a.

Chapter 15

1. Jodi L. Lukkes, Maxim V. Mokin, Jamie L. Scholl, and Gina L. Forster. "Adult rats exposed to early-life social isolation exhibit increased anxiety and conditioned fear behavior, and altered hormonal stress responses." *Hormones and Behavior* 55, no. 1 (2009): 248–56. doi:10.1016/j.yhbeh.2008.10.014.

2. Sergio M. Pellis, Vivien C. Pellis, and Brett T. Himmler. "How Play Makes for a More Adaptable Brain: A Comparative and Neural Perspective." *American Journal of Play* 7, no. 1 (Fall 2014): 73–98. https://files.eric.ed.gov/fulltext/EJ1043959.pdf.

3. Peter Gray. *Free to Learn: Why Unleashing the Instinct to Play Will Make Our Children Happier, More Self-Reliant, and Better Students for Life*. Basic Books, 2013.

4. Robert Root-Bernstein Lindsay Allen, Leighanna Beach, Ragini Bhadula, Justin Fast, Chelsea Hosey, Benjamin Kremkow, Jacqueline Lapp, Kaitlin Lonc, Kendell Pawelec, Abigail Podufaly, and Caitlin Russ. "Arts Foster Scientific Success: Avocations of Nobel, National Academy, Royal Society, and Sigma Xi Members." *Journal of Psychology of Science and Technology* 1, no. 2 (October 2008): 51–63. doi:10.1891/1939-7054.1.2.51.

5. Nala Rogers. "To Win a Nobel Prize in Science . . . Make Art?" Inside Science. October 5, 2018. https://www.insidescience.org/news/win-nobel-prize-science-make-art.

6. "Convention on the Rights of the Child." United Nations Human Rights. November 20, 1989. https://www.ohchr.org/en/professionalinterest/pages/crc.aspx.

7. Jessica Lahey. "Recess Without Rules." *The Atlantic*. January 28, 2014. https://www.theatlantic.com/education/archive/2014/01/recess-without-rules/283382/.

8. Institute of Medicine; Food and Nutrition Board; Committee on Physical Activity and Physical Education in the School Environment; Harold W. Kohl III and Heather D. Cook, editors. "Physical Activity, Fitness, and Physical Education: Effects on Academic Performance." *Educating the Student Body: Taking Physical Activity and Physical Education to School.* Washington, DC: National Academies Press, 2013.

9. Peter Gray. "Declining Student Resilience: A Serious Problem for Colleges." *Psychology Today*. September 22, 2015. https://www.psychologytoday.com/nz/blog/freedom-learn/201509/declining-student-resilience-serious-problem-colleges.

Chapter 16

1. Shaozheng Qin, Christina B. Young, Xujun Duan, Tianwen Chen, Kaustubh Supekar, and Vinod Menon. "Amygdala subregional structure and intrinsic functional connectivity predicts individual differences in anxiety during early childhood." *Biological psychiatry* 75, no. 11 (2014), 892–900. doi:10.1016/j.biopsych.2013.10.006.

2. S. Schindler, L. Schmidt, M. Stroske, M. Storch, A. Anwander, R. Trampel, M. Strauß, U. Hegerl, S. Geyer, and P. Schönknecht. "Hypothalamus enlargement in mood disorders." *Acta Psychiatrica Scandinavica* 139, no. 1 (September 19, 2018). doi:10.1111/acps.12958.

3. Christopher G. Davey, Michael Breakspear, Jesus Pujol, and Ben J. Harrison. "A Brain Model of Disturbed Self-Appraisal in Depression." *American Journal of Psychiatry* 174, no. 9 (2017): 895–903. doi:10.1176/appi.ajp.2017.16080883.

4.   Heath D. Schmidt and Ronald S. Duman. "The role of neurotrophic factors in adult hippocampal neurogenesis, antidepressant treatments and animal models of depressive-like behavior." *Behavioral Pharmacology* 18, no. 5–6 (2007): 391–418. doi:10.1097/FBP.0b013e3282ee2aa8.

5.   Hitesh C. Sheth, Zindadil Gandhi, and G.K. Vankar. "Anxiety disorders in ancient Indian literature." *Indian Journal of Psychiatry* 52, no. 3 (2010): 289. doi:10.4103/0019-5545.71009.

6.   Peter P. Hinshaw. "Historical Perspectives on Mental Illness and Stigma." *The Mark of Shame: Stigma of Mental Illness and an Agenda for Change.* Oxford: Oxford University Press, 2007.

7.   Hippocrates. "Book II: Section 16: Case I." *Of the Epidemics.* 400 BCE.

8.   Robert C. Abrams. "Late-life depression and the death of Queen Victoria." *International Journal of Geriatric Psychiatry* 25, no. 12 (2010): 1222–29. doi:10.1002/gps.2467.

9.   Sven Bremberg. "Mental health problems are rising more in Swedish adolescents than in other Nordic countries and the Netherlands." *Acta Paediatrica (Oslo, Norway: 1992)* 104, no. 10 (2015): 997–1004. doi:10.1111/apa.13075.

10.   G.L. Klerman, P.W. Lavori, J. Rice, T. Reich, J. Endicott, N.C. Andreasen, M.B. Keller, and R.M. Hirschfield. "Birth-cohort trends in rates of major depressive disorder among relatives of patients with affective disorder." *Archives of General Psychiatry* 42, no. 7 (1985): 689–93. doi:10.1001/archpsyc.1985.01790300057007. Also see,
Martin Seligman. *Learned Optimism: How to Change Your Mind and Your Life.* New York: Random House, 1991.

11.   Jean M. Twenge, Brittany Gentile, C. Nathan DeWall, Debbie Ma, Katharine Lacefield, and David R. Schurtz. "Birth cohort increases in psychopathology among young Americans, 1938–2007: A cross-temporal meta-analysis of the MMPI." *Clinical psychology review* 30, no. 2 (2010): 145–54. doi:10.1016/j.cpr.2009.10.005.

12.   "Mental Health Disorder Statistics." Johns Hopkins Medicine. 2021. https://www.hopkinsmedicine.org/health/wellness-and-prevention/mental-health-disorder-statistics.

13.   J.M. Twenge. "The age of anxiety? The birth cohort change in anxiety and neuroticism, 1952–1993." *Journal of Personality and Social Psychology* 79, no. 6 (2000): 1007. doi:10.1037//0022-3514.79.6.1007.

14.   Katherine M. Keyes, Dahsan Gary, Patrick M. O'Malley, Ava Hamilton, and John Schulenberg. "Recent increases in depressive symptoms among US adolescents: trends from 1991 to 2018." *Social psychiatry and psychiatric epidemiology* 54, no. 8 (2019): 987–96. doi:10.1007/s00127-019-01697-8.

15. T. Fleming, J. Tiatia-Seath, R. Peiris-John, K. Sutcliffe, D. Archer, L. Bavin, S. Crengle, and T. Clark. *Youth19 Rangatahi Smart Survey, Initial Findings: Hauora Hinengaro/Emotional and Mental Health*. New Zealand: The Youth19 Research Group and The University of Auckland and Victoria University of Wellington, 2020.

16. Catherine K. Ettman, Salma M. Abdalla, Gregory H. Cohen, Laura Sampson, Patrick M. Vivier, and Sandro Galea. "Prevalence of Depression Symptoms in US Adults Before and During the COVID-19 Pandemic." *JAMA Network Open* 3, no. 9 e2019686 (September 2020). doi:10.1001/jamanetworkopen.2020.19686.

17. Matthias Pierce, Holly Hope, Tamsin Ford, Stephani Hatch, Matthew Hotopf, Ann John, Evangelos Kontopantelis, Roger Webb, Simon Wessely, Sally McManus, and Kathryn M. Abel. "Mental health before and during the COVID-19 pandemic: a longitudinal probability sample survey of the UK population." *The Lancet Psychiatry* 7, no. 10 (July 2020): 883–92. doi:10.1016/S2215-0366(20)30308-4.

18. George A. Mensah, Gina S. Wei, Paul D. Sorlie, Lawrence J. Fine, Yves Rosenberg, Peter G. Kaufmann, Michael E. Mussolino, Lucy L. Hsu, Ebyan Addou, Michael M. Engelgau, and David Gordon. "Decline in cardiovascular mortality: possible causes and implications." *Circulation research* 120, no. 2 (2017): 366–80. doi:10.1161/CIRCRESAHA.116.309115.

19. Andre Burguiere, Christiane Klapisch-Zuber, Martine Segalen, and Francois Zonabend, editors. *A History of the Family, Volume I: Distant Worlds, Ancient Worlds*. Belknap Press: 1996.

20. Sally C. Curtin and Melonie Heron. "Death Rates Due to Suicide and Homicide Among Persons Aged 10–24: United States, 2000–2017." *NCHS Data Brief* 352 (October 2019): 2. https://www.cdc.gov/nchs/data/databriefs/db352-h.pdf.
    Also see,
    Ruch et al. "Trends in Suicide."

21. Danielle C. DeVille, Diana Whalen, Florence J. Breslin, Amanda S. Morris, Sahib S. Khalsa, Martin P. Paulus, and Deanna M. Barch. "Prevalence and Family-Related Factors Associated with Suicidal Ideation, Suicide Attempts, and Self-Injury in Children Aged 9 to 10 Years." *JAMA Network Open* 3, no. 2 e1920956 (2020). doi:10.1001/jamanetworkopen.2019.20956.

22. Robyn A. Cree, Rebecca H. Bitsko, Lara R. Robinson, Joseph R. Holbrook, Melissa L. Danielson, Camille Smith, Jennifer W. Kaminski, Mary Kay Kenney, and Georgina Peacock. "Health Care, Family, and Community Factors Associated with Mental, Behavioral, and Devel-

opmental Disorders and Poverty Among Children Aged 2–8 Years—United States, 2016." *Morbidity and Mortality Weekly Report* 67, no. 50 (December 2018):1377–83. doi:10.15585/mmwr.mm6750a1.

23. National Center on Birth Defects and Developmental Disabilities and Centers for Disease Control and Prevention. "Data and Statistics on Children's Mental Health." CDC. Last reviewed March 22, 2021. https://www.cdc.gov/childrensmentalhealth/data.html.

Chapter 17

1. Stephen W. Porges. "Neuroception: A Subconscious System for Detecting Threats and Safety." *Zero to Three* 24, no. 5 (May 2004): 19–24. ERIC Number: EJ938225.

2. CBC News. "Shea Heights hero finds strength to lift vehicle off injured boy." CBC. September 28, 2015. https://www.cbc.ca/news/canada/newfoundland-labrador/shea-heights-hero-finds-strength-to-lift-vehicle-off-injured-boy-1.3246481.

3. Matthew Diebel. "Man sets fire to spider at gas pump, sparking blaze." *USA Today*. September 26, 2015. https://www.usatoday.com/story/news/2015/09/26/man-causes-fire-at-gas-station-after-trying-to-burn-spider-as-he-filled-his-car/72903236/.

Chapter 18

1. Ken K.Y. Ho. "Diet-induced thermogenesis: fake friend or foe?" *Journal of Endocrinology* 238, no. 3 (2018): R185–91. doi:10.1530/JOE-18-0240.

2. Julia J. Rucklidge, Rebecca Andridge, Brigette Gorman, Neville Blampied, Heather Gordon, and Anna Boggis. "Shaken but unstirred? Effects of micronutrients on stress and trauma after an earthquake: RCT evidence comparing formulas and doses." *Human Psychopharmacology* 27, no. 5 (2012): 440–54. doi:10.1002/hup.2246.

3. Cindy Gellner. "Should I Be Worried If My Child Gets Sick Too Often?" Transcript of an interview conducted December 28, 2015. Updated May 17, 2018. https://healthcare.utah.edu/the-scope/shows.php?shows=0_5nzgsffm.

Chapter 19

1. Firdaus S. Dhabhar. "Effects of stress on immune function: the good, the bad, and the beautiful." *Immunologic Research* 58, no. 2 (2014): 193–210. doi:10.1007/s12026-014-8517-0.

2. Valerie Strauss. "Why pushing kids to learn too much too soon is counterproductive." *The Washington Post*. August 17, 2015. https://www.washingtonpost.com/news/answer-sheet/wp/2015/08/17/why-pushing-kids-to-learn-too-much-too-soon-is-counterproductive/.

3. Jon Simpson. "Finding Brand Success In The Digital World." *Forbes*. August 25, 2017. https://www.forbes.com/sites/forbesagen-cycouncil/2017/08/25/finding-brand-success-in-the-digital-world/#7d952ddd626e.

4. Daniel J. Levitin. "Organizing Our Social World." *The Organized Mind: Thinking Straight in the Age of Information Overload*. New York: Plume, 2014.

5. Carl E. Schwartz, Christopher I. Wright, Lisa M. Shin, Jerome Kagan, Paul J. Whalen, Katherine G. McMullin, and Scott L. Rauch. "Differential amygdalar response to novel versus newly familiar neutral faces: a functional MRI probe developed for studying inhibited temperament." *Biological Psychiatry* 53, no. 10 (2003): 854–62. doi:10.1016/s0006-3223(02)01906-6.

6. Lilianne R. Mujica-Parodi, Helmut H. Strey, Blaise Frederick, Robert Savoy, David Cox, Yevgeny Botanov, Denis Tolkunov, Denis Rubin, and Jochen Weber. "Chemosensory Cues to Conspecific Emotional Stress Activate Amygdala in Humans." *PloS One* 4, no. 7 e6415 (July 2009). doi:10.1371/journal.pone.0006415.

7. "World is angry and stressed, Gallup report says." BBC News. April 26, 2019. https://www.bbc.com/news/world-48063982.

8. John M. Darley and C. Daniel Batson. "'From Jerusalem to Jericho': A study of situational and dispositional variables in helping behavior." *Journal of Personality and Social Psychology* 27, no. 1 (1973): 100–08. Doi:10.1037/h0034449.

Chapter 20

1. V.J. Felitti, R.F. Anda, D. Nordenberg, D.F. Williamson, A.M. Spitz, V. Edwards, M.P. Koss, and J.S. Marks. "Relationship of childhood abuse and household dysfunction to many of the leading causes of death in adults. The Adverse Childhood Experiences (ACE) Study." *American Journal of Preventive Medicine* 14, no. 4 (1998): 245–58. doi:10.1016/s0749-3797(98)00017-8.

2. Victoria Williamson, Cathy Creswell, Pasco Fearon, Rachel M. Hiller, Jennifer Walker, and Sarah L. Halligan. "The role of parenting behaviors in childhood post-traumatic stress disorder: A meta-analytic review." *Clinical Psychology Review* 53 (2017): 1–13. doi:10.1016/j.cpr.2017.01.005.

3. Erin P. Hambrick, Thomas W. Brawner, and Bruce D. Perry. "Timing of Early-Life Stress and the Development of Brain-Related Capacities." *Frontiers in Behavioral Neuroscience* 13 (August 2019): 183. doi:10.3389/fnbeh.2019.00183. Also see,

Erin P. Hambrick, Thomas W. Brawner, Bruce D. Perry, Kristie Brandt, Christine Hofmeister, and Jen O. Collins. "Beyond the ACE Score: Examining relationships between timing of developmental adversity, relational health and developmental outcomes in children." *Archives of Psychiatric Nursing* 33, no. 3 (2019): 238–47. doi:10.1016/j.apnu.2018.11.001.

4.   Oprah Winfrey and Bruce D. Perry. *What Happened to You? Conversations on Trauma, Resilience, and Healing.* Flatiron Books, 2021.

5.   Michael D. De Bellis and Abigail Zisk. "The biological effects of childhood trauma." *Child and Adolescent Psychiatric Clinics of North America* 23, no. 2 (2014): 185–222. doi:10.1016/j.chc.2014.01.002. Also see,

M.D. De Bellis. "Developmental traumatology: the psychobiological development of maltreated children and its implications for research, treatment, and policy." *Development and Psychopathology* 13, no. 3 (2001): 539–64. doi:10.1017/s0954579401003078.

6.   Bruce D. Perry. *The Boy Who Was Raised as a Dog: And Other Stories from a Child Psychiatrist's Notebook—What Traumatized Children Can Teach Us About Loss, Love, and Healing.* New York: Basic Books, 2007.

7.   Felitti et al. "Relationship of childhood abuse."

8.   Jessie R. Baldwin, Avshalom Caspi, Alan J. Meehan, Antony Ambler, Louise Arseneault, Helen L. Fisher, HonaLee Harrington, Timothy Matthews, Candice L. Odgers, Richie Poulton, Sandhya Ramrakha, Terrie E. Moffitt, and Andrea Danese. "Population vs Individual Prediction of Poor Health From Results of Adverse Childhood Experiences Screening." *JAMA Pediatrics* 175, no. 4 (2021): 385–93. doi:10.1001/jamapediatrics.2020.5602.

9.   R. Yehuda, M.H. Teicher, R.L. Trestman, R.A. Levengood, and L.J. Siever. "Cortisol regulation in posttraumatic stress disorder and major depression: a chronobiological analysis." *Biological psychiatry* 40, no. 2 (1996): 79–88. doi:10.1016/0006-3223(95)00451-3.

10. Felitti et al. "Relationship of childhood abuse."

11. Karlen Lyons-Ruth, M.H. Teicher, R.L. Trestman, R.A. Levengood, and L.J. Siever. "Borderline symptoms and suicidality/self-injury in late adolescence: prospectively observed relationship correlates in infancy and childhood." *Psychiatry Research* 206, no. 2–3 (2013): 273–81. doi:10.1016/j.psychres.2012.09.030.

12. Montagu. *Touching.*

13. Robyn L. Bluhm, Peter C. Williamson, Elizabeth A. Osuch, Paul A. Frewen, Todd K. Stevens, Kristine Boksman, Richard W.J. Neufeld, Jean Théberge, and Ruth A. Lanius. "Alterations in default network

connectivity in posttraumatic stress disorder related to early-life trauma." *Journal of Psychiatry & Neuroscience: JPN* 34, no. 3 (2009): 187. http://jpn.ca/vol34-issue3/34-3-187/.

14. Bluhm et al. "Alterations in default network connectivity."

15. Janina Fisher. *Healing the Fragmented Selves of Trauma Survivors: Overcoming Internal Self-Alienation.* New York: Routledge, 2017.

16. Kim L. Felmingham, Richard A. Bryant, and Evian Gordon. "Processing angry and neutral faces in post-traumatic stress disorder: an event-related potentials study." *Neuroreport* 14, no. 5 (2003): 777–80. doi:10.1097/00001756-200304150-00024.

17. S.L. Rauch, B.A. van der Kolk, R.E. Fisler, N.M. Alpert, S.P. Orr, C.R. Savage, A.J. Fischman, M.A. Jenike, and R.K. Pitman. "A symptom provocation study of posttraumatic stress disorder using positron emission tomography and script-driven imagery." *Archives of General Psychiatry* 53, no. 5 (1996): 380–87. doi:10.1001/archpsyc.1996.01830050014003. Also see,
L.M. Shin, R.J. McNally, S.M. Kosslyn, W.L. Thompson, S.L. Rauch, N.M. Alpert, L.J. Metzger, N.B. Lasko, S.P. Orr, and R.K. Pitman. "Regional cerebral blood flow during script-driven imagery in childhood sexual abuse-related PTSD: A PET investigation." *The American Journal of Psychiatry* 156, no. 4 (1999): 575–84. doi:10.1176/ajp.156.4.575.

18. Bessel van der Kolk. *The Body Keeps the Score.* New York: Penguin Books, 2014.

19. Bridget L. Callaghan, Andrea Fields, Dylan G. Gee, Laurel Gabard-Durnam, Christina Caldera, Kathryn L. Humphreys, Bonnie Goff, Jessica Flannery, Eva H. Telzer, Mor Shapiro, and Nim Tottenham. "Mind and gut: Associations between mood and gastrointestinal distress in children exposed to adversity." *Development and Psychopathology* 32, no. 1 (2020): 309–28. doi:10.1017/S0954579419000087.

20. B. van der Kolk, M. Greenberg, H. Boyd, and J. Krystal. "Inescapable shock, neurotransmitters, and addiction to trauma: toward a psychobiology of post traumatic stress." *Biological Psychiatry* 20, no. 3 (1985): 314–25. doi:10.1016/0006-3223(85)90061-7.

21. Judith McFarlane, Jacquelyn Pennings, Lene Symes, John Maddoux, and Rene Paulson. "Predicting abused women with children who return to the abuser: Development of a risk assessment tool." *Journal of Threat Assessment and Management* 1, no. 4 (2014): 274–90. doi:10.1037/tam0000025.

22. E. Alison Holman, Dana Rose Garfin, and Roxane Cohen Silver. "Media's role in broadcasting acute stress following the Boston Marathon bombings." *Proceedings of the National Academy of Sciences of the*

United States 111, no. 1 (2014): 93–98. doi:10.1073/pnas.1316265110. Also see,

Beth E. Molnar, Ginny Sprang, Kyle D. Killian, Ruth Gottfried, Vanessa Emery, and Brian E. Bride. "Advancing science and practice for vicarious traumatization/secondary traumatic stress: A research agenda." *Traumatology* 23, no. 2 (2017): 129. doi:10.1037/trm0000122.

23.   Alayna Schreier, Jessica K. Pogue, and David J. Hansen. "Impact of child sexual abuse on non-abused siblings: A review with implications for research and practice." *Aggression and Violent Behavior* 34 (May 2017): 254–62. doi:10.1016/j.avb.2016.11.011.

24.   R. Yehuda, J. Schmeidler, E.L. Giller Jr., L.J. Siever, and K. Binder-Brynes. "Relationship between posttraumatic stress disorder characteristics of Holocaust survivors and their adult offspring." *American Journal of Psychiatry* 155, no. 6 (1998): 841–43. doi:10.1176/ajp.155.6.841.

25.   Yehuda et al. "Relationship between posttraumatic stress disorder characteristics."

26.   Brian G. Dias and Kerry J. Ressler. "Parental olfactory experience influences behavior and neural structure in subsequent generations." *Nature Neuroscience* 17, no. 1 (2014): 89–96. doi:10.1038/nn.3594.

Chapter 21

1.   Christina Bethell, Jennifer Jones, Narangerel Gombojav, Jeff Linkenbach, and Robert Sege. "Positive Childhood Experiences and Adult Mental and Relational Health in a Statewide Sample: Associations Across Adverse Childhood Experiences Levels." *JAMA Pediatrics* 173, no. 11 (2019): e193007–e193007. doi:10.1001/jamapediatrics.2019.3007.

2.   Sue C. Bratton, Dee Ray, Tammy Rhine, and Leslie Jones. "The Efficacy of Play Therapy with Children: A Meta-Analytic Review of Treatment Outcomes." *Professional Psychology: Research and Practice* 36, no. 4 (2005): 376. doi:10.1037/0735-7028.36.4.376.

3.   Caroline Case and Tessa Dalley. *The Handbook of Art Therapy*. Routledge, 2014.

4.   Renée Emunah. *Acting for Real: Drama Therapy Process, Technique, and Performance*. Routledge, 2013.

5.   Daniel J. Levitin. *This Is Your Brain on Music: The Science of a Human Obsession*. Penguin Random House, 2006.

6.   Leslie Bunt and Brynjulf Stige. *Music Therapy: An Art Beyond Words*. Routledge, 2014.

7.   Michael H. Thaut and Gerald C. McIntosh. "Neurologic Music Therapy in Stroke Rehabilitation." *Current Physical Medicine and Rehabilitation Reports* 2, no. 2 (2014): 106–13. doi:10.1007/s40141-014-0049-y.

8.   Janelle Nimer and Brad Lundahl. "Animal-Assisted Therapy: A Meta-Analysis." *Anthrozoös* 20, no. 3 (2007): 225–38. doi:10.2752/089279307X224773.

9.   Ainat Rogel, Alysse M. Loomis, Ed Hamlin, Hilary Hodgdon, Joseph Spinazzola, and Bessel van der Kolk. "The impact of neurofeedback training on children with developmental trauma: A randomized controlled study." *Psychological Trauma: Theory, Research, Practice and Policy* 12, no. 8 (2020): 918–29. doi:10.1037/tra0000648.

10.   Q. Li, K. Morimoto, A. Nakadai, H. Inagaki, M. Katsumata, T. Shimizu, Y. Hirata, K. Hirata, H. Suzuki, Y. Miyazaki, T. Kagawa, Y. Koyama, T. Ohira, N. Takayama, A.M. Krensky, and T. Kawada. "Forest bathing enhances human natural killer activity and expression of anti-cancer proteins." *International Journal of Immunopathology and Pharmacology* 20, no. 2 Suppl 2 (2007): 3–8. doi:10.1177/03946320070200S202.

11.   Hiromitsu Kobayashi, Chorong Song, Harumi Ikei, Bum-Jin Park, Juyoung Lee, Takahide Kagawa, and Yoshifumi Miyazaki. "Population-Based Study on the Effect of a Forest Environment on Salivary Cortisol Concentration." *International Journal of Environmental Research and Public Health* 14, no. 8 (August 2017): 931. doi:10.3390/ijerph14080931.

12.   V.J. Harber and J.R. Sutton. "Endorphins and exercise." *Sports Medicine* 1, no. 2 (1984): 154–71. doi:10.2165/00007256-198401020-00004.

13.   Pim Cuijpers, Suzanne C. van Veen, Marit Sijbrandij, Whitney Yoder, and Ioana A. Cristea. "Eye movement desensitization and reprocessing for mental health problems: a systematic review and meta-analysis." *Cognitive Behaviour Therapy* 49, no. 3 (2020): 165–80. doi:10.1080/1650 6073.2019.1703801.

14.   Linda Geddes. *Chasing the Sun: The New Science of Sunlight and How it Shapes Our Bodies and Minds.* Pegasus Books, 2019.

Chapter 23

1.   Peter Scharff Smith. "The Effects of Solitary Confinement on Prison Inmates: A Brief History and Review of the Literature." *Crime and Justice* 34, no. 1 (2006): 441–528. doi:10.1086/500626.

2.   Melissa McGlensey. "21 People Describe What Sensory Overload Feels Like." The Mighty. February 11, 2016. https://themighty.com/2016/02/people-explain-what-sensory-overload-feels-like/.

3.   Roianne R. Ahn, Lucy Jane Miller, Sharon Milberger, and Daniel N. McIntosh. "Prevalence of parents' perceptions of sensory processing disorders among kindergarten children." *American Journal of Occupational Therapy: Official Publication of the Americamn Occupational Therapy Association* 58, no. 3 (2004): 287–93. doi:10.5014/ajot.58.3.287.

4. Liberty. *Reducing stress in schools.*

5. Nationwide Children's Hospital. "Smoke alarms using mother's voice wake children better than high-pitch tone alarms: Including the child's first name in the alarm message does not improve the effectiveness of the alarm." *Science News.* October 25, 2018. https://www.sciencedaily. com/releases/2018/10/181025084038.htm.

6. "Police chases: Avoid pursuing fleeing youths, says Judge Becroft." RNZ. October 24, 2019. https://www.rnz.co.nz/news/national/401675/ police-chases-avoid-pursuing-fleeing-youths-says-judge-becroft.

7. Stephen W. Porges. "Reducing auditory hypersensitivities in autistic spectrum disorder: preliminary findings evaluating the listening project protocol." *Frontiers in Pediatrics* 2 (August 2014): 80. doi:10.3389/ fped.2014.00080.

8. "Calmer." Flare Audio. https://www.flareaudio.com/pages/calm-er-life.

Chapter 24

1. "Leading Perspectives on Disability: A Q&A with Dr. Stephen Shore." The Lime Network. https://www.limeconnect.com/opportunities_ news/detail/leading-perspectives-on-disability-a-qa-with-dr-stephen-shore.

2. S. Hossein Fatemi, Kimberly A. Aldinger, Paul Ashwood, Margaret L. Bauman, Charles D. Blaha, Gene J. Blatt, Abha Chauhan, Ved Chauhan, Stephen R. Dager, Price E. Dickson, Annette M. Estes, Dan Goldowitz, Detlef H. Heck, Thomas L. Kemper, Bryan H. King, Loren A. Martin, Kathleen J. Millen, Guy Mittleman, Matthew W. Mosconi, Antonio M. Persico, John A. Sweeney, Sara J .Webb, and John P. Welsh. "Consensus paper: pathological role of the cerebellum in autism." *Cerebellum (London, England)* 11, no. 3 (2012): 777–807. doi:10.1007/s12311-012-0355-9.

3. Elysa J. Marco, Leighton B.N. Hinkley, Susanna S. Hill, and Srikantan S. Nagarajan. "Sensory Processing in Autism: A Review of Neurophysiologic Findings." *Pediatric Research* 69 (2011): 48–54. doi:10.1203/PDR. 0b013e3182130c54.

4. Steven Stagg, Li-Huan Tan, and Fathima Kodakkadan. "Emotion Recognition and Context in Adolescents with Autism Spectrum Disorder." *Journal of Autism and Developmental Disorders* (October 7, 2021). doi:10.1007/s10803-021-05292-2.

5. Søren Dalsgaard, Søren Dinesen Østergaard, James F. Leckman, Preben Bo Mortensen, and Marianne Giørtz Pedersen. "Mortality in children, adolescents, and adults with attention deficit hyperactivity disor-

der: a nationwide cohort study." *Lancet (London, England)* 385, no. 9983 (2015). doi:10.1016/S0140-6736(14)61684-6.

6. A.J. Zametkin, T.E. Nordahl, M. Gross, A.C. King, W.E. Semple, J. Rumsey, S. Hamburger, and R.M. Cohen. "Cerebral glucose metabolism in adults with hyperactivity of childhood onset." *The New England Journal of Medicine* 323, no. 20 (1990): 1361–66. doi:10.1056/NEJM199011153232001.

7. Ronald C. Kessler, T.E. Nordahl, M. Gross, A.C. King, W.E. Semple, J. Rumsey, S. Hamburger, and R.M. Cohen. "Patterns and predictors of attention-deficit/hyperactivity disorder persistence into adulthood: results from the national comorbidity survey replication." *Biological Psychiatry* 57, no. 11 (2005): 1442–51. doi:10.1016/j.biopsych.2005.04.001.

8. Martijn Arns, Sabine de Ridder, Ute Strehl, Marinus Breteler, and Anton Coenen. "Efficacy of neurofeedback treatment in ADHD: the effects on inattention, impulsivity and hyperactivity: a meta-analysis." *Clinical EEG and Neuroscience* 40, no. 3 (2009): 180–89. doi:10.1177/155005940904000311.

9. Klaus W. Lange. "Micronutrients and Diets in the Treatment of Attention-Deficit/Hyperactivity Disorder: Chances and Pitfalls." *Frontiers in Psychiatry* 11, no. 102 (February 26, 2020). doi:10.3389/fpsyt.2020.00102.

10. Jasmine M. Brown, Roger Bland, Egon Jonsson, and Andrew J. Greenshaw. "A Brief History of Awareness of the Link Between Alcohol and Fetal Alcohol Spectrum Disorder." *The Canadian Journal of Psychiatry. Revue canadienne de psychiatrie* 64, no. 3 (2019): 164–68. doi:10.1177/0706743718777403.

11. Lynn K. Paul. "Developmental malformation of the corpus callosum: a review of typical callosal development and examples of developmental disorders with callosal involvement." *Journal of Neurodevelopmental Disorders* 3, no. 1 (2011): 3–27. doi:10.1007/s11689-010-9059-y.

12. E.M. Armstrong and E.L. Abel. "Fetal alcohol syndrome: the origins of a moral panic." *Alcohol and Alcoholism (Oxford, Oxfordshire)* 35, no. 3 (2000): 276–82. doi:10.1093/alcalc/35.3.276.

Chapter 25

1. Shamard Charles. "Social media linked to rise in mental health disorders in teens, survey finds." NBC News. March 14, 2019. https://www.nbcnews.com/health/mental-health/social-media-linked-rise-mental-health-disorders-teens-survey-finds-n982526.

2. Keyes et al. "Recent increases in depressive symptoms among US adolescents."

3.   Andrew K. Przybylski, Amy Orben, and Netta Weinstein. "How Much Is Too Much? Examining the Relationship Between Digital Screen Engagement and Psychosocial Functioning in a Confirmatory Cohort Study." *Journal of the American Academy of Child and Adolescent Psychiatry* 59, no. 9 (2020): 1080–88. Doi:10.1016/j.jaac.2019.06.017.

4.   Oliver Lindhiem, Charles B. Bennett, Dana Rosen, and Jennifer Silk. "Mobile technology boosts the effectiveness of psychotherapy and behavioral interventions: a meta-analysis." *Behavior Modification* 39, no. 6 (2015): 785–804. Doi:10.1177/0145445515595198.

5.   Jonathan A. Mitchell, Daniel Rodriguez, Kathryn H. Schmitz, and Janet Audrain-McGovern. "Greater screen time is associated with adolescent obesity: a longitudinal study of the BMI distribution from ages 14 to 18." *Obesity (Silver Spring, Md.)* 21, no. 3 (2013): 572–75. Doi:10.1002/oby.20157.

6.   "Guidelines on Physical Activity, Sedentary Behaviour and Sleep for Children Under 5 Years of Age." World Health Organization. https://apps.who.int/iris/bitstream/handle/10665/325147/WHO-NMH-PND-2019.4-eng.pdf.

7.   Yiren Kong, Young Sik Seo, and Ling Zhai. "Comparison of reading performance on screen and on paper: A meta-analysis." *Computers & Education* 123 (August 2018): 138–49. Doi:10.1016/j.compedu.2018.05.005.

8.   Elizabeth J. Ivie, Adam Pettitt, Louis J. Moses, and Nicholas B. Allen. "A meta-analysis of the association between adolescent social media use and depressive symptoms." *Journal of Affective Disorders* 275 (October 2020): 165–74. Doi:10.1016/j.jad.2020.06.014.

9.   Scott Meech. "Cyber Bullying: Worse Than Traditional Bullying." TechLearning. May 1, 2007. https://www.techlearning.com/news/cyber-bullying-worse-than-traditional-bullying.

10. T.R. Nansel, M. Overpeck, R.S. Pilla, W.J. Ruan, B. Simons-Morton, and P. Scheidt. "Bullying behaviors among US youth: Prevalence and association with psychosocial adjustment." *JAMA* 285, no. 16 (2001): 2094–100. doi:10.1001/jama.285.16.2094.

Chapter 26

1.   Christa Fouché, Kim Elliott, Stuart Mundy-McPherson, Vanessa Jordan, and Tricia Bingham, reviewers. "The Impact of Youth Work for Young People: A Systematic Review for the Health Council of New Zealand and the Ministry of Youth Development." Health Research Council of New Zealand and the Ministry of Youth Development. July 2010. https://www.myd.govt.nz/about-myd/publications/youth-work-syst-rev-final-final.pdf.

2. David J. DeWit, David DuBois, Gizem Erdem, Simon Larose, Ellen L. Lipman, and Renée Spencer. "Mentoring Relationship Closures in Big Brothers Big Sisters Community Mentoring Programs: Patterns and Associated Risk Factors." *American Journal of Community Psychology* 57, no. 1–2 (2016): 60–72. doi:10.1002/ajcp.12023.

3. Charles J. Gelso, Dennis M. Kivlighan, and Rayna D. Markin. "The real relationship and its role in psychotherapy outcome: A meta-analysis." *Psychotherapy* 55, no. 4 (2018): 434. doi:10.1037/pst0000183.

4. Ian McCafferty. "In Safe Hands: Massage & PTSD." American Massage Therapy Association. May 24, 2016. https://www.amtamassage.org/publications/massage-therapy-journal/massage-and-ptsd/.

5. "Principle 11—Disclosure of personal information." Privacy Commissioner. 2013. https://www.privacy.org.nz/the-privacy-act-and-codes/privacy-principles/limits-on-disclosure-of-personal-information-principle-11/.

Chapter 27

1. Marco Schlosser, Terje Sparby, Sebastjan Vörös, Rebecca Jones, and Natalie L. Marchant. "Unpleasant meditation-related experiences in regular meditators: Prevalence, predictors, and conceptual considerations." *PLoS One* 14, no. 5 (May 2019): e0216643. doi:10.1371/journal.pone.0216643.

2. Mark R. Lepper, David Greene, and Richard E. Nisbett. "Undermining Children's Intrinsic Interest with Extrinsic Reward: A Test of the 'Overjustification' Hypothesis." *Journal of Personality and Social Psychology* 28, no. 1 (1973): 129. doi:10.1037/h0035519.

Chapter 29

1. Julianne Holt-Lunstad, Timothy B. Smith, and J. Bradley Layton. "Social relationships and mortality risk: a meta-analytic review." *PLoS medicine* 7, no. 7 (July 2010): e1000316. doi:10.1371/journal.pmed.1000316.

2. Bethell et al. "Positive Childhood Experiences."

3. Burguiere et al. *A History of the Family*.

4. Jon Younger. "High-Demand Soft And Hard Skills For Freelancers And Other Professionals." *Forbes*. February 15, 2020. https://www.forbes.com/sites/jonyounger/2020/02/15/high-demand-soft-and-hard-skills-for-freelancers-and-other-professionals/#1f9a853c61ba.

Chapter 30

1. Ruch et al. "Trends in Suicide."
2. S. Hackett, P. Branigan , and D. Holmes. "Harmful sexual behaviour framework: an evidence-informed operational framework for children and young people displaying harmful sexual behaviours." London: NSP-CC, 2019. https://www.icmec.org/wp-content/uploads/2019/04/harmful-sexual-behaviour-framework.pdf.

Chapter 36

1. R.A. Neimeyer. "Searching for the meaning of meaning: grief therapy and the process of reconstruction." *Death Studies* 24, no. 6 (2000): 541–58. doi:10.1080/07481180050121480.
   Also see,
   George A. Bonanno and Scott O. Lilienfeld. "Let's be realistic: When Grief Counseling is Effective and When It's Not." *Professional Psychology: Research and Practice* 39, no. 3 (June 2008): 377. doi:10.1037/0735-7028.39.3.377.

Chapter 37

1. Liz Gordon. "The empty nest is refilled: the joys and tribulations of grandparents raising their grandchildren." Auckland: Grandparents Raising Grandchildren Trust (NZ). 2016. https://www.grg.org.nz/site/grg/The%20empty%20nest%20is%20refilled%20-%20Research%20Report.pdf.
2. Harriet Hodgson. *So, You're Raising Your Grandkids! Tested Tips, Research, & Real-Life Stories to Make Your Life Easier.* WriteLife Publishing, 2018.
3. Gordon. "The empty nest is refilled."

Chapter 40

1. Lucas Reilly. "19 Smart Facts About Albert Einstein." Mental Floss. March 14, 2019. https://www.mentalfloss.com/article/573985/albert-einstein-facts.

About Familius

Visit Our Website: www.familius.com

Familius is a global trade publishing company that publishes books and other content to help families be happy. We believe that the family is the fundamental unit of society and that happy families are the foundation of a happy life. We recognize that every family looks different, and we passionately believe in helping all families find greater joy. To that end, we publish books for children and adults that invite families to live the Familius Ten Habits of Happy Family Life: *love together, play together, learn together, work together, talk together, heal together, read together, eat together, give together,* and *laugh together.* Founded in 2012, Familius is located in Sanger, California.

Connect

Facebook: www.facebook.com/familiustalk
Twitter: @familiustalk, @paterfamilius1
Pinterest: www.pinterest.com/familius
Instagram: @familiustalk

*The most important work you ever do will
be within the walls of your own home.*